Routed to Heaven

How Near-Death Experiences, Afterlife Testimonies
And Heavenly Insights Can Help You Live With Intention

JULIE BONN BLANK

North Beach Books

~~~

Library Cataloging Data
Names: Bonn Blank, Julie (Julie Bonn Blank)
Routed to Heaven: How Near-Death Experiences, Afterlife Testimonies
And Heavenly Insights Can Help You Live With Intention/ Julie Bonn Blank
(9in × 6 in.)
ISBN-13: 979-8-9944532-4-7 (paperback)

Key Words: Christian Memoir, Christian Nonfiction, Devotional, Bible Study, Christian Living, End Times, Near-Death Experience, Life Purpose

Library of Congress Control Number: 2026902258
~~~

Dedication

To Jesus

For taking me on a journey and meeting me there. I will never forget.

To Randy and Renee Kay

For the safety, shelter and sanity that helped launch my wet-winged flight to seek every wounded soul—bringing Heaven, Hope and Healing to them with Light and Truth. And for quickly and deeply discerning the real me. May my eyes always scan for other returnees and opportunities as you have done, so that our Jesus-impact is a billion-fold.

I thank my God every time I remember you. In all my prayers for all of you, I always pray with joy because of your partnership in the gospel from the first day until now, being confident of this, that He who began a good work in you will carry it onto completion until the day of Jesus Christ.

Philippians 1:3-6

Why 'Routed To Heaven' Stays With You

A MUST READ!

Looking into the eyes of Jesus' changes you forever as it did for Julie Bonn Blank during her personal NDE. That change is seen in this remarkable book in the gift that Jesus imparted to her to be able to peer deep in the soul of others and overcome past traumas and tears. Surely a book that will inspire, comfort, and aid! A must read!! **B W Melvin, author of *A Land Unknown: Hell's Dominion*** and ***Heaven Beckons***

TIMELY & LIFESAVING!

As someone who had a very similar encounter, I can tell you that this book is a beautiful library of heavenly encounters that will change your life. We are living in a very important time when Heaven is meeting earth, and this book is part of the fulfillment of Jesus's prayer: that the Father's will would be accomplished on earth, as it is in heaven. **-Gabe Poirot, YouTuber & Author of *18 Days in Heaven***

I CAN ONLY IMAGINE!

Routed to Heaven is both comforting and courageous. Through powerful stories of those who have encountered Heaven through near-death experiences, Julie invites readers to see how intentionally and uniquely God reaches each of us—meeting us exactly where we are and in the way that will make the greatest impact. What sets this book apart is Julie's heaven-minded mission manifesto—an eternal-minded roadmap she weaves through every chapter. As she identifies ten common blocks that arise when we seek answers, she gently challenges readers to confront them. Her description of Heaven as a golden kaleidoscope of glory is unforgettable. With thoughtful "pause and ponder" reflections at the end of each chapter, I found myself drawn into a profound examination of my own life and faith. Whether you have questions about Heaven, unresolved anger toward God, or a desire to take an honest inventory of your spiritual journey, this book is for you. **Cherie Denna, Women's Pastor & Award-Winning Author (2025 Selah Award in Memoir, 3rd; 2024 Golden Scroll Award in Memoir, 2nd; 2024 Christian Market Book of the Year; 2024 Christian Indie Award in Memoir, 3rd)**

PEACE, CONNECTION & COMFORT!

Routed to Heaven is a touching anthology that highlights near-death experiences and the profound insights they offer about the afterlife, the Divine and how to bring the wonder, glory and serenity of Heaven to a spiritual walk here on earth. Julie Bonn Blank's compilation aims to inspire readers by presenting stories that evoke feelings of peace, beauty, and a deeper connection with God. These narratives can provide comfort to those grappling with questions about life after death and the nature of Heaven. **Pam Farrel, bestselling author of 60+ books including *Glimpse of God's Glory: One Woman's Near-Death Experience***

LIFTED MY EYES!

Routed to Heaven by Julie Bonn Blank stirred my heart and lifted my eyes toward the hope of Heaven. I was really blessed by the book. It's a topic I've struggled with in the past, but she made it so approachable. Through moving testimonies and thoughtful devotional insights, this book invites readers to live each day with eternity in mind and in joyful anticipation of the glory to come. **Karen Barnett, 2025 ACFW Carol Award Winner & Author**

MASTERFUL & BRILLIANT!

I count it among my greatest blessings to know Julie and to call her friend. She has inspired me, challenged me, and reminded me what wholehearted devotion to Jesus looks like in action. I have no doubt that this book will do the same for you. This book is a masterful tapestry. **Randy Kay, Author of *Heaven Stormed, Heaven Encounters,* and *Revelations From Heaven,* Host of *Revelations From Heaven,* and Pastor of *My Family***

THIS WILL AWAKEN YOUR HEART!

Routed to Heaven isn't just a collection of divine encounters and miraculous stories—it's a faith-filled guide that points the way to transformation. Through inspiring testimonies, Scripture, and her thoughtful reflections, Julie shows how we can overcome life's obstacles and live intentionally with eternity in mind. This book will awaken your heart to Heaven even as you walk daily in God's presence on earth. **Twila Belk, Author, Speaker, Encourager**

24-KARAT GOLD NUGGETS FROM GOD!

Routed To Heaven takes an in-depth look at how God intervenes in ordinary people's lives in a supernatural and **extraordinary** way. These testimonies will not only uplift and excite you as you read them, they will beckon you to acknowledge that in reality there is far more to life than what we see here on this earth and that the spirit realm is just as real, if not more real than our earthly existence.

Julie could have stopped right there and this would have been an excellent book simply for the testimonies, but she doesn't! It is clear God then divinely guided her to take those testimonies and mine from them spiritual truths and concepts that are given to you the reader, so that instead of just reading about someone else's testimony, these 24 karat gold nuggets of God-inspired wisdom can be part of your story as well! **Bruce Van Natta, author of *A Miraculous Life* and founder of Sweet Bread Ministries**

EXPERIENCE HEAVEN, HOPE & HEALING!

Sister Julie's new book *Routed to Heaven* shows the hand of God upon individuals who went to Heaven and came back changed! She brings her vision statement to life in these pages: To impact lives for the Kingdom by bringing Heaven, hope, and healing to others. You, the reader, will experience Heaven, hope, and healing, to prepare our hearts and live daily for eternity! There is no better investment in this brief, so-called life! **Steve Kang, Founder and Pastor at *Revive the Nations*, Irvine Onnuri Church, Church Planter at *Send Network SBC***

WILL INCREASE YOUR FAITH!

I really enjoyed reading this book because I personally have never had a Heavenly visitation. But I got to see what happened, what one might look and feel like, as a reader in all of these stories. I know they are real. This book increased my faith. **Kerri Pomarolli, Author, Speaker, Comedian**

A CAPTIVATING READ!

I wanted to tell you that it really is a captivating read and I love the layout. The reflection or study portions are very helpful in processing and applying the information that proceeds them. I pray that God will continue to use your experiences to encourage and bless others, especially those who are experiencing doubts or disillusionment. I enjoyed this book! **Doug Timmons, Lead Pastor, Crossroads Church**

Landmarks Of The Eternal

Foreword by Randy Kay

The first time Julie Bonn Blank appeared on our show, *Revelations From Heaven*, I knew I was speaking with someone truly extraordinary. As she shared her remarkable afterlife experience with our audience, her authenticity shone through every word. But what struck me most wasn't just her incredible journey to Heaven—it was the evident transformation that had taken place in her heart.

Julie's story begins in crisis: a severe allergic reaction that caused her heart to stop in an ambulance. What happened next changed everything. Clinically dead, she found herself in Heaven, standing with Jesus, viewing those breathtaking orange glass panels dancing in kaleidoscope patterns, feeling His overwhelming love, and receiving a mission: 'There is still so much work to be done.' He sent her back—but not before leaving an indelible mark on her soul that would redirect the entire trajectory of her life.

What you hold in your hands is not merely parts of Julie's story, though hers alone would be worth the read. This book is a masterful tapestry woven with over twenty near-death and afterlife accounts from people whose lives intersected with eternity. You'll meet Jason, who sat on Jesus' lap and was healed as a toddler after clinical death. You'll encounter Pam, who experienced God's glory during a medically induced coma that took her to Heaven's gates. You'll walk alongside Dawn, who was ejected from a plane and coached through survival by the Holy Spirit. And you'll meet many others whose testimonies confirm the reality of Heaven, the power of God, and the urgency of this moment in history.

But *Routed to Heaven* offers something beyond inspiration—it provides a roadmap. Julie has brilliantly structured this book as both validation and activation. Each powerful testimony is followed by her insightful reflections that address the very real blocks preventing us from living with eternal intentionality: fear, grief, trauma, unforgiveness, guilt, mental health struggles, waiting on God's timing, tribulations, strongholds, wounds and spiritual warfare.

Julie has created a practical framework—what she calls a 'Heaven-Minded Mission Manifesto'—to help you discover your unique purpose and live it out with boldness. Through each chapter, she guides you through essential tools: deep prayer, pre-praise, knowledge, service, the power of belief, love, gratitude, restoration, worship, and the often-overlooked gift of the Holy Spirit. She teaches you not just to survive these end times, but to thrive in them with Kingdom impact.

I've had the privilege of interviewing hundreds of people who have experienced Heaven, and I can tell you that Julie stands apart as a Kingdom leader of the highest caliber. Her heart beats in rhythm with God's purposes. Her faithfulness to His calling is exceptional. And her willingness to be transparent about her own struggles—from surviving domestic abuse to losing her job, from medical crises to the painful journey of watching some of her family walk away from faith—makes her message all the more powerful and accessible.

Julie doesn't write from an ivory tower. She writes from the trenches, where she has ministered for years through Cascade Christian Writers, ARMS (Abuse Recovery Ministry Services), and now through her expanding work in her own ministry. Her ministry encompasses abuse recovery, writing mentorship, speaking, and healing prayer. She leads with humility, serves with joy, and pours out the living water that flows through her—just as God showed her friend Patti in a vision: Julie as a pitcher that pours and pours yet never runs dry.

What makes this book particularly timely is Julie's willingness to address the controversial and the supernatural. She doesn't shy away from discussing spiritual warfare, deliverance, the gift of tongues, or the reality of Hell. In an age when much of the church has become sanitized and comfortable, Julie boldly proclaims the full counsel of God. She's moved from her conservative roots into a deeper understanding of the Holy Spirit's power—not through rebellion, but through obedience to God's clear leading.

The 'Pause & Ponder' sections at the end of each chapter turn reading into transformation. Julie doesn't just want you informed; she wants you activated. She's asking the hard questions: What blocks are preventing your mission? What do you need to surrender? How will you live differently knowing that Heaven is real and time is short?

As you read *Routed to Heaven*, you'll discover that this book addresses a critical gap in Christian literature. We have plenty of books about Heaven, and we have books about finding your purpose, but few successfully bridge both worlds. Julie has done exactly that—showing us not only the glorious reality that awaits but also how that reality should radically alter how we live today.

I've watched Julie pour herself into this work with a dedication that can only come from someone who has truly died, met Jesus face to face, and returned with a message. She writes with the urgency of one who knows time is short and the authority of one who has glimpsed eternity. Her practical tools for overcoming blocks are born from her own hard-won victories and her years of ministry helping others find freedom.

Julie is more than an author—she is a spiritual warrior, outfitted with the full armor of God and ready for battle. Whether she's leading abuse recovery groups, mentoring writers, praying healing over the sick, or penning words that carry the weight of Heaven, she operates from one central truth: Jesus is Lord, Heaven is real, and we were made for eternal impact.

I count it among my greatest blessings to know Julie and to call her friend. She has inspired me, challenged me, and reminded me what wholehearted devotion to Jesus looks like in action. I have no doubt that this book will do the same for you.

Read this book if you've ever wondered whether your life has greater purpose. Read it if you're stuck in fear, grief, or unforgiveness. Read it if you need hope that Heaven is real and worth everything. Read it if you're ready to stop merely existing and start living with the end—and the Beginning—in view.

The Master is calling. The harvest is ripe. And as Julie so beautifully demonstrates through her own journey and the journeys of those she's gathered here, when we surrender completely to His purposes and live with Heaven in view, our lives become extraordinary testimonies of His grace and power.

Don't just read this book—let it transform you. Let it awaken you to the eternal reality that surrounds us. Let it propel you into the mission God has uniquely designed for you.

Heaven is watching. Your time is now.

Randy Kay
Author of *Heaven Stormed, Heaven Encounters,* and *Revelations From Heaven*, Host of *Revelations From Heaven YouTube,* and Pastor of *My Family*

Heaven Calls

In the year that King Uzziah died, I saw the Lord, high and exalted, seated on a throne; and the train of his robe filled the temple. Above him were seraphim, each with six wings: With two wings they covered their faces, with two they covered their feet, and with two they were flying. And they were calling to one another: 'Holy, holy, holy is the Lord Almighty; the whole earth is full of his glory.' At the sound of their voices the doorposts and thresholds shook and the temple was filled with smoke. 'Woe to me!' I cried. 'I am ruined! For I am a man of unclean lips, and I live among a people of unclean lips, and my eyes have seen the King, the Lord Almighty.'

Then one of the seraphim flew to me with a live coal in his hand, which he had taken with tongs from the altar. With it he touched my mouth and said, 'See, this has touched your lips; your guilt is taken away and your sin atoned for.' Then I heard the voice of the Lord saying, 'Whom shall I send? And who will go for us?'

And I said, 'Here am I. Send me!'

Isaiah 6:1-8

Ushered In

Once upon a time, she stood in front of Him, head bowed to her chest in awe and respect. He had already lifted her off her knees and now raised her chin with His fingers and looked deeply into her eyes, compassion overspilling from His own. 'My child, your journey has just started. Get wisdom. Though it cost all you have, get understanding. Do not just write it, say it. Bring healing and Heaven to my people.' (1)

Her eyes filling at both the unspeakable honor of being chosen and the deep love shining from His face—her hands shaking—she stammered her very next thought. 'Y-Yes, my Lord. But h-how?'

He stepped back, waving His hand, and with a surge from her toes to face that she felt to her very soul, she stepped back at the sudden lightweight additions wrapping around her body. Her eyes flew down, widening. The new laced-up boots shouted sturdiness for the most rugged trails, and would stabilize her weak ankles over all terrain. The belt around her waist glowed, shiny with braided light. She understood that it would stay radiant—as long as she sought and spoke the very truths He imparted. People would see her Belt of Truth first, might even question it—and concentrate there as they discerned her words and actions.

It would become a major focus to ensure that the belt stayed in top condition.

A plate of gleaming metal covered her chest—guarding very essential organs. She understood then that He would protect her. Although the writing on the plate was upside down, she read it anyway. She whispered, 'No weapon formed against you shall prosper.' (2)

She stretched her arm out. It now held a lightweight, sturdy shield—firmly connected but seemingly alive, silver rippling. As she clenched it tightly, raising it higher, it sent prickles of energy up her arm that traveled through her whole body. She would draw essential strength from the shield—as long as she followed through with consistent undertaking.

In her other hand, a flaming sword with a double edge rested. She lifted it in wonderment—it outshone the most eye-catching earthly lightsaber. Electric warmth traveled through her hand, up her arm, around her body, somehow blending in with the shield's energetic strength in perfect unity. No pain—just an invigorating spark—and a swift confidence that she could accomplish whatever He asked. And she would. With divine assistance, the sword would anticipate and prepare her for each battle ahead. In awe, she whispered. 'May I battle well, my Lord. For You alone.'

'You will battle for their souls, bringing eternal healing,' He replied very gently. She nodded quickly, drawn to His eyes with deep blue ocean depths and flames in the pupils. Her smile reached her ears. His seemed to wrap around eternity.

On her legs? Her usual denim. She quirked one eyebrow. Really? Perhaps she should ask for knee pads. Or at least shin guards! Didn't her legs also need protection? Reading her thoughts, He grinned. 'You won't need those.'

'Alright. I trust You. Always.'

And then with another wave of His hand, she felt a light weight cover the top of her head and roll down her neck, yet somehow leaving her face open and free to the warmth around her. 'You've worn this for a long time, daughter. This is not just your protection, but a reminder that your identity is in me. Not in what you've done, nor what has happened to you. You belong to Me. I will guide. Now, Julie—go.'

***

After I returned from Heaven the first time (you can read the story in Chapter One), each day and moment became more precious. Time is short, I knew. And I still needed to stir up impact.

But what exactly did that mean?

Most readers admit to skipping book introductions. I tend to read them—if they capture my attention. And after mulling over what to place in this introduction section for a couple of months, God returned me to Heaven. My armor-outfitting experience there quickly became specific, vivid, and impactful—and this time, I saw Jesus! We met in the big meadow with a nearby tree. And I still do not remember a hug, but I know I will get that first someday because He knows what that means to me. I despised returning, earth-bound once again. But obviously, I did, and as I opened my eyes and bolted to a sitting position, He was repeating, 'No weapon formed against you will prosper…' and I was speaking it aloud in tandem. A beautiful, transcendent duet. And then He whispered, 'There's your introduction.'

Yes, Sir! Oh wait, including the 'once upon a time'?

Sure enough—cliché as it is.

I returned from my first trip to Heaven with only partial memories. Truly I thought the events I chronicled in Chapter One held the full experience. A fast trip to Heaven resulted in some incredible sights and His quickly spoken sentence highlighting my Heaven-Minded Mission Manifesto.

You will learn that He revealed more of my journey at very distinct and needed times.

I hope as you read this book, you will choose to start living very intentionally in this last season of days, as I have.

Because He did not just call me. He selected you too. We hold the title of 'His Squad' in this last season of days. He specifically is raising us up, and if you are on earth, you still have a job to accomplish. He expects results from me and you.

Each chapter includes a newly-written near-death or afterlife account. I interviewed the people and wrote most of them, but a few are the original account from the author—the only edits sought to provide clarity, gather more of the story, or match the format of the rest of the book.

Let's chat about story genuineness—always a question when people cite accounts regarding the supernatural. I am super pleased that most of the stories hailed from people I know personally or am professionally affiliated with.

It is very important to me that I am only passing on the truth. As a directive not just from my Lord but as a personal value, keeping my Belt of Truth shiny remains essential. The stories within this book have been verified in at least one (but many have more than one) of the following ways:

- I personally know and have a relationship with the person reporting the story.
- I have a professional and ongoing relationship with the person through a trusted organization.
- The person is closely connected to a person I have a relationship with.
- I spent time with the reporting person, getting to know them as I prayed and discerned.

God brought clarity as I moved through the collection process. With some stories, He waved the yellow pause flag or full stop red flag. I followed His direction and did not include those stories. And other green-flag stories await the second book.

Each story included has the go-ahead not just from me, but from Him.

After each account is a reflection from me about a topic. The first few chapters focus on the initial tools you will need as you seek to create your Mission Manifesto for living intentionally. We then move into chapters of ten specific blocks that may occur as you seek answers. I hope you choose to pray about these potential blocks and any others God suggests. Sometimes we think there are no hurdles, when in actuality, they exist. I ran into that little blip in my own journey. But God knew.

The last part of the book includes ten tools I encourage you to utilize when determining and carrying out your Manifesto. He spoke clearly to me throughout—I can honestly say that I only remain a vessel here. A go-between to vault these messages to you. All Bible verses are sourced using the NIV version unless otherwise indicated. There is also a Companion Study Guide for either personal or group study, if you wish to go deeper.

Think of your Heaven-Focused Mission Manifesto as a personal mission or value statement. It is flexible. It may include your core values or your beliefs—which provide the 'whys.' It may mention your gifts and talents (see Chapter Two). Or perhaps you want it to just state your focus or goals.

It is important to write it down because as you move into implementation, you will need to not just pray about opportunities—but much as a board of directors might do—you will also desire to ensure that all your activities fit your direction. We are told in James 2:15-26 that our purpose should determine our priorities. This is especially helpful as others start asking you to do many things!

Implementation should include all three components: Asking, Seeking, and Knocking (the action part). (3) In James 1:5, He assures us that when we ask for wisdom, He provides. He promises to answer—in His timing, of course, but then expects you (within the gifts and talents He provided you) to follow through in honoring Him and others through your Mission Manifesto.

If you are curious, or desire an example, here is mine: **To impact lives for the Kingdom by bringing Heaven, hope, and healing to others.** Everything I work toward and accomplish passes that test of connecting to my Manifesto.

I assume you chose this book because you know the Lord and want to either read about people's experiences or learn what He has for you next. But if you do not know the Lord as your Savior, please still continue reading. Jeremiah 29:11-13 says, "For I know the plans I have for you,' declares the Lord, 'plans to prosper you and not to harm you, plans to give you hope and a future. Then you will call on me and come and pray to me, and I will listen to you. You will seek me and find me when you seek me with all your heart."

Long my favorite verse, it is wildly appropriate for this book and for my journey this past year. I will be praying for you as you proceed.

'The beginning of wisdom is this: Get wisdom. Though it cost all you have, get understanding' (Proverbs 4:7).

… 'Do not be afraid, Daniel. Since the first day that you set your mind to gain understanding and to humble yourself before your God, your words were heard, and I have come in response to them' (Daniel 10:12).

'My people are destroyed from lack of knowledge' (Hosea 4:6).

PART ONE: FOUNDATIONAL FRAMEWORK

Chapter One

He Carried Me Back From Heaven

Julie Bonn Blank

It started with a pounding heartbeat that I could not calm. Lightheadedness made me woozy. My Apple Watch medical alert flashed red numbers. My mouth felt filled with cotton. Some body functions failed, and as my ability to think plummeted, a black cloud hovered around my vision.

Alone, I stumbled around the house—and clearly heard the Lord tell me to treat it like an allergic reaction.

I had not changed anything recently in my intake except to clean up my diet. I doubted this supposed allergy. Reactions, although common to me, usually presented much differently.

'This is an allergic reaction.' I heard it distinctly again, in my head. I shuffled to my backpack purse in the kitchen and downed most of my oral rescue meds. Then I returned to the couch, longing to lie prone. Around me, the walls shifted and my bookshelves grew wavy. I felt sleepy—but each time I started to tilt my head to a couch pillow, I heard, 'Do *not* go to sleep.' I smothered the yearning and pulled my weak muscles to a sitting position four times. Turning on the television, I tried to focus on the news to stay awake. But each channel brought an odd feeling – like I had seen all the broadcasts before.

I verbally answered the Lord twice. Boy, good thing my neighbors could not hear me talking to myself.

The effectiveness of the meds started slacking off on the job. Maybe I should call 911. I tried to text my husband, Bill—failing because my hands trembled so badly. I finally sent it in two text messages. 'Really sick. Might be reaction. Come home?'

Calling 911 drifted through my mind again. For the second time, I argued myself out of it. Surely the meds would kick in soon. For several years now, I had fought allergic reactions and often severe ones—certainly, I could handle this one as well. I started texting my daughter and my parents but became unable to finish. My whole body had started shaking like my garden boxes during earthquake rumblings.

Weird. This felt like some kind of shock.

'Julie, treat this as an allergic reaction.' Out loud this time—and much more insistent. Now I grew confused—I swallowed my pills! Hadn't He seen me? It dawned slowly through the thick fog my brain resided in. God meant my EpiPen!

I rummaged through my purse, finally dumping the contents on the counter. My EpiPen rolled under a barstool. The plants on my windowsill started to dance.

I had never stuck myself with the injectable before. I usually made it to the ER in time. But I finally admitted that something felt different this occasion. I sensed myself balancing on the edge of a humongous cliff, with one leg dangling over. And He Who Spoke maintained an insistence and firmness in His tone I had never heard before.

The devil had fought to take me and my three ministries down for a few years now. He attempted almost everything possible. Except for annihilating me.

Was this his work?

I scrambled for my reading glasses as I could not see the instructions on the EpiPen sticker. I stabbed myself in the thigh—right through my jeans. Because the instructions said I could. Right?

I counted to ten aloud, slurring my words, and yanked it out. I tossed it on the side table, reminding myself to move it later for safety. Once a mother ... right?

A few minutes later, my heart rate calmed a bit and the bookshelves stopped weaving. But I became unable to remain upright. Who attached twenty-pound weights to my legs? The trembling never stopped—and my eyes still refused to focus.

Time to punch three numbers on my phone.

The 911 operator wanted more information. Unable to form a coherent sentence, I managed 'Have allergies. Took EpiPen,' and her pace picked up. She assured me that medics were only a couple of miles away.

The EMT guy arrived at the front door. I met him there, but not without a serious attempt to collapse on our stairs.

'I have a better idea. Take my arm. I can treat you better out here than on your stairs.'

As foggy as everything remained, I clearly heard his words.

He heaved me up, surrounded me with his arms, walked me outside, pushed me up into the ambulance, and strapped me down.

I hate being strapped down or confined—but it barely registered. Gratefulness filled me.

No voice told me to stay awake. I passed out at least four or five times. Each time, it started with a gray cloud when my eyes closed, then faded to a pinpoint black.

Psalm 23 ran through my head multiple times each time

I regained consciousness. I tried to focus on only that. Despite my faith and the care God had provided so far, fear continued to rise. I had not slipped off the cliff yet but understood how close I had wavered.

And still dangled.

'Though I walk through the valley of the shadow of death, you are with me, Oh Lord. Dear Jesus, my family has already had so much loss. My kids lost their dad. My husband lost his first wife. My parents lost their son. My brother, his brother. I need to stay here, please. Heal me, Jesus. Though I walk through the valley of the shadow of death. I will not fear… I will not fear… I will not fear.'

The first time I opened my eyes after a fade-to-black, I asked the EMTs' names. After all, they had asked for my phone wallet and knew mine—no need to be rude. Each time I awoke, our cul-de-sac trees moved in the breeze outside the window. 'Why are we still at my house?'

The ambulance grew small, and everywhere I looked, shiny metal gleamed. The walls pressed in more.

I wanted to cry—but energy quickly shortened as my body drained resources. Romi drew blood out of a vein in my hand, told his partner to run a lab test, and administered Benadryl and steroids but never really answered me. Or rather, I likely passed out again before he could.

When I awoke again, Romi noted my watch flashing and grabbed my wrist. He struggled to get my arm out of my sweater to get the cuff on my other arm. I blacked out halfway through that effort.

He later told me that he hesitated to administer more epinephrine because my heart already sped along like a commuter train on the way to work. And I could not think coherently enough to tell him that my heart usually gallops with allergic reactions in the initial stages. Epi brings it down.

Each time I headed to passing-out mode, he called my name and asked questions, sometimes jostling my shoulder or arm. I mumbled back before fading again, halfway through my sentence.

At one point, the driver apparently popped back to help. I did not see him, but the voice differed this time. Again, gray hovered at the edges of my vision. 'What do you do for work, Julie?'

I tried to explain my calling in writing, overseeing Cascade Christian Writers, advocating for domestic violence victims and a goal to bring hope and healing to all traumatized people.

He chuckled. 'You aren't under any stress at all!'

Answering their questions took a great deal of effort and focus. My eyes closed, and I felt my head fall to the side yet again.

But this time, there was no grayish-black—only a semi-solid gold cloud. What was that? I tilted my head like a pet hopeful for a treat. God gave me the sometimes-burdened bequest of intense curiosity, much to other people's chagrin. Trying to unpuzzle this dullish gold cloud quickly became my new focus.

Noting a still silence, peace flowed around me and through me—usually I feel a bit quiet-opposed. But you know how muted the outside world becomes when wearing a good pair of earplugs or noise-cancelling earphones? That is the closet description I can provide. Stark stillness filled the environment—so vast that it felt gigantic. I could not even hear a sigh, a yawn, or a breath—but then again, maybe I was not breathing.

I felt bubbled in soundproof, soft cotton. Cocooned in warmth, enveloped somehow and yet not enclosed. The claustrophobia from the ambulance melted away. Metal replaced with silk. It felt a comfortable 73-75 degrees.

Rays of light sprang up behind the gold cloud. They reached far and wide with brilliance and multiple layers of strength. I felt they received a calling—a mission they joyfully hastened to fill. They danced.

Staring at the gold cloud that was a bit solid yet bordered with shifting, scalloped edges, I noted movement behind it. Shapes. Slowly, the cloud faded a bit, and the figures became more prominent. People!

A smile simmered—an urge to shout and say, 'Hello there!' I, the extrovert, prioritized walking over to meet them.

But when I tried to step forward, two living, breathing squares of jeweled glass snapped into place, blocking my view. They fell from the sides—met in the middle. Came from above—settled on the ground. As I describe this, it is the first time I remember the ground. Lucious grass tickled my toes with velvety softness. The panels before me touched, but never settled into stillness.

I do not remember blinking as they danced. There was no desire or need to blink.

The colors mimicked mostly orange from the light shining behind, but also yellow and pink with faint purple. The triangular, individual pieces moved in a kaleidoscope pattern. A flower flashed within the glass, then another popped up—with white pearls and back onyx embedded, shifting, moving, spinning. The flowers held no mouth on their pretty faces yet smiled at me. They welcomed me in a beautiful, synchronized routine created just for me.

The colors were unlike any seen before, my eyes fixated on the radiant circus performing in front of me—a piece of astounding art indeed.

I tried to step forward but could not. Greeting the people was not in the plan after all. Not a good sign! But unable to generate sadness, I just felt star-blasted. And curious.

Awareness flooded me finally. I did not stand alone. Someone stood nearby. Those paneled gates were not performing for me. With a mighty wave of recognition and awe, I realized that Jesus stood to my right.

Gracious, how long had He stood there? How could I not have known? I wanted to turn my head and see Him face-to-face, throw myself into His arms, fall to my knees, sing praises. Thank Him. I had no idea which should come first!

But unable to do any of that, I stood frozen.

'Not yet, Julie,' He confirmed in a rich, beautiful baritone voice that still gives me shivers when I remember. It is hard to explain how safe I felt when I heard His voice. How singled out and adored. How memorable and unique. Everything I had journeyed through, reached for, strived for, longed for—lived *here*. My home was here! This was where I was created to reside.

I knew I could talk and walk with Him 24/7 and it would never be enough. That goofy Earth had never held my true home.

Then, my Lord grew sad. I felt the weight tug in my heart. He said, 'Go! There is still so much work to be done.'

He was sending me away! Without even a hug!

The next words bubbling up were, 'Yes, Lord,' but as soon as He said, 'Go,' I headed backward in what felt like a vacuumed vortex at a hundred miles per hour. Yet I heard the rest of the sentence. Although I never felt Him pick me up or an initial touch, He held me on the way back down.

Back in the ambulance, I opened my eyes. Romi turned away from pushing more steroids into my IV, scrambling to find something. 'Go now! Quickly!' he called to his partner.

My gaze moved to the heart paddles next to me, waiting. Having previously seen the damage they cause on other people—a fuzzy thankfulness filled me.

My right hand, the one closest to the silver wall of the ambulance, felt snugly held in a slightly larger one, although no one was there.

'Hi there!' Romi called cheerfully as he turned back. I believe my lip twitched, but I could not answer. All my faculties felt far away—creating a disconnected jolt. My whole body felt stunned.

I grew Earth-chilly very fast. And I felt a bit like one does when waking after sleeping a long time but not exactly. More like one might feel waking up from being dead, I suppose. As I struggled to adjust, my right hand was gently, yet firmly, squeezed. Turning my head, I saw nothing but the side of the ambulance again. My Lord had stayed with me! I wanted to ask Romi if he felt Jesus there too. Did those who accompanied me know about Heaven?

My body continued to struggle. I passed out more times in the ambulance, on the gurney in the hospital hallway, and in the room when I received one—but I did not visit Jesus in Heaven again. Instead, He hung out with me. My head-dropping experiences returned to the gray cloud, then pinpoint black.

When the medical team finally stabilized me and I could talk, I jabbered about orange glass panels, flowers, and my Lord to Bill, who had just arrived. I could not believe where I had been.

A few days later, my primary doctor's office confirmed my flatlining premiere.

Recovery from an afterlife experience does not register on the scale of easy peasy. But Jesus did not leave when I was discharged from the hospital—I felt His imminent presence for the next week. He knew I would hanker for Him and He prepped me. When I grew ready, His constant companionship slipped away, although I still feel Him close often in prayer, scripture reading, and worship—and now extremely close again as I obey in writing this book, praying over others, and accepting prayer from believers who walk close to Him.

I did not hear the praise, worship, songs, angels or loved ones as others have in Heaven. That I remember, anyway. The only thing I heard in the deep resonating womb of silence was His voice, which is wildly appropriate. There remained no doubt where He wanted my focus.

Lately, He assures me that we discussed more things. As I write these chapters, He brings other memories—and those delicious tidbits are included within. I am so excited that He gave me permission to share more happenings with you.

Reflection With Julie: Magnetic Megaphone

I have found some near-death and afterlife experiences featuring God speaking aloud. But most mention that if God, angels, or others in Heaven speak, it occurs telepathically. This makes sense when you consider our acute hearing there and the thousands of conversations, praises, and prayers that transpire simultaneously. Some friends say they heard it all at once, yet it was not convoluted, confusing, or irritating. Each conversation, song, and prayer made sense. What an incredible God we serve!

When my allergic reaction first threatened, He spoke in my head—and I knew His voice. When it became urgent, it resonated out loud. He had to get through to me somehow!

The Lord spoke aloud to me first in my late twenties. I had curled up in a zone of desperation after a life-impacting car accident. My husband at the time was permanently disabled—our three kids basically had two disabled parents. At least for a few years. I struggled to freelance and pay our bills, provide caregiving, keep my sanity, be a good mama—all in tremendous, daily pain. There were times I depended on pain pills to get through. I still depend on my chiropractor and massage therapist.

One day, I truly felt fed up. When catching a few minutes alone in the restroom, I stared in the mirror as tears poured down my cheeks.

And aloud, I heard, 'Julie, you are going to be OK.'

My tears stopped instantly. What? I looked around the bathroom nervously. My eyes flew back to the mirror as a giggle bubbled out. Sure enough, He had spoken. One of my kids then knocked at the door, asking who was in there with me!

When I returned from Heaven, I hit a deep-study of scriptures and researched Heaven books with every spare moment—often up to four hours a day. Keeping a spreadsheet, which grew to a massive workbook, I recorded specific events as well as things Jesus, God, the Holy Spirit, or angels voiced to people during their Heaven experiences.

I searched for mutuality and potential messages in those commonalities for all of us. I ached to know God more deeply and not just from the scriptures—although, of course, that played a huge part.

Lost cause! At least His vocal portions. I still add new accounts. Many commonalities surface as I practice investigative journalism. But it turns out that our Lord speaks just like us. He says what He needs to say to each individual and appears, at times, to even vary the linguistics. And like us writers, He sometimes says a bunch. He has voiced, 'Hey,' to me and to others. He uses current and past slang—although of course it is never derogatory. One of my online friends wonders whether He speaks in the dialect of Bible Times or other time periods to people from those eras.

That would not surprise me at all.

This last Sunday in church, when I questioned why He seemed quiet about a certain situation, He immediately said silently, 'I have answered you two ways. First, this way, and secondly, this way…'

Sometimes, it seems so hard to listen.

As you consider how God wants you to live intentionally in this season, know that He may also speak to you through His Word, and the wisdom of other people who walk close to Him. I encourage you to discern. He will never advise you to dismiss others (unless it is in the form of setting boundaries for your own health) and He will not instruct in any way against His scriptures. Pay close attention, weighing what you hear. Consider the following verses:

'…and that you may love the Lord your God, listen to his voice, and hold fast to him. For the Lord is your life…' (Deuteronomy 30:20, second part).

'Listen, listen to me, and eat what is good, and you will delight in the richest of fare. Give ear and come to me; listen, that you may live. I will make an everlasting covenant with you, my faithful love promised to David' (Isaiah 55:2-3, second part of verse 2).

'I will listen to what God the Lord says; he promises peace to his people, his faithful servants—but let them not turn to folly' (Psalm 85:8).

Numerous verses in the Bible talk about listening to/for

Him, using our knowledge and research—and seeking wisdom from others. I use the following method to help discern His voice from my desires.

First, I spend time in prayer about the specific question. Second, I pursue all the verses I can find that may apply (often, Bible folks were in similar straits). Third, I connect with a circle of people who know me well and love the Lord. I often find that they all agree (or remain neutral) when a particular move is right for me. Sometimes this is a different set of people, depending on the question. And always, nuggets of impact and wise words occur within the process that I heart-hold. Fourth, I take my time, if the circumstances allow that. That registers at annoying at times, but it is not always necessary. Obviously, in situations of Him speaking, medical emergencies or perhaps a time that He provides the same message over and over again—I do not need to consult with others.

I just need to obey. You know how that goes.

My dad taught my siblings and me that God answers 'yes,' 'no,' and 'maybe.' If I am not getting a firm yes or no, it is likely a maybe, which means, 'Wait a while. This is not the right time, place, people, or circumstances.' All four of those components should be present to make a decision a correct one. In my youth, this often became a frustrating process. But in my adulthood, and perhaps because of where some of my decisions sent me, remembering this serves me well.

We were never meant to navigate Earth alone. The answers we chase, the direction we crave, the peace our souls long for—all of it is found in Him. We were all created to reside with Him in Heaven forever—even those of us who have sometimes charged ahead in our earthly lives without Him. When we choose a route without seeking His counsel, forward gears may still grind because He is gracious, but they will never quite settle into park. Instead, we feel only restlessness, an incompleteness—a sense that we misplaced something. Eventually, it might even roll us backward. When we pause, lean in, and invite Him into the process, clarity surfaces. The pieces fit. Never doubt that He holds the map—and leads with wisdom, grace, and perfect timing.

'Plans fail for lack of counsel, but with many advisers they succeed' (Proverbs 15:2).

'My sheep listen to my voice; I know them, and they follow me' (John 10:27).

Pause & Ponder

1. Consider the ways God speaks to you.
2. Jot down how you discern His voice.

Chapter Two

I Talked To Jesus In Glory

Pam Farrel

I have Diabetes 1.5, which is rare and challenging to regulate. After dealing with consistently rising A1c for several years, my endocrinologist prescribed a new medication, but supply chain issues delayed it. I planned to start it after returning from a speaking engagement in Texas, so I packed only my current meds and headed to a conference for Christian Creatives.

During a flight layover, I felt excruciating shoulder pain. I bought some over-the-counter meds, but the pain worsened, causing severe nausea. I prayed for strength to reach the restroom and then barely made it to the plane. Upon arrival at my destination, my friend noticed my distress. 'I assume it's from carrying my backpack,' I assured her. 'I'll take some Tylenol PM tonight and I'm sure it will be better tomorrow.'

But it wasn't.

I pushed through the conference with a variety of over-the-counter meds, ice, and prayer. The ministry team prayed for me, and I received temporary relief during worship and my speaking sessions. Grateful for God's grace, I completed the work.

As I returned home, the pain became unbearable. I could hardly carry my bags and needed help at the airport. When my husband, Bill, picked me up, I was sobbing.

At sunrise the next morning, we visited urgent care. The X-rays showed a break of my upper rib, which needed rest.

Despite the stronger meds provided, the pain persisted, and my gut blocked up. My system became toxic. One hot day, I felt freezing under several blankets. Dizziness and nausea overwhelmed me. My heart raced, and I gasped, 'I think I'm having a heart attack!'

Interestingly, I didn't feel fear. Or anxiety. Instead—I felt an overwhelming urge to pray.

Bill looked concerned. 'I'm taking you to the ER.'

But I felt a supernatural peace.

On our arrival, Bill explained my family history of heart attacks. They moved me to ICU. Two doctors arrived. One told me to slow my breathing.

I tried, to no avail. 'I can't!'

Bill added, 'She's diabetic.'

I had developed Diabetic Ketoacidosis (DKA), which occurs when the body can't produce enough insulin—leading to dangerous ketone buildup. I was quickly intubated, put on eleven IV lines, and placed in a medically induced coma, which is safer than a diabetic coma but still risky. Fortunately, I received immediate care, avoiding the grim statistics of DKA fatalities.

Around 4 a.m., the doctors sent Bill home. 'Get some rest. We are stabilizing her with the medically induced coma. When she wakes—if she wakes—she will need you rested.' The doctor tried to reassure him, 'I'll do my best to keep her alive. I'll call if anything changes.'

Reluctantly, he left and drove home. He told me later that he prayed through tears. 'Dear God, I know Pam will be okay, whether she goes to You or stays. I trust Your will. But I and the kids and grandkids love her, so Father, please, don't let my phone ring tonight.'

After a little rest and a lot of prayer, Bill reached out to our sons. Their reactions varied—some wept, some expressed anger, while others declared faith, trusting God for a miracle. Bill then contacted other family, friends, and colleagues, sending requests for prayer far and wide.

When entering the coma, I was ushered into God's presence. Words fall short in describing the beauty, majesty, and peace I encountered. There was no fear—only a sense of divine tranquility, flawless beauty, and ultimate peace beyond understanding. It was like a black velvet canvas shimmering with golden light—living, radiant light that reflected God's presence.

I saw thousands of angels, radiant and graceful, dancing before Heaven's gates. The angels' beautiful wings sparkled with shimmering gold. I felt timeless—lost in the splendor.

I sensed Jesus—my Wonderful Counselor, Mighty God, Everlasting Father, and Prince of Peace. Though I did not see Him physically, I felt His presence all around me, wrapping me in peace and provision.

God's Word became vivid and alive as cherished verses seemed to materialize. In His presence, the truth of God's Word became dynamic—the Scriptures came to life. Verses like John 1:1 filled my soul. 'In the beginning was the Word, and the Word was with God, and the Word was God.'

It felt as though I was standing beside Joseph when the angel declared Jesus' birth.

I was not just with God—I was enveloped by Him. It reminded me that He had been with me—through my conference, illness, the ER, the ICU, and now in Heaven. My soul recognized the Savior I had known and pursued all my life—yet He was far greater than I ever imagined.

My heart overflowed with awareness of Him, my Immanuel. I spoke to Him not with my voice but through a deep mind-to-mind connection. I felt the full magnificence of God—Father, Son, and Spirit.

We held many conversations on a wide variety of topics. I pondered my eternal destiny several times.

'Am I dead, Lord? Is this Heaven?' I felt very content—

acknowledging that I had fought the good fight. I was ready to stay in His presence, if that was His will. I praised Him for my family's faith, confident of their strength without me. Though I longed to meet my soon-to-be-born grandsons and pour more faith into my kin, I trusted God completely. His will, not mine.

Jesus assured me that I was alive, showing me the closed gates of Heaven. 'It's not yet your time to enter.'

As I looked around again, I marveled. Dancing angels transformed into a golden mountain range with rivers of gold flowing down. The hands of people I loved gathered endless treasure at the base.

'What does that mean, Jesus?'

He reminded me of my daily prayer of Ephesians 3:20 at 3:20 p.m: 'Now to Him who is able to carry out His purpose and do superabundantly more than all that we dare ask or think (infinitely beyond our greatest prayers, hopes, or dreams), according to His power that is at work within us.'

His voice warmed respectfully. 'This vision is a glimpse of the abundant answers to those prayers from His Heavenly perspective.'

Jesus's presence was a restful reminder of Psalm 16:11. 'You make known to me the path of life; you will fill me with joy in your presence, with eternal pleasures at your right hand.'

While I marveled at the beauty and glory around me, I felt only joy and bliss—knowing this place offered eternal pleasure, ultimate contentment, and fulfillment.

'Lord, this is so incredible. Are you preparing me to stay with you? I could live in this love.'

I sensed the divine response, 'You do live in my love! You have the fruit of my Spirit.' Images of love, joy, peace, and more filled my mind. Then He said, 'But I have more for you to do. It's time to go back.'

My eyes flickered open, and I returned to the earthly realm, in the ICU. I felt both grateful to be alive and humbled by my time in His glorious presence. The beeping machines signaled my return to consciousness, alerting the nurses. My mind raced. Why couldn't I talk? I was just communicating with Jesus.

A nurse rushed in, surprised. 'You probably want to know what happened.' She explained the ventilator and that my hands were restrained to prevent me from pulling the tubes out.

I gestured for the whiteboard I saw across the room and wrote a happy face and heart with an arrow pointing to her. To my surprise, the nurse teared up. 'No one ever thanks us.'

Just then, Bill walked in, his relief evident as he grinned. 'Thank you, Jesus! You're back! You're going to be okay! You are writing and bossing people around! It's you!' Our hearts rejoiced as he embraced me, kissed my forehead, and prayed thanksgiving over me.

I had 24 more hours on the ventilator to ponder the glorious experience. I asked Bill to take a photo with me holding the whiteboard that read, 'Thx for praying!' He sent it to my praying friends and family. I jotted a note asking Bill to set up my computer tablet to play worship music because worship had filled Heaven.

I knew my path ahead would lead to strength and recovery as I worshipped my way to wellness. Some of my first words to Bill, a day later, were, 'I love you. I need to share what God gave me while I was in a coma.'

Still, now a few years later, the first instant that I close my eyes, I again see those lovely golden angels and the gates of Heaven. Like the Apostle Paul, I say, 'I am hard pressed between the two. My desire is to depart and be with Christ, for that is far better. But to remain in the flesh is more necessary on your account.' (4)

My first quiet time at home once I was released captured the purposeful marching orders from God's throne to my heart: 'For You delivered me from death, even my feet from stumbling, to walk before God in the light of life.' (5) I felt Him say, 'I am not finished with you yet. I want you to walk before Me in the light of the living—to bring My life-giving messages of hope, peace, joy, and salvation far and wide.'

That confirmed purpose and motivation is the beat of my heart, and in every breath I take.

Reflection With Julie: Priceless Purpose

You will note a common theme with Pam's story and my story. His work is incomplete—so we skedaddled back to Earth to finish the job. Many others in the 'near-death or afterlife club' share this.

He needs you on the job, too, or you would not be here. He said to me, 'There is still *so* much to be done.' It is not just an assignment for us and others who have returned. Your commission may not focus directly on winning souls—but He needs you on the time clock of your specific calling during this season. Perhaps you feel already rooted, or you are just now probing. Maybe you thought you were set—and are now beginning to puzzle. Perhaps whispers of 'the last days' are creating fresh yearning to live with more eternal intention.

Prepare for anything as you and He walk together—and as you read this book. Most I have met who return from Heaven experience a profound examination of their lives, and often a new focused target. I jog along right next to you—as I am still discovering all that God intends for me as well. More revelations arrive each day!

You can obtain this target focus without punching your

Heaven ticket. I want to help you thrive—live like you have traveled to Heaven and back and now are pursuing and enjoying the unique and (maybe startling) changes that Jesus has for you.

Let's work on it together.

God says to offer ourselves to Him as those brought from death to life. Trust me, when you travel there and back, this new perspective directly from Heaven could easily become an obsession. My day feels largely askew if I fail to complete my two or so hours of scripture time.

How do we start? Well, we all have gifts and talents, and using them equals worship. It is, in fact, the ultimate form of worship. And guess what, using them in Heaven also equals worship. He provided those gifts and talents to you for life! All of life! We will not pew-sit in Heaven all day, although there are gathering times. We will also rest, although there is no official dark night schedule. God excels in creativity, my friends.

My spiritual gifts assessments remained consistent through the years. In youth group, I landed at fifty percent leadership and fifty percent mercy—a combination I felt worked well. Shouldn't every leader display mercy? Seemed basic to me.

Twenty-five years later, I tested the same. I must also note that I attended a conservative church both times and likely skimmed over any questions relating to anything slightly woo-woo. You know, like prophecy.

I recently retested. After my trip to Heaven, exhortation, leadership, mercy and teaching are exactly even, with service one point behind. Prophecy and giving also show numbers this time, for the first time ever. It appears God added or enhanced gifts as part of my Heaven journey and afterwork. Perhaps a topic for a future chapter!

Personality tests are often somewhat skewed, especially

when someone hails from trauma or abuse. While leading abuse recovery groups, I sometimes see confusion when an attendee completes a test. I normally consider the section with the highest mark to be the prominent personality—sometimes one might have two areas somewhat even across. However, when someone experiences abuse, parts of their personality repress to survive. If they are still healing or still in abuse, I view close-to-even percentages across most or all the categories instead.

When I have grown to know someone or lead them in a group, my guess of their personality type is usually accurate, but I completely missed the mark with my now friend, Robyn, a long-term group member. For this round, we completed the animal personality test developed by Dr. John Trent and Gary Smalley. (6) And as she read her results (which were somewhat stretched across categories, but indicated a Golden Retriever as primary), her eyebrows scrunched and she started tapping her pen on the table. She looked up at me, frowning. 'This isn't me, though.'

'Tell me more about that.'

'I'm a Lion.'

A Lion is a natural-born leader. Was she sure? She seemed very fitting of a Golden Retriever, who is loyal, often compliant, and a peacemaker. Interesting!

Robyn continued, 'And I had a dream ten years ago. In the dream I went to visit my sister and when I walked in, this sickly-looking lion ran to me. The whole family kept asking 'Do you like our new golden retriever?' and I argued. I told them it was a Lion, not a Retriever—but no one believed me.'

Robyn had struggled with her very controlling and addicted husband for over thirty-two years, greatly subduing her true personality in order to survive. And sure enough, as she worked hard on healing, her inner Lion appeared in group.

Her ongoing personality tests also reflected those changes. She was not a Golden after all, but a very unhealthy Lion.

What a blessing it became to see her leadership skills fine-tune as she realized 'stuck' no longer defined her, and that she could choose good things, set boundaries, and heal that personality. I quickly encouraged her to use those gifts with confidence! As Robyn moves forward from group, God continues to set leadership opportunities in front of her. I am so excited to see where He guides her!

Years ago, I interviewed for a job position with a faith-based organization. They required all applicants to complete a personality test. As I visited the CEO's office afterward to discuss my results, as well as some weaknesses my personality often holds, I explained how I had worked on those things. He said thoughtfully, 'There is one thing these personality tests don't take into account.'

I bit the bait. I am Curious Julie, after all. 'What's that?'

'The working of the Holy Spirit in someone's life.'

So true!

Ephesians 4:16 says: 'From Him the whole body, joined and held together by every supporting ligament, grows and builds itself up in love, as each part does its work.' This indicates that when we do not use our talents and gifts, we deprive the family of God.

Consider also the following verses:

'All who are skilled among you are to come and make everything the Lord has commanded' (Exodus 35:10).

'For we are God's handiwork, created in Christ Jesus to do good works, which God prepared in advance for us to do' (Ephesians 2:10).

'Each of you should use whatever gift you have received to serve others, as faithful stewards of God's grace in its various forms' (1 Peter 4:10).

'Do not offer any part of yourself to sin as an instrument of wickedness, but rather offer yourselves to God as those who have been brought from death to life; and offer every part of yourself to him as an instrument of righteousness' (Romans 6:13).

Perhaps you completed personality tests and spiritual gifts assessments recently (I recommend both) and if so, you can discern how God gifted you. But if you have not, many years have flown by since, or if you think your results might have slipped sideways on your life-track due to trauma or drama, please implement this step as you seek to live with intention.

The beautiful truth is this: there is a piece of the Kingdom—of ministry, of mission—that only you can carry. A life only you can live, and an astonishing story only you can declare.

And you do not need to be a Lion or travel to Heaven and back to impact. Our Lord only needs your willingness—a readiness to believe your presence here is no accident waiting to happen. A belief that if He desired you at Home, He already would have summoned. Are you willing to leap into the space God designed with you in mind?

Beloved, no one else can take your place in His story. You matter—more than you realize. You are intended for impact. Your earthly work for Him is watched and adored by the Heavenlies. Live like daughters and sons of the Most High King.

Because that is what you are.

'What no eye has seen, what no ear has heard, and what no human mind has conceived—the things God has prepared for those who love him' (1 Corinthians 2:9).

'To one there is given through the Spirit a message of wisdom, to another a message of knowledge by means of the same Spirit, to another faith by the same Spirit, to another gifts of healing by that one Spirit, to another miraculous powers, to another prophecy, to another distinguishing between spirits, to another speaking in different kinds of tongues, and to still another the interpretation of tongues. All these are the work of one and the same Spirit, and he distributes them to each one, just as he determines' (1 Corinthians 12:8-10).

Pause & Ponder

1. With a space here on Earth that only you can fill, what might living intentionally mean for you?
2. Consider taking a personality test and spiritual gifts assessment if you have not completed those recently. (7) Contemplate things you enjoy doing. God gives us a desire for fulfilling His plan for us, even if we start out with shaking knees.
3. Write out any thoughts regarding your Heaven-Minded Mission Manifesto.

Chapter Three

I Returned To Earth For A Do-Over

Jeff Schmidt

I was seventeen when I made a foolish mistake. While obsessed with the power of driving, I received an opportunity one evening to drive a more powerful car than ever before. That entire day, alone at home, I had withstood deep nervousness—like something unfortunate waited just around the corner.

I should have taken it as the warning it was meant to be.

After visiting a friend, I headed home in this powerful vehicle. On a stretch of long road marked highway speed, I accelerated too quickly—beyond the limit.

I saw no other vehicles, but as I sped, others quickly appeared. Choosing to pass, I let up on the accelerator slowly just as I started to pass the first one, and—unaware of my rapid approach—the driver suddenly veered into my lane on the left.

Zero reaction time resulted.

Instantly, I left my body, soaring upward to a type of meeting room. I sensed, but not with my physical eyes, a round table surrounded by 'family-like' people. They waited to discuss my dire situation far below. They must be my deceased ancestors watching over me—it never occurred to me that they might be angels.

In this other dimension, time didn't matter. There was no sense of panic or frankly, any emotions at all—just a rational discussion and somewhat of an interview.

One spokesperson led, but the others also asked questions, and I believe I shared opinions.

Amazingly, I did not feel any judgement whatsoever, only concern. Stressing that the last thing I desired was to hurt or kill another person, I waited for my fate. At one point, I talked them out of taking responsibility, shouldering all the fault. The team seemed resolute in protecting me.

We sorted out all the possible scenarios of where I could have turned, and only one way—a hard right and off the road at high speed, if done in time—could have prevented the accident.

Was I getting a retake? Even if it meant losing control and flipping over several times, it seemed worth a shot. The accident was one hundred percent my fault. I felt ready to pay—even if it meant my death. Down there, it had recently rained. With wet grass on the hilly embankment to the right, maybe my car would slide this time instead of flip.

That rain was a gift from God, I told the group.

I *was* getting a retake! Once confident in our decision, I remember proclaiming 'I'm ready' and instantly landed back in my body with my hands positioned on the steering wheel.

No adjustment time arrived with me. I cranked the steering wheel to a rigid right and missed the other vehicle by only inches. Careening off the road almost sideways, time stood still. Graced with that downhill grass slope, I hung midair before landing the car hard on its side, the upright tires spinning. As suspected, the wet grass prevented an out-of-control landing. The car slipped instead of flipped.

I must have passed some life test to be given such mercy. This event caused me grow up in an instant! To this day, four-plus decades later, I believe death intended to strike but instead, history shifted.

A moment of accelerated fun could have resulted in a long period of sorrow and shame for more than one family. And for me—there may have very well been consequences eternally.

Taking full responsibility instantly caused, I believe, a reversal of my timeline. Had I argued with the committee or defended myself, the results would have tipped the other direction.

God gave me life as a gift—and I had almost squandered it. Instead, He appointed me a do-over.

Afterward, my life no longer felt like mine. With an eternal shift of priorities, I chose to dedicate my regained time to create a God-centered life. A momentum arose in me to discover spiritual truth, always feeling God's presence and grace in the process.

I focused on creating an attitude of becoming a filial child—one more attended with one's parents (God and the Lord) over oneself. Disappointments often led to deep repentance, creating a grateful environment for spiritual growth that effectively counteracted any complaint.

At times, dark spirits tried to attack with doubt and fear of the unknown. With my spiritual eyes, I often simply saw small dark beings with selfish intent. They aggressively attempted to pull my energy and the many days of efforts away. That became sufficient motivation to infiltrate the core of understanding of the deep heart of the Creator. Because, why were they so worried?

Preparing an attitude to properly connect each day, I overcame the dark attacks. Each day became an experience with the Creator beyond rituals or simple beliefs—more of a skin touch relationship with my own Father. Who, I discovered, is not an abstract God at all—but full of intense love, immense grace, and personal care. The basic sense that we are in the 'parent-child' relationship that Jesus taught is overwhelming when considered and experienced deeply.

I gave my utmost to live a life in response to God's call daily. Starting with being an empty vessel each morning without ego allowed me to maintain that relationship long term for the most part. My goal is to preserve that lifestyle to the end.

Abundant blessings follow the path of creating a filial child's life. Such a path is opposite of the world's ways and takes much effort daily to maintain—but is fulfilling to a great degree!

Long ago, animals were used as offerings—then the only begotten Son became an offering. Today we, with full sincere faith, recognize our true purpose when becoming a living offering, wherein, we voluntarily find a way to live for others on the frontlines, advancing God's plan.

My favorite line in hymns growing up was 'Here am I, send me, send me.' It captured the path of the plot I sought, always willing to die for God if needed. But in the end, those extreme conditions were not necessary.

I learned to give Him my first, purest form of love. My second love form to others in everyday experiences. As long as I journey sincerely in that child-parent relationship, serving others, practicing gratitude, and kicking those evil spirits to the curb when they show up, I feel great love and connection from Him. Regardless of my changing circumstances, this method brings me great spiritual fruit and maturity in God's love.

Reflection With Julie: Clashing Combat

As you work on your Mission Manifesto, remain aware of Satan's mostly-invisible minions. I have always called them that—call them whatever you prefer. The scriptures name them demons. And although some may prefer that I downplay this chapter, I must kindly refuse. God asked me for bold-speak throughout this book and I will obey, even about evil.

For if I do not, we would all miss a major component of why sometimes we cannot view our Heaven-Minded Mission Manifestos, or get stuck in fulfillment.

We often imagine spiritual warfare as a distant battle—a

clash of good and evil, or angels and demons somewhere out there. But more often, it shows up quietly and strategically: as the temptation we carry a weak spot for, doubt when we're about to speak truth, hesitation when we proceed with our calling, greed or pride when things are looking up, fatigue when we're ready to serve, division between team members when focused on purpose, shame when we feel unworthy, distraction when the Holy Spirit asks for pinpoint focus, conflict with needed unity, and numerous other examples.

It is not random!

You may have already guessed the exact time period I sustained a demon-enhanced hit, although I had been feeling very strong. Once when discerning a certain part of this book with someone, I took care of that one quick. It helped that the other person also recognized it. And then last night and today, when I determined to write this chapter.

Someone tried to waylay this portion. And I mean someone-with-a-small-s-this-time.

It started last night with an email that set me on edge. I responded briefly, and the person continued their tirade. Writing out another whole email, I determined that I was reacting instead of responding and deleted it.

As I perused other activities, the Holy Spirit coached me on the hidden happenings behind the person's email. Reflecting, I gave thanks and sent back a friendly email based on that instead—which to task-oriented me seemed rather off topic! It did not even address the initial questions. Ha ha. Should I have been so surprised when they responded positively and gratefully? No—the coaching had floated down for a reason.

Listen carefully and well. Then implement what the Holy Spirit shares.

Today, I felt a little return of the anxiety I gained from my past abuse that God previously healed. Note the progression.

It started yesterday but registered slight, and I chalked it up to my very active imagination. Until today when it sideswiped me with a little more punch and I clued it up. I received two additional emails challenging other people's near death and afterlife experiences. Then a third verbal confrontation from elsewhere after weeks of no wordy-warfare whatsoever.

No, he did not give up with trying to kill me off a year ago.

Sometimes well-meaning believers can unintentionally become instruments—not by intent, but through words spoken in rapid haste, judgment passed without grace, or actions accomplished without spiritual discernment.

Last week, I read an article on a well-known Christian internet site. An authority in many Christian's minds. As an opinion piece, the author wrote that God desires healing to become normalized in our congregations and society.

Beautiful article. Brutal comments.

I mean, wow, I even read one from one well-meaning brother (I assume) who insisted the answer bordered on the obvious: God did grant those gifts 'back then' but they were temporary.

OK. I respect his opinion.

Will there be more? Yes! It reminded me to prepare each step of the way.

Should I skip this chapter? Absolutely not! Stubborn is my middle name. Here I go!

These challenges do not pose random resistance—they target you and your Manifesto and rate as very, very personal. Do not interpret it as any less. When we walk in mission and purpose, we step onto a battlefield.

Do not forget about or downplay the resistance.

But do not ever let it scare you off from living your Mission Manifesto.

Satan truly is a loser. And I suppose he will poke at me for calling him that but I do not care. Do you realize that we as Christians, who have received God's same power, have more authority than Satan and his minions? If not, look up the verses I footnoted and plaster them to your heart. It is the truth! (8)

My first introduction to spiritual warfare was via Frank Peretti as a teenager. At home, I guess it was just something we did not talk about. Or at youth group. In his fiction book *This Present Darkness,* (9) he presented each sin and doubt that besot us as individual demons. Although he persisted dramatically in the descriptions, making an awfully good suspense story that kept me hooked—he also showed amazing scenes of Christians who tired of the tirade and chucked these things out, far away.

Wow! We have power! I learned to call these entities out, and that because I believe in Jesus, they must obey. No choice there!

I have pitched them out many times since.

Many near death and afterlife experiences depict hell. My focus does not linger there although I have read some accounts. You may choose to read some, but please know they excel in horrific and terrifying—apt to raise your compassion level to new heights. Some near-death and afterlife survivors felt pulled to hellish dimensions. Some teetered on the brink of Heaven or saw Hell nearby. Other stories recount Jesus reaching down and plucking them out of hell as they call for Him. (10)

Of course, we cannot guess the stories of those who remain in hell but with scriptures and testimonials, we can surely imagine the horror of eternal life there. Many stories of returnees also recount the worst part by far—separation from Love. From God. (11)

You do not want to reside there for eternity—no matter how much the desires of your flesh remain satisfied here on earth. It is never worth the trade.

Do you know that Satan fights hard for your soul and even if you belong to Jesus, he may still try? Especially if you desire to make Lord-impact. Check out I Peter 5:9.

Satan told B W Melvin (now a speaker and author) that he would receive half his kingdom if he decided to 'be like them.' (12) Steve Kang, a former Buddhist now turned pastor and speaker, was told by Satan, who sent an angel of light, that if he sacrificed himself, he would receive 50,000 less years of hell. Steve went on to attempt suicide by cutting himself from his stomach to his neck and spent time in ferocious hell until his mother and her prayer warriors prayed him out of it and back to earth. (13) Missionary Ruthellen Davison Carlton visited Heaven and not only saw and heard demons bidding for her spirit as it rose to Heaven, but experienced an energetic battle between demons and angels as it sought to return to her body. A vicious weather storm began on earth when her spirit succeeded but she then experienced ten seizures, only five of which she remembers. (14)

Satan remains a liar. (15) He wants you to believe that he has your best interests at heart, that his ways bring fulfillment, joy, and peace. And of course, we even agree sometimes as we follow his decrepit map and wander through pleasurable sin and the resulting valley of dismay.

But truly, my friends, he wears that charm and smooth exterior only temporarily—most likely as he sways you to the dance floor and keeps tempo as he waltzes smoothly along. The reality is he then attempts to lure you off the floor and into his domain so he can say, 'What? You thought you were special? No, you will suffer the exact same as those already here. You were but a pawn. One more soul stolen from the King. This is part of my revenge package, you see. Thanks for helping me out.'

We also have a true master of the ultimate disguise upcoming. The scriptures warn us that the anti-Christ will wear many 'redeeming' features many people will fall for:

- False miracles - 2 Thessalonians 2:9, Revelation 13:13.
- Smooth words, charisma, and convincing (will likely be well-spoken) - Daniel 11:32, Revelation 13:5.
- Visually impressive and deeply admired by us - Daniel 7:20.
- Appearance of unifying us all together and appearing to be our savior - 1 Thessalonians 5:3, Daniel 9:27.
- Will either claim to be divine or deny Christ, or both - 1 John 2:22, Matthew 24:24.

Hey! Are we vibing on aligned wavelengths? The antichrist will boast stark similarities to Lucifer. Likely high-ranking, charming, and most dangerous of all, positively persuasive. A bit like a well-practiced narcissist. It figures that the king of the darkness would choose one with kindred traits.

Have no doubt if you ever stand in front of this person who is actually a scary creature underneath, your very human side will likely say, 'Um ... wow!' (insert starry gaze here) and maybe even lose your place in the script. 'He's well spoken. Look at the miracles! He even healed my nephew … and finally, world unity! Potential peace…'

Many will lean—and fall. Eventually, the antichrist openly opposes God. In fact, Revelation 13:7 says that he is given permission to wage war against and conquer us. A bit like Job, but worse. Wowsa.

Now is a good time to shore up those boundaries and barriers, my friends. He sends his minions to do the prep-work, and it is our job to waylay them so our Mission Manifestos from the Lord are not delayed, reduced or cancelled entirely.

Let's remember the following:

- Satan has brawn but not more power than God, and therefore not more power than what God has given you as a believer. (1 John 4:4, Job 1:12, Isaiah 54:17)
- He is not omnipresent. He is not everywhere because the Bible states in Psalm 139:7–10 and Jeremiah 23:23–24 that only our Lord is omnipresent.
- He is not omniscient. He does not know everything—only what is released to him to know. (Job 1:6–12, Luke 4:1-13)
- Until the very end when he is banished, he will never stop trying to end the Lord's missions and our God-ordained manifestos. (1 Thessalonians 2:18, 2 Corinthians 4:4, 1 Peter 5:8)
- He and his minions will come disguised. Satan often blinds unbelievers. (2 Corinthians 11:14–15, 2 Corinthians 4:4, Revelation 13:11–14)
- Hell is Satan's kingdom—but also his future prison. The Bible presents it as a place of judgment, separation from God, and conscious suffering. (Revelation 20:14–15, Mark 9:43–48)
- We are to be sober, watchful, and prepare by wearing the full armor of the Lord. (Ephesians 6:10-17, 1 Thessalonians 5:6, 1 Corinthians 16:13)

Jeff sensed the minions in his life after he incurred a life-changing experience bringing sensitivity, knowledge and gratefulness. The minion king learned something too: with all Jeff sought to learn and the amount he now welcomed the almighty God into his life, the more dangerous this Jeff-human became. Satan had better create largish efforts to tow in doubt, discouragement, and anything else possible to accost this man from his own spiritual growth and from sharing his story! And he had better proceed with urgency!

Jeff recognized the efforts and continues to derail them with the power Jesus gave him.

Do not be discouraged or fearful, my friends. The enemy may prowl, but he is not in control—God is. In Romans 8:11, we learn if you have accepted Him as Lord of your life, the same Spirit that raised Jesus from the dead now lives in you. We are not fighting alone. Nor are we powerless. James 4:7 reminds us to resist the devil, and he will flee.

Walk boldly forward, knowing that the very strength of Heaven runs through you.

You are needed on the frontlines.

'For our struggle is not against flesh and blood, but against the rulers, against the authorities, against the powers of this dark world and against the spiritual forces of evil in the Heavenly realms' (Ephesians 6:12).

'The angel of the Lord encamps around those who fear him, and he delivers them. Taste and see that the Lord is good; blessed is the one who takes refuge in him' (Psalm 34:7-8).

Pause & Ponder

1. How has Satan attempted to halt or waylay your Mission Manifesto or what you think your Manifesto might include?
2. What will you do the next time he attempts to do this?

PART TWO: MISSION MANIFESTO MOATS

Chapter Four

I Didn't Want To Live Anymore

Dawn Caldwell De Wulf

Note: this story discusses suicide.

The darkness wholly enveloped me—precisely what I wanted. The sadness, pain, and what I now know was grief had become so intense, so all-encompassing, that I just wanted the darkness to swallow me up and silence the noise. All the noise.

Amidst the breakdown of my first marriage to a man I had been with since age 15 and with whom I had five amazing daughters, I found myself in a pit—a dark pit with seemingly no end. Every day engulfed me with pain, and I just wanted it to end. As much as I loved my daughters, I had become convinced they would be better off without me. The world would be better off without me.

On that day, two days before Christmas, I ingested every medication I found in the house. I swallowed whole bottlefuls at a time—my blood pressure medication, pain medication, cold medication, cough syrup—anything and everything.

I crawled under the bedcovers and waited for the darkness to swallow me. No one would miss or grieve me. For what had I ever done to impact anyone else? Words from the evil one and others had long ago convinced me. It became time to do something about it.

I lay in my bed for several hours, the battle continuing to rage in my mind with zero relief. Finally, as I sank into a dark, black cloud—it enveloped me. I discerned faint noises…my former husband, my daughters and cars. But they were so far away.

Good! That is where they belonged.

I do not understand what happened next. I saw a faint glow—like a blush from the beginnings of a fire. It grew brighter and brighter but never so intense that it hurt my eyes.

Warmth gradually surrounded me.

Being a fog, rain, and winter kind of girl, I hate heat. My dream weather resides in Scotland. Moody. Mysterious.

The complete opposite of this—and yet I loved it.

The light and warmth grew until they were perfect. The warmth rushed all the way through my body. There are no words for it, but it felt like perfect peace, joy, love, and contentment—all of the best emotions and feelings you can dream of all at once.

Clarity rushed in with the warmth. I knew where I stood!

Revelation 21:23-24 says this about Heaven: 'The city does not need the sun or the moon to shine on it, for the glory of God gives it light, and the Lamb is its lamp. The nations will walk by its light, and the kinds of the earth will bring their splendor into it.'

And the colors. Revelation describes streets and a city of pure gold, the city walls' foundations encrusted with every kind of precious stone—jasper, sapphire, emerald, ruby, pearl, and every other gem.

I did not see stones. But no words in English fully encapsulate the breathtaking array of colors. Every color on earth and many more—no names exist. The colors glimmered and glowed from deep inside whatever the object was, surrounding me and embracing me along with the light and warmth. I felt like I rested inside one of those kaleidoscope toys we all had as children but millions of times more beautiful.

I wanted to stay forever. Knowing there was no pain or

sadness here, I knew if I stayed that those feelings would never return.

After enjoying Heaven for a while, I became aware of other people. I knew so many of them without even seeing their faces—recognizing them just by their presence.

The only face I saw was one that then moved close to me. It was my grandma, my Mimi, my mom's mother.

I felt her embrace me, although not physically. She was stunning. Gorgeous. If I were to guess her age, I would say early to mid-30s, even though I did not know her then. Regardless, I immediately recognized her.

Before she passed away shortly after my senior year in high school, she had experienced massive health problems and struggled most days to breathe. Emphysema (although she had never smoked), weakened her. I remember her bent over and frail.

But here she glowed with a vibrance—completely at peace.

Mimi shared that I needed to return. It was not audible, but I heard her. 'You can't stay. Your work isn't done yet. You have more to do.'

But why would I want to go back to the uncertainty? The shattered pieces of my life? The pain? No, I did not want to go back. But I knew I had to. Mimi told me, and she would not lie.

I soaked up the light for a bit longer and then slowly saw it fading away until it was down to a tiny pinhole. It disappeared.

Back in the earth darkness, pain and struggle surrounded me.

I wish I could say that those moments became my rock bottom, but that would be a lie. I reached many, many more over the next 14-15 years until I completely surrendered my desperate need for control over to God. I look back on this experience often, and during difficult times, I can still feel just a bit of the joy and peace I experienced that dark December day.

God has a greater purpose for my life. He made that clear. And my desire to end my own life did not stop His plan. He saw so much beyond that.

Looking back in Revelation 21, I love to read verse 4. It says, 'He will wipe every tear from their eyes. There will be no more death or mourning or crying or pain, for the old order of things has passed away.'

These words are true and trustworthy. I have experienced them.

Reflection With Julie: Third-Strike Sins
Potential Block: Guilt

Perhaps a remorse-wall detours you from discovering your path to intentional living. As I struggled to discover His path for me, some major past sins weighed heavily. I forgave other people involved—but no grace existed in my heart for me. I felt my Lord's gentle correction. By not absolving myself, I placed Julie on a pedestal above He who had already forgiven me.

Big oops!

My friend, if you seek His forgiveness, you are purged. Period. Arising doubts or plaguing sorrow hail straight from Satan, who tucks just enough truth into the folds of the lie to convince you that you are undeserving of God's unfailing mercy.

Perhaps you grew up with the belief that suicide is unforgivable. When we choose to snuff out a life that God knitted together and cherishes, we grab this final earthly decision and hold it tightly, clenching our hands closed. Not Your choice, God! Mine!

That seems pretty unforgivable.

There are many additional Near-Death or Afterlife accounts of suicide attempts, and those experiences fail to indicate a wrathful God who ships a suicide victim into the horrors of hell. Not only did Dawn visit Heaven when she tried to end her life, author and speaker Ana Christina saw and spent time with her sister in Heaven, who committed suicide. (16)

And here, I must reserve a moment to reassure you how beloved you are to me and to God. Although suicide seems like an answer for some at difficult times and many of us have worn those shoes, His heart is for you to live abundantly until He calls you Home. He has crafted an earth-plan that only you can fulfill. Please reach out for help if you are considering this extreme route or feel yourself at risk to head there.

Scripture is clear that a continual hardening of the heart remains the only unforgivable sin. But then, is that truly unforgivable? Not if someone then softens their heart, choosing to tune in. I John 1:9 clearly states He is faithful to forgive and to cleanse us from *all* unrighteousness. The scriptures instead indicate that situation to mean 'eternal hardening'—someone who chooses to never see the truth.

Let's consider David's words in Psalm 139. David often grieved and struggled to stay in a good mental state:

"You have searched me, Lord, and you know me. You know when I sit and when I rise; you perceive my thoughts from afar. You discern my going out and my lying down; you are familiar with all my ways. Before a word is on my tongue you, Lord, know it completely. You hem me in behind and before, and you lay your hand upon me. Such knowledge is too wonderful for me, too lofty for me to attain. Where can I go from your Spirit? Where can I flee from your presence? If I go up to the heavens, you are there; if I make my bed in the depths, you are there. If I rise on the wings of the dawn, if I settle on the far side of the sea, even there your hand will guide me, your right hand will hold me fast. If I say, 'Surely the darkness will hide me and the light become night around me,' even the darkness will not be dark to you; the night will shine like the day, for darkness is as light to you. For you created my inmost being; you knit me together in my mother's womb. I praise you because I am fearfully and wonderfully made; your works are wonderful, I know that full well. My frame was not hidden from you when I was made in the secret place, when I was woven together in the depths of the earth. Your eyes saw my unformed body; all the days ordained for me were written in your book before one of them came to be." Psalm 139:1-16

Many of us struggle to see our Lord in dark times. Trusting Him morphs into a choice. Sometimes, we skedaddle the other way like an airhorn has blown and the world's marathon started without us. I certainly have! And yet, in Psalm 139:16, we learn that He already observed each day of our life (and need I say, death). In Luke 15:3–7, He divulges sprinting after the one wandering sheep-kiddo because of His intense love for that one. He speaks of the Shepherd's joy in discovering the wanderer and shouldering it all the way home.

He finds and reaches for us because just as our lives remain incomplete without Him—He also lacks when missing one of us. When Randy Kay stood in Heaven, the Holy Spirit whispered to him why humankind exists. 'We created you because we desired a family.' (17) Although God could certainly score an award for the most children, the large number of us does not decrease our value to Him.

Near Him in Heaven, I felt like His one and only. And we could enjoy all the time we desired, if we chose to take it, and if I had experienced a remain-here blessing. Although Jesus carries the COO title, He was not engrossed in answering others' prayers or accompanying them along a path (although I am sure He actually was because He seems to be multiple places simultaneously). He was not directing the angel choir. He was not engaged with scheduling the next ten angelic interventions or providing tours to the newly-arrived. He did not shoo me to get a move on so He could complete His to-do list for the day and email it to the Boss.

No, He directed me back so I could tend to mine.

He felt sad to send me back—I perceived that to the deepest corner of my soul. He cannot wait for a Julie-hug! I was the only one who mattered to Him—and that is exactly how it will one day feel for you too.

I know now that if we truly knew, *really* understood, how deeply God adores us, how constantly His eyes rest on us, how fiercely He manages and redirects for our good, then even the hardest days would not unravel us. Of course, painful happenings still ache and sting. And downright hurt. A guarantee. But those moments and days would not topple us if we truly wised up, because we stand on something stronger than circumstances and pain. Our Foundation remains a solid rock of anchoring adoration and love.

We are His warriors!

If we saw ourselves the way He views us, we would stop doubting our worth in the stormy gales, refuse to fear, trust Him, and begin striding through the tough times with confidence, hand in hand with the One who never lets go. We would feel His intense love-ray in the middle of the trying times and rest in it, turning our face to the warmth while the world battles on around us.

One day, when the time is right, He will take your hand, look into your eyes with pure devotion, smile hugely, and welcome *you* home. Until then, my friend, know His deep and unfailing love for you—just as you are. And, carry on with confidence as you seek His next steps.

'So do not fear, for I am with you; do not be dismayed, for I am your God. I will strengthen you and help you; I will uphold you with my righteous right hand' (Isaiah 41:10).

'God does not dwell on our sins any more than I, as a human parent, dwelt on my children's wrongdoing…forgiveness is never withheld.' Madeleine L'Engle (18)

Pause & Ponder

1. Consider your darkest days and how God showed up in them.
2. Think of what might be blocking your steps forward and address them.

A Jesus Hug, Image Courtesy of Julie Bonn Blank

Chapter Five

I Went To The Brink And Back—Twice

LeaAnn Nielsen Swinney

Note: This story discusses suicide ideation, abuse, alcohol/drug use, and food disorders.

My mother did not think much of me. Sometimes she portrayed the best mom in the world, and other times, she revolved into the meanest. My dad teetered back and forth, too. One minute, he laughed and cracked jokes, and the next, he stayed behind a closed door for days.

I believed I was a bad child. I always paid penance for some sin, and my mother's yelling reverberated in my nightmares. Since I performed nothing correctly, I felt grateful to Mrs. G., a teacher at my small Christian school, who encouraged my writing. She and school became my safe place.

When my brothers and sister were born, I think Mom attempted improvement. She and Dad started attending church, and she worked toward being the perfect wife. She sewed all our clothes, created gingerbread houses, and drove in the carpool, but there was a problem—she never eased up on me. We played the perfect family well—nobody understood the abuse at home.

As a teenager, I started noticing boys. One night at the skating rink, an older boy kept looking at me, and I was so hungry for attention that I fell for it. The next day, we went on a walk and he took advantage of me on the cold ground. The police and medical people brought kindness. But the other kids did not, and one very low night I attempted suicide and ended up in the hospital having my stomach pumped.

Mom and Dad eventually divorced. Mom drank, cheated on Dad, and beat my sister and me. I cut my hair, and she became unable to drag me around by it anymore. Turning to drugs, it did not take long to become addicted. I also chose the wrong friends. Shortly after, I began to starve myself.

Being sick and tired grew old fast.

My boyfriend at the time tried everything to encourage my addiction, but surprisingly, Mom helped me. Now involved in Narcotics Anonymous, I started to make positive strides. A different man, Stan, who was supposed to be a one-time thing, gave me a ride home each day. I spent every night with him, then every day. He drank a lot—but that seemed normal to me. He treated me well when he was not drinking, and I overlooked the rest. We eventually married.

Shock arrived when I got pregnant, but we decided to keep the baby. Months later, I awoke in pain—she wanted out. The paramedics and my mother-in-law delivered her. But sadly, eight days later, I called 911 because I woke up from our little nap, but she never did. The same paramedics who showed up to welcome her into this world showed up to take her out.

I was devastated.

People said some very mean things, and that eating disorder expanded. I became obsessed with food and not eating it. With no control over my baby's death or my husband and how he treated me, food intake felt like the only thing I could control.

I developed anger with God. Mom told me and others that God grew jealous of my baby, Krystal, and wanted her for Himself.

Thankfully, we later birthed two additional girls, both healthy.

Stan worked long hours, drinking when not working. I managed the girls, worked, and exercised, always watching my weight. When my husband struggled or experienced extra stress, the drinking and control worsened. My anger at God increased. What had I done to deserve all of this? Why had He not stepped in?

We traveled to Ecuador for a very late honeymoon and had a great time. But the fun abated when I struggled to breathe well. We traveled home and a week later, I landed in the hospital with what they thought was an Ecuador bug. After every test and no answers, one night I started hallucinating—or so I thought.

I became very warm, but not uncomfortable. It was cozy, and a bright light beamed everywhere. Enclosed in quiet, a soft womb-like presence, any noise would have seemed loud. I felt safe, peaceful, and profoundly loved—like nothing could hurt me again. Relishing it, my contentment scale rose off the charts.

I wanted to rest there forever.

Seeing wings, I then felt them brush against my shoulders, feeling much like a hug. I still look for pictures of those wings, but nothing comes close.

In what must have been only seconds or moments, but felt longer, I opened my eyes back in the hospital bed, and suddenly, medical staff rushed me down the hall to obtain an echocardiogram at 2:00 in the morning.

As a child, rheumatic fever had destroyed a heart valve and damaged another. My trip to Ecuador pushed me over the edge—I was drowning in fluid. After open-heart surgery and recovery, I left Stan, starting over with a new home and job thanks to my brothers and their wives. But then came a call: Stan had cancer. I dropped everything to return home. Soon after, I fell ill too. Finances crumbled, and we nearly lost the house.

One night, I felt a strange headache. In the morning, I collapsed on my right side. Stan called 911—he strongly suspected a stroke. I remember nothing of the brain surgery, but I remember God.

This time, there was no immediate bright light, but there was warmth, and I wanted to stay yet again. It was so cozy that I really detested returning. I mean, this was my second visit. Really? How many visits before the 'real thing' could one get?

The light grew as Jesus welcomed me. I felt safe in His presence. He knew me so well.

He kissed me on the cheek. A moment frozen in time I will never forget. 'It's not your time,' He explained gently.

Back home I went.

The bleeding stroke gave me only fifty percent chance of living, and I relearned how to walk, eat, read, and write over months of recovery. Returning home from rehabilitation, nothing was the same. In just a few years, I lost both parents, endured repeated surgeries, and slipped into deep depression. Stan turned to drinking instead of support, even after his cancer remission.

With Stan's drinking out of control again, we fought constantly. He would not let me eat, and he scared me every night. An old friend I once blocked reconnected, and my siblings helped move me to a safe group home.

I have since experienced another stroke, and two heart valves have been replaced.

But after my Heaven visits, I am no longer angry with God for the loss of my daughter, my strokes, my abusive marriage, and everything else. It would be easy to remain angry and bitter—I elect not to.

I also still struggle with the food issue sometimes. But I am choosing to put my trust in Him. I know He will get me through. Without Him by my side, I would never have made it this far.

Reflection With Julie: Course (De) Construction
Potential Block: Tribulations

I once wrote an article for *Leadership Magazine* called 'The Job Family.' It guided ministry leaders on walking alongside families who experience ongoing trials and trauma. How did I know what to write? Because for at least eighteen years of my adult life, my family and I walked through one major trial after another. Over time, I noted weariness and quiet frustration in our ministry leaders'—and even friends'—responses. They did not know what to say anymore.

And honestly, I understood.

I felt beyond help.

As LeaAnn mentioned, when I first reached out after years (we developed a friendship at that Christian school), she grew fearful and blocked me. Not only did I work in the domestic abuse industry, as a fellow survivor, I recognized and honored the repercussions in her. As is common for one experiencing overwhelming trauma, she grew defensive and shut me down.

We texted for hours when she felt safe with me again. After forty years, our synergy still hummed. We talked about safeguards, such as blocking her bedroom door at night and erasing all her phone messages. Behind the scenes, her safety plan became an active project.

Trials, and especially ongoing heavy issues that seem never-ending, can waylay us from discovering our Manifesto and living intentionally.

On the opposite highway, I have seen many times when multiple trials in one person's life lead to an outpouring of ongoing ministry, impact, and sometimes even healing. If you rest in a continual ditch of ongoing physical or emotional pain, I am so sorry. I know how discouraging and difficult that is. You are a true champion, but please remember that Jesus even needed help carrying His cross to the hilltop. Seek assistance and please be encouraged. Your story, even if convoluted, can transform to immense and beautiful results as you remain faithful! Lamentations 3:31-32 says, 'For no one is cast off by the Lord forever. Though he brings grief, he will show compassion, so great is his unfailing love. For he does not willingly bring affliction or grief to anyone.' Psalm 18:19 is one of my favorites, written by David after he was relentlessly pursued by King Saul. 'He brought me out into a spacious place. He rescued me because he delighted in me.'

Continue to chase Jesus. Pursue Him with passion. Know that He is fighting for you.

LeaAnn, and many of us, led a worldly-colorful life at one point which tends to launch a question people wonder about but hesitate to ask. Are trials caused by sin? Some of them, yes. Many of our trials take the main stage as an effect of our sinful decisions, or someone else's sin. But no, not all are caused by bad decisions—we live in a world where King Minion reigns. Where sin, darkness, pain, demonic influence, the occult and anti-God thinking rules the majority.

But I will never, ever be that one who says, 'I'm so sorry that you have cancer. What about the sin in your life?' I do not believe this correlates, and I hope you agree. Trials are tools Satan delights in using because they are so very effective. Continual adversity and misery can easily stop us from living with intention and ministering to others.

Fortunately, my Lord fights for us all if we reside in His family.

I deduced no clue that LeaAnn's struggles grew so enormous in our years apart and that she visited Heaven twice. In the days after my first visit to Heaven, as I was home recovering, worshipping, praying, crying, already missing Heaven, and attempting frantically to journal and draw what I experienced, we texted.

And now, she remained there for me—offering comfort and understanding when I needed it the most.

Is that not just like our Father? He does not waste our pain when we willingly give it to Him.

He carefully enacted your very life and placed you here to complete the work He deemed for only you to accomplish. But at some point, especially if you experience multiple struggles and life changes, you might feel summoned to another avocation. Something much more tender and powerful: the ministry of presence.

As I write today, my friend LeaAnn is recovering from another heart surgery. She lives in a group home and receives caregiving. She may never be able to step out and help run VBS, shuttle people to appointments, or volunteer for a meal service. But she does a bang-up job of encouragement right where she lives, not just to me, but also to stroke sufferers and people who struggle with traumatic brain injuries.

The number of people with trials and trauma who visit and return from Heaven (and sometimes Hell) who then begin a ministry, numbers in the astounding range. As I head-review the almost forty Heaven books I have brain-devoured this past year, most of the authors now serve in ministry and many of the people they feature in their books also took this step. In the book, *A Miraculous Life: True Stories of Supernatural Encounter with God,* (19) Bruce Van Natta shares many stories that led to his ministry. After suffering childhood sexual abuse, he received a close hug from Jesus. Later in life, God pulled him out of addiction. Then came the day when he was crushed by the front of a truck, that portion weighing ten to twelve thousand pounds, and as his spirit watched from above, two eight-foot angels inserted their arms under the truck, touching his body and protecting him from further damage. After he healed, he and his wife felt highly motivated to begin in ministry, and God guided each step, at times the path seeming twisty and wayward. Like me, they sometimes questioned and took matters into their own hands, sliding off the track. But God fulfilled all His promises as they then chose to obey.

In one of the most profound stories I have ever read, Samaa Habib, a former Muslim, entered Heaven after a bomb exploded nearby, killing her friends. Although her encounter with Jesus is one to read for sure, what impacted me the most is that Samaa experienced God's astounding protective measures throughout her entire life, even as a child, during extraordinary events. In a country controlled by communists when professing Christians received beatings from their families, experienced shunning and often death, His hand on her remained incredibly evident. She received a choice in Heaven, stay or come back and win more souls for His kingdom. Samaa chose earth—and increased soul-conversion. (20)

Perhaps you are not meant to start a ministry—that is a-OK if God agrees. Sometimes, your greatest impact is not in the tasks you accomplish, but in the quiet ways you show up. You might become the steady voice in someone's storm, the one who speaks truth over the shouted lies. You may be the gentle validation that reminds someone they are not crazy or alone. Perhaps you will become the listening ear when no one else is really hearing, or the warm hug that expresses more support than words ever could. Maybe you will walk alongside them on their twisty-trail, providing just a touch or word at the crooked corner spots and when a flash flood threatens.

It becomes a privilege to walk beside someone in their pain. Never underestimate how He might use your prayers, heart, voice, or hands to help someone else rise. My Lord is the master at turning pain into purpose and He can do that in your life, and their life.

We carry the hope we receive. And whether other's trials are occasional or seem to be taking over in this stage of their lives, we reside here to remind others through our actions what a friend we have in Jesus.

'Praise be to the God and Father of our Lord Jesus Christ, the Father of compassion and the God of all comfort, who comforts us in all our troubles, so that we can comfort those in any trouble with the comfort we ourselves receive from God' (I Corinthians 1:3-4).

'My comfort in my suffering is this: Your promise preserves my life' (Psalm 119:50).

Pause & Ponder

1. Have trials and hard times pulled you away from Jesus, or closer to Him?
2. Is there a block in your life that is a deterrent to the discovery or fulfillment of your Manifesto?
3. Spend some time pondering how you conquered, are surmounting or will crush those blocks and how they then can be used to benefit other people.

Chapter Six

He Planted An Army Around My Home

Lea Peters

Our youngest child was barely three months old when the military assassinated the president of Burundi in an attempted coup d'etat. Although their planned coup failed, the death of the president threw the country into civil war.

We had served in Central Africa as missionaries for six years—civil unrest and political chaos felt common. But that was nothing like the Burundian coup attempt. That morning, we awoke to the sounds of gunfire and mortar rounds. Although originating from well over a mile away, they shook the light fixtures in the house.

Our three children were too young to understand and comprehend the changes. Schools closed, phone lines were cut, and it became unsafe to leave our home. We huddled inside while the military drove up and down the street, giving each other the 'thumbs up' sign, signifying a successful mission.

The capital city of Bujumbura, where we lived, slowly returned to a semblance of normalcy as the Vice President took over duties of the President. At the same time, an ethnic civil war embraced the countryside. The military retained firm control of the capital but could not control the rest of the country.

As violence and chaos swept over Burundi, displaced Burundians flooded into the city by the tens of thousands. They set up tents and makeshift cardboard shacks to live in wherever they found room.

Not two years had passed since we first planted our church in Bujumbura. How could we minister if the battle zone came any closer? What about the children? Wouldn't ramifications hit them the hardest?

We remained in constant prayer for the safety and emotional well-being of our children. But when other foreigners living in Burundi (who were not Christians or missionaries) decided to remain there with their children, we felt we should also endure. Our church family needed us.

Bujumbura remained calm, but after two years of fighting in the countryside, the rebels surrounded the city.

On a Thursday, I dropped our four-year-old daughter off at her preschool next door to our house. Although we heard gunfire, it was still several kilometers away as it had remained for weeks. I took little notice of it until later in the morning when it suddenly sounded closer. A ton of cars started driving by the school next door and I decided to retrieve our daughter.

At our front gate, I saw multitudes of parents searching for their children. A man in military uniform, whose child attended our daughter's school, approached.

'What's happening?' My voice hitched and broke.

'The rebels are attacking the city, ma'am. They will raze the city to the ground!'

My husband raced out of the gate to pick up our oldest son from his school—thankfully, less than two kilometers away.

All three children soon gathered in our home. We kept them away from the windows as scary tracer bullets, rockets, grenades, and other weaponry exploded everywhere.

As the fighting enveloped the city, church members—with now only destroyed homes—sought refuge. Soon sixteen fellow believers slept on our living room floor. We spent many hours praying together and watching and listening to the war pass by our house.

Two days later, we dared to travel to the church building.

Surrounded by military, the church looked relatively

unscathed. But they denied us entrance—it was too dangerous. We circled the back roads and around the church, finally pulling up to the rear entry. Guards in a tank parked on that side allowed us entry.

Empty bullet casings littered the floor—a few of the benches housed bullet holes. The church guard had hidden underneath the wooden platform during the night of fighting.

As I stood in the doorway overlooking the inner city, images usually seen only on television broadcasts surrounded me. Mothers and small children fled with bundles on their heads, houses burned, and gunshots rang out sporadically. Decimated homes from bombs crumbled. Several large sections of streets, now leveled to the ground, suffered damage all in the name of tribalism.

Although our congregation had shrunk from over five hundred to only fifty-six, we stood in the church and declared refusal to flee—no matter the challenges ahead. God had called us to Burundi, and we felt no direction from Him to leave.

The desperate situation of those displaced by the war grew significantly. For several years, we headed out daily in teams to minister to the children in the displaced camps by supplying them with food and emergency medical care. We fed over one thousand children daily.

Meditating on God and His Word became my only escape from the fear that often gripped my heart. I even started reconsidering our decision—my mind desperately wanted to flee. Our children lived in a war zone!

One afternoon when gunfire seemed reduced, I allowed two of the kids to play in the walled back yard as the youngest napped inside. I watched through the window as my daughter played with her toys and my son rode on his bicycle.

But then, gunshots rang just outside the front wall of our home. I raced to the back yard. Plucking my 10-year-old son off the bicycle, I tucked him under one arm, hoisted my daughter under the other, and ran inside the house.

Was it not time to abandon God's call? How much living on the edge could we do? Praying daily, sometimes several times a day, I scoured the Heavens for assurance that our decision to obey and stay remained the correct one.

Sleep often evaded me. We usually awoke to the familiar sound of gunfire and grenades.

Until one night, when I awoke to singing.

I pulled myself out of bed and walked down the hallway. Drawing near to the living room, I opened the door. Light shone through the curtains, and a cool draft flowed through the house. A breeze passed by my face and I felt the peace of God's presence. The windows on both sides of the room radiated light.

Through the curtains, I saw silhouettes of angels.

I stumbled quickly across the room, feeling no fear. God's presence grew stronger the closer to the window I came. Opening the curtains, I gasped. Angels surrounded the entire perimeter of our home. Standing shoulder to shoulder, they shone brightly, lifting their hands in praise.

I knelt. I sensed someone standing next to me and felt a smooth fabric brush my right hand. Jesus Himself was with me, and His armies stood guard outside. I wanted to remain there forever. Such intense comfort filled my heart as I heard God's voice reassure me: 'Your family and the church will be fine.'

Fear vacated that night as my eyes and heart opened to the multitude protecting us. I don't remember how long I stayed in the living room, but for months afterward, I watched those angels follow us, ministering to us while the world splintered. I learned that the ones who walk beside me have intense strength straight from Him. And I know now that every night as I lay down—an army stands guard outside my window.

Reflection With Julie: The Terror Tunnel
Potential Block: Fear

Fear can motivate change, or become the very conduit that grabs us tightly, holding us back from our Manifesto. It often persists as the reason we choose stagnancy, sin, hurting others, and ourselves too.

The reality is, we give fear a lot of power and authority in our lives.

When Lea and her family lived in a war zone, they feared the potential impact of hostile clashes, injuries, death, and potential supply shortage. They feared becoming imprisoned. They frequently became apprehensive when considering abuse and mistreatment from the enemy.

At times, they grew scared for their lives.

Claustrophobia grasps its squeezing tendrils on me more than I like to concede. When my kids were young, I could not enter the play tunnels at the fast-food restaurant, even when they called. Even when they felt stuck or another kid teased them. Once, one offspring got bopped on the head by a playmate and I still could not enter. Instead, I poked my head (slightly) inside and instructed my child on how to get to me.

A few years ago, I sprinted out of the underground tunnel leading to the base of Niagara Falls. I failed to run far, because I was forced to wait my turn for the elevator. As I almost hyperventilated, I realized that both my husband and our friends had followed me closely back to the elevator in solidarity. They must have run too! You can laugh—I am cracking up.

My maternal grandma loved agate rocks. Years back, many washed up on the Oregon Coast. Her garage rock polisher spun them into beautiful treasures with glassy, soft surfaces. I often ran my hands through full agate-holders like butter, sour cream and whipped cream containers. The cool, smooth feel of the now-polished rocks comforted me.

How does this relate to fear? Please, keep reading.

I love agates too, but now they hide more. Or perhaps my grandma truly did collect them all. Fact—I love all rocks. My husband once had to cut me off when we visited my folks in Arizona and I kept stuffing more rocks into the backpack he carried. My parents later requested my presence and the watching of 'The Long, Long Trailer' with Lucille Ball. (21) Hilarious!

When I discovered that agates wash up at 'The Tunnel Beach' (22) that some call 'The Secret Beach' on the Oregon Coast, I started pining for a day trip. But I ran into one gigantuous issue—it was called a secret for a reason. Accessing the beach requires a little hike through a tunnel. And the burrow grows pretty 'tunnel-like.'

Well, if my own kid who felt stuck in a tunnel could not motivate me, whatever would? Apparently, a longing to find an agate memorial in honor of my grandma, who I lost at thirteen. And a desire to conquer this fear.

Off we meandered, hubby promising to lead the way and hold my hand if needed.

I refuse to drag you through all the muck, but know I almost declined when I saw the tunnel. But then determined to film my victory, because surely doing that would distract me (not), and could make a nice reel (it did). Tucking in close behind Bill, I drew in many deep breaths.

'Ready?'

I nodded. 'Charge!'

Moments later, I fell behind as he became a cartoon road runner. I attempted a jog. Alas, large (lovely) boulders lined the sandy tunnel path and required clever dodges. The walls narrowed dramatically. I finally viewed light ahead, focused on it, and burst out on the other side, thanking God and throwing my arms up in victory.

The beach practically shouted respite and relief as I then threw my arms around Bill, who tried to apologize for leaving me behind. No worries! I made it!

We grappled along as I scoured the ground between the larger rocks for agates, but although I watched others picking up what must be the elusive stones, we failed to discover even one!

Perching on a log an hour later, we watched the waves incessantly peak, roll and slide onto the sand before retreating to their ocean home. Was it worth the trepidation? Maybe. I believe I temporarily conquered a ~~monster~~ large fear. But bummer! I sighed. 'Thank you, Jesus, for the beauty around us, the peace here and the company.' I squeezed Bill's hand, and then we tossed some non-agate rocks into the ocean while chatting with other beachcombing rockhounds.

My head whipped to the right when I saw a teenager gather up the biggest agate ever! And then a lady wandered by casually, holding a full baggie of them.

What?!?

I felt happy for them—I promise.

Just disappointed for me. Where were those other beaches I read about with a tendency to house them? One in California where I could scoop them up by the cupful?

With Bill still 'neighboring,' as the kids and I call it, I started back toward the tunnel, and a moment later, wandered off the rocky path. Sitting on a large rock near the tree line, my gaze slid to the sand.

AH! There it lay! A big agate about the size of the palm of my hand—hiding amongst the larger boulders, nestled in. My hand swooped down and snatched it up as I yelled to Bill. Gorgeous rock! I knew the real reason God and Grandma provided it—because I threw on some backbone and stumbled through that tunnel anyway.

My reward gleamed in my hand as I held it tightly.

My fear of close spaces or even my anxiety the three times I hovered close to punching my permanent Heaven ticket seems minimal compared to Lea and her family who literally lived in a war zone. True perspective clears up so much fog, doesn't it?

Fear, as enlarged apprehension, can rate as good and God-given because it can create an urgency to act. Healthy fear becomes handy in times when a bear might lumber out from behind a tree, someone nearby needs medical help, or a person on the road drives aggressively. The body increases cortisol and adrenaline when risk increases and reduces other body functions as a lifesaving measure.

However, more often fear involves the enemy lying and us giving him too much cred. He embroils something truly small into massive proportions—often life-impacting. Although usually a lie, fear becomes our truth when we allow that. And then it grows, due to the enemy's whispers and our focus-choice. Fear, as it hails from Satan, thrives in shadows.

Did I really think that the tunnel might collapse or squeeze the air out of my lungs? Or what? And what if it did? Heaven awaits! Honestly, it becomes eye-opening to attempt pinning the reason for this huge fear to the tarmac—everything I think of seems really dumb. So, consider that in regards to your fear. Take it apart and dive in. Consider what is beneath it, besides the enemy. Is it a fear of disappointing people? A dread of rejection? An unease regarding safety? Fear of repercussions, because that happened in the past? A fear of punishment from others or God? The angst of potentially not being good enough? A desire to enlist self-perfection? Why?

What scary trepidation holds you back from the intentional living that God requests of you? Maybe it feels like a beach tunnel—dark, long, cold, drippy, uncertain, closing in.

But God does not lead us into tunnels to abandon us. He guides us through them. And on the other side is light. Clarity. Obedience. Growth. Freedom. Peace. Impact. Treasure!

You do not have to see the whole way through. In fact, we usually cannot. Our view remains chronically dim and will not expand until Heaven. You must choose to trust the One who walks beside you.

I also assure you of additional security patrol. Guardian angels are assigned to you. The most common near-death and afterlife accounts indicate that *one to three* of them watch over you, honor you, and even look up to you as you are created in the image of God. They seize their assignments with joy. We do not honor them above the Lord or even alongside the Lord, but you may see some here (and will for sure when you arrive in Heaven). Or, like Lea, you might catch a sneak-view of a whole multitude especially called to protect you and yours. If you fine-tune your ears and spiritual eyes, you may sense their presence here on Earth. He often sends them. (23)

Step into a tunnel with me today, friend. Conquer a fear. And when it gets a bit harrowing in the middle, grab for our Jesus. He surrounds us despite our fears and within our anxious thoughts. The dark, drippy tunnel will not last forever. However, the waiting surge He wants you to generate for Him will have eternal provision for others – and for people beyond them.

You've got this.

'For who is God besides our Lord? And who is the rock except for our God?' (Psalm 18:31)

'The angel of the Lord encamps around those who fear him, and he delivers them' (Psalm 34:7).

'Have I not commanded you? Be strong and courageous. Do not be afraid; do not be discouraged, for the Lord your God will be with you wherever you go' (Joshua 1:9).

Pause & Ponder

1. During this time of fear, Lea focused on scripture mediation, as well as prayer. How does meditating on God's words help you? Does it help with your fears?
2. What fears have held you back? What is one fear you will commit to work on conquering and how will you do that? Consider praying the following prayer.

Prayer to Release Fear

Dear Lord,

I know that fear is not from You. Knowing Your deep love for me, I understand that fear is the last thing You desire for your children, just as we cringe thinking of our family members being afraid.

Lord, I have attempted everything in my power to control my fear and it still returns. I recognize now that this is a work of Satan and his demons. I also understand that as Your child, I have the power to demand that they cease. So today, right now, in the name of Jesus, I demand that any spirits of fear, including rejection, unworthiness, danger, consequences, disappointment, ________ (add any others) and any other fear I've identified as a block be cast far from affecting me.

In their place, I take on:

A **shield of faith**—knowing that You have not left me;
A **mantle of courage**—knowing I can do all things with You;
An **unmovable anchor**—as I trust Your strength, and
A **sword** with the power of an almighty God—Who guarantees His presence and protection.

Thank You, Jesus, for releasing me from fear.

Amen.

Chapter Seven

I Was Ejected From A Plane

Dawn M. Andresen

Three friends and I headed out for breakfast in a bit of an unusual but fun fashion. We were flying to Wisconsin in a 4-seat Cessna 180 with floats.

It would be fun, right?

Why was I hesitating?

As I walked down to the dock where the plane waited, I halted briefly. I probably shouldn't go. Why was I doing this? The night before, my friends had partied. Would the alcohol affect them this morning?

I pushed it out of my mind and climbed in. The pilot greeted me, mentioning that he'd flown since he was a young boy and remained accident-free.

Well, that wouldn't last.

I shook my head fast. Where did that come from? So weird! My eyes wandered to the plane's dash where I caught the numbers 12:34. I blew out a big breath. Those numbers had pranced into my life daily for many years, in that order, and not just on clocks. My youngest daughter had mentioned a few months before that maybe it highlighted the time I would eventually die.

I should really get out of the plane!

But I did not leave. I was now cornered in my seat. Besides—my friends would express concern about me being over-dramatic. Sighing, I grimaced and reached back for my seatbelt. Unfortunately, both the backseat seatbelts lay tucked down behind the seats, so the two of us in back could not buckle up. Fighting some unease, I shrugged at my seatmate,

Shawn, once again chastising myself for thinking the worst possible scenario—a crash.

We took off and gained altitude. I looked out the window and noticed the tree line just ahead. Did the pilot see that? He pulled up on the yoke. We wobbled a bit but still hovered below the trees.

The pilot slumped over the wheel. Oh no! Was he still drunk?

Time seemed to slow. The oddest noise filled the small interior. The plane leaned hard to the side. I barely found time to glance over to the side door—which was gone! My unbuckled friend and I tumbled toward the opening with the speed of gravity.

The actual fall escapes my memory. God's grace perhaps.

I hit my head and landed on something really hard—tumbling repeatedly. In the lake and now underwater, I panicked.

I had never been a skilled swimmer.

A calm voice filled my head. 'Relax your muscles. You will float to the top. Relax.'

I focused intently. Fighting against the instinct to battle the water with my limbs, I let go, calming my muscles instantly. Floating up, I popped above the surface and spit out my gum. Chewing it may have saved my life—I had not gasped or swallowed water.

'Help!' I screamed, drawing more air into my aching lungs. 'Help me!'

My jacket and heavy boots threatened to pull me back down. Mid-October in the middle of lake meant limited time. My body began shivering with intensity, as if to prove that reality.

'Relax,' I heard again.

Treading water, I peered around—the shore rested in the

distance. Too far to swim. I saw part of the float from the plane and Shawn also treading water some ways away.

I screamed again.

'Relax. You need to conserve your energy.'

The insistent Holy Spirit apparently wanted me alive. I started to pray like I have never appealed before. Asking Jesus to forgive me became the first priority. I then prayed to see my loved ones again, to hold my unborn grandson, and for my very life.

I did not feel done yet.

As I prayed, I felt my body slowing down. Hypothermia arrived with a quiet vengeance. Parts of my body numbed—I could no longer feel them. And I became unable to think or process clearly. I struggled to hold my head above water and knew it would not stay there long.

I tried to remove my boots.

'Leave them on. Conserve your energy—it is keeping you afloat.'

I sighed. Was I supposed to give up? Die out here in the middle of a lake after falling fifty or sixty feet from a plane?

Finally sliding under the water, peace enveloped me. This must be the end, then. But I felt safe, held, and peaceful.

Unknown to me, a first responder and paramedic who lived at the edge of the lake had witnessed the accident. He yelled for his neighbor and called 911 before running to his boat.

My body jerked as he yanked my arm. He pulled me out by my arm and long hair. My eyes opened slowly, and I saw Shawn already in the boat as we sped off toward the shore—she made it too. Gratefulness filled me as my eyes shuttered again. With divine timing, the ambulance pulled up just as we reached the bank of the lake.

In the ambulance, I grew very confused as my body shifted

into shock. They kept asking questions and the words made no sense. I tried to answer, my responses mumbled and jumbled. I could at least still pray in my head. I shivered violently as I asked God to help me and wondered what would happen next.

The EMT cut off my clothes to scan visually for damage and tried to be reassuring.

Once at the hospital, I felt alone but reminded myself that God was truly with me. He had just saved my life, after all. They wrapped me in heated blankets and activated an internal warmer. Eventually, I warmed and they rolled me off for a full body scan. No visible injuries showed up.

With excruciating back pain, I could not move. But after warming, I remembered clearly and tried to explain what had occurred.

Although I had no internal injuries, the scan revealed a black spot on my left lung. Once I stabilized, they admitted me for two days of tests and rest, then discharged me.

A month before the needed lung surgery, they extracted tissue samples—it was non-cancerous. During the actual surgery, the doctor removed part of my rib and a small section of the lung. The biopsy showed histoplasmosis which can spread and become fatal.

My doctor told me that falling out of a plane and getting hypothermia saved my life.

It slowed down my reactions and movements, making me unable to panic—and the adrenaline traveled right to my heart and kept it beating. The Holy Spirit helped me safeguard the needed adrenaline. And of course, the scan at the hospital caught the black spot when I had felt no pain or symptoms.

After Shawn and I tumbled out, the plane landed in a field. Because the pilot and my friend up front wore seatbelts, they remained uninjured. But the landing caused the back of the plane to slam the rear seats forward. If Shawn and I had been buckled in, we would have been crushed.

Jesus ejected me instead.

Before the accident, I led a shallow spiritual life—walking with Him mostly only as needed.

I knew without a doubt that He had never left, even as I lived superficially. And as He uses me in the life of my children, seven grandchildren, and neighbors—it has grown obvious that He ejected me for a very good reason.

Reflection With Julie: Divine Delays
Potential Block: Waiting

Waiting on God's timing is arduous sometimes, no doubt about it. Over two years ago, I sprouted abundant allergies at my day job. At about the three-hour mark of working, my voice would turn hoarse and I started choking on food (even my safe foods) like a pelican trying to swallow a fish. As my throat swelled, I could not stop hacking.

My cohorts at ARMS/Abuse Recovery Ministry Services adored me, as I cherished them, and they adapted. Reducing my office hours, I worked mostly from home. But eventually unable to tolerate any hours at the office, I switched to only working at home. Seriously, my allergy doctor kept writing letters: 'My patient must be in a controlled environment or she goes into anaphylaxis…'

With a staff of only six full-timers, I knew the impact of someone's absence—we always scrambled a bit when one of us vacationed or attended conferences.

This home schedule held water, but only until the bucket leaked. A year later, my Lord said, 'Turn in your notice. It's time to go.'

This prompted sheer confusion. I must have misheard or misinterpreted.

He persisted, and my spirit dipped into a steep pothole as I distinguished confirmation from a few other sources. After talking to Bill and a few others, I turned in a wide notice with intent to start job searching—holding zero idea of what came next—and knowing they would gladly retain me for as long as possible. They always had before.

I mused the 'why' because if you have not deciphered this in me, I sometimes mimic a two-year-old darting around asking 'why' about everything. Perhaps God wanted me only working part time so I could finish book three in my trilogy? That commitment needed completion before starting this book—and I ached to write about Heaven!

Surprise then pride rose when I experienced the final and devastating affirmation. My supervisor, who walks closely with the Lord, felt the equivalent! Time to go, Julie! They needed my director position working fulltime at the office.

I expected them to bargain my notice with tears and pleas.

Emotionally, I had planned to stay forever—well, until retirement anyway.

Stupid human nature—full of pride and sin. So, what did this writer scratch into the next scene? Ah, shucks, I am almost embarrassed to share. I scrambled to save my job, even though God clearly directed me to depart. I loved my coworkers and the ladies in recovery from abuse. And did they not remember that conferences and speaking gigs already graced my calendar for the next year? That more leader's curriculum needed written?

What about a job share situation where someone else worked half my hours in the office?

Despite my bargaining endeavors, my supervisor firmly placed her mama hardhat on and implemented a tough love program—on me. Having heard from God also, she would pry my fingers from the back bumper of the car as she drove the whole organization away from me if needed.

And she did. I doubt it was easy. Things grew weird—hurtful incidents occurred, confusing me more. After years of knowing her and serving with these programs, I felt untrusted. I sensed oppression—the very mountain we taught against! What had I done to cause this new suffocating environment?

Throughout the tough love moves, she kept saying very strange things like 'I don't know what is ahead for you, Julie. But it's going to be awesome!' and 'Just you wait. God is up to something.'

Uh huh.

How was this better?! It was part of my responsibility to partially pay our expenses at home.

The evening I walked out of the building for the last time, sleep evaded me. Sitting at the dining room table, I sobbed, feeling alone and still extremely perplexed.

'Julie, you have everything you need to go forward.'

I heard that clearly. But aloud, I asked, 'What?'

As in, would you please repeat Yourself?

Silence ticked. Several beats later, I asked, 'Wait, do you mean the advanced abuse recovery program I was writing? That's even more confusing, Jesus. I changed my mind on the programming, remember? I don't want to start—a *thing*. An organization. We already have a good ARMS. It will make a very good devotional book when I'm done with the Heaven book. Just guide me, please—I don't get it.' I sighed.

'You've received the best of the best in your training and experiences.' He threw this thought in my head.

Truth. It includes hundreds of hours of abuse training from the best faith-based people in the business. Hundreds of hours of leading groups and training facilitators. Years of advocacy work.

Agitated, I stood and stomped to the kitchen to retrieve my

water glass. Surely, He was not calling me to begin a new ministry? Ugh!

As time passed, I shoved *that book* out of my mind. And my Lord mastered His vagueness. 'Just keep writing,' became the mantra. At every job interview and new potential client meeting, He clearly told me this was not the 'forward' He intended. Even my many coaching clients dried up. When I questioned, pleaded, groveled, complained…whatever, He said patiently, 'Just keep writing, Julie.' And once, post interview as I was leaving, He repeated, 'Julie! Go home and write!'

'I am writing!' I squeaked as I wrapped fiction book three. And then, like a little kid, 'But I'm sad! I miss them all. And we need me to earn money…'

Whine, whine, whine.

'I know your needs. I feel your sadness. Write.'

I lunched with former co-workers and blast it all, I kept slipping into phrases like 'Well, when we do this…I mean when *you all* do this…'

One was kind enough to say, 'It is 'we.' You will always be a part of us!'

Ha ha. God, please bless Tricia who recognized my struggle and loved me anyway. Even with the passing of several months, I still scrambled to release this job from my heart, even though the last days with my boss and the board delivered a whole lot of difficult. I missed the team, the tasks, praying with people so many times a day, and I longed for the heart-fulfillment received when helping women who tripped in the shoes I once wore.

'Knock it off, Jules.' I coached myself for about the hundredth time. Then mumbled, 'God's got something else. Just obey. Let it go.'

Six months later, I sit here typing like a Gen Z gamer. It is hard to believe all that God has sketched in my life—and the additions He continues to color with vivid strokes. My scribbles include months of praying, pleading, pulling closer to my Lord, studying Him and Heaven, working on my health, finally getting diagnosed, writing like a wild woman about to die again…and now apologizing to my former boss. Truly, our lovely catch-up conversation included much laughter. Although I probably should send her this chapter to read before it goes to print!

Jesus also orchestrated a specially-timed event for Dawn. How deeply He loves her! In this extreme situation, He ejected her from a plane, safely into water versus land, and coached her through potential danger and a sure death, to pull her close to Him and ensure that lung spot was seen and addressed. A spot that caused no symptoms, pain, or hint of something amiss.

Our Lord viewed her role post-accident and knew that after her incident, she would choose living with intentionality—sowing seeds of His love into little lives, weaving His concepts throughout their vast experiences, and most of all—praying diligently for them.

Those kids will reshape stories going forward.

During this time, I met with a new prayer warrior friend, Hannah. At the time, I am afraid I spewed a bit of frustration, not knowing what God intended next and stress-struggling. When she prayed for me, she brightened. 'I see you as a warrior—in armor.'

Sound familiar? Yes, the Heaven memory God gave me for this book's introduction, many months later, also featured a Julie-warrior. Because God confirms it when He provides direction or steers one to His Waiting Room.

Hannah explained more of what she heard when she

prayed. 'That job was one peak of one mountain, Julie. You know how we think we view a summit ahead but it is just another hill? You thought it was your summit, but God is giving you another mountain journey, and another summit.'

I had just met Hannah. In fact, this was the first time I saw her in person.

Later, she texted me. 'I wish I could draw.'

That drew a laugh. 'Why is that?'

'I wish I could draw how I saw you. Because you weren't just a warrior. You were a formidable warrior. Big, outfitted, strong, ready.'

God intends for each one of us to turn the tide. That is why you picked up this book and now read late into the night, yes? You feel a tickle. The softest caress of greater things to come – while sensing that He desires more from you. And perhaps even holds expectations of you.

I understand the magnificent frustration that perching on the edge of the seat in His Waiting Room causes. I echo your experience of launching up from that dumb, hard plastic chair, expertly pacing the floor, and peering out the windows, hoping for the next step to soon saunter around the corner. But when He is quiet (or in this case for me, limited in His answers), *draw close and wait expectantly.*

I have learned the extremeness of my Lord. Because I know His heart.

He will do whatever necessary to snag your attention when you are needed for plans that in this last season of days will increase. Perhaps He even popped this book into your hands when you planned on reading a favorite suspense author instead. Seriously, He will draw you to the lowest grounds financially, remove any security you relied on, adjust your life so it feels challenging and perhaps even appear desolate, show you the supernatural or perhaps even pull you up to Heaven for a quick visit.

His plans are worth the wait. I promise and double pinky guarantee. Take a deep breath if you are in His Waiting Room. Several people told me (independently) to make sure to rest during this time period.

Each time, I replied or thought, 'Huh?' but in the past few weeks, as the fog starts clearing, I understand a tad bit more. God was preparing to ramp things up—using me for a piece of that impact. And I needed to be prepared in return.

Rest in the sometimes annoying waiting room. Draw close and prepare spiritually. When He raises the gate, He needs you spiritually steady, super strong and running at full force.

'Be patient, then, brothers and sisters, until the Lord's coming. See how the farmer waits for the land to yield its valuable crop, patiently waiting for the autumn and spring rains. You too, be patient and stand firm, because the Lord's coming is near' (James 5:7-8).

'Wait for the Lord; be strong and take heart and wait for the Lord' (Psalm 27:14).

Pause & Ponder

1. Is there an area of your life that you feel you are waiting on God? What is that?
2. What facets of it are under your control and what will you commit to do during the waiting period?

Artwork © Jessica Smith Art. Reproduced with permission.
For more of the artist's work, visit www.jessicasmithart.shop.

Chapter Eight

He's Saving A Greenhouse For Me
Laura M.

When I was very young, I dreamed of frolicking and playing in a field not on earth, and it stretched on forever. I woke up feeling different, more alive somehow, and discounted the experience as just a weird thing.

But I never forgot it.

And then I traveled back.

I struggle with anxiety, depression, and health issues. At the age of 12 or 13, Mom and I attended a prayer meeting where people prayed or worshipped independently.

Bowing my head, I felt lifted into the air. Weirdness overload! I heard every sound around me—especially the prayers—and still felt Mom next to me. But a second location dawned. I was visiting two places at once!

On arrival, I viewed a pathway and gate. I skipped toward it, knowing I was in Heaven. The clear gate (not gold colored) melted in and out of my vision. When it faded into view, it stood wide open. I remember feeling a little befuddled, but I knew to follow the path, so I complied.

When I walked through the gate, I entered a super bright room blaring with intense warmth. I could not see a thing but heard voices. In my head, the Holy Spirit said, 'Welcome. Look around and make yourself familiar.'

Should I look up? No, I might burn and die. I kept my eyes down and saw Jesus' feet. And what was this? I wore a long dress with layers and layers of colors—it went on forever.

I never wore dresses on earth because I had been told I don't look like a girl, and now I have body image issues. So, why wear a dress?

I tripped on the train a bit, and He assured me, 'You're beautiful and loved. You are in a dress because you are worthy of that beauty, no matter how you are feeling.'

Although there was no music, we danced. I felt like I was about age 7 again!

I remember getting a tap on the shoulder and being escorted out. We moved into the grassy field that stretched on for miles. Nostalgia rose. A repeat from years ago—in my dream. It felt familiar, quiet, serene, and peaceful. Feelings are very intense in Heaven—more so than I ever felt on earth. Joy filled me as we walked.

I saw unusual plants with huge fruit. Soon, we ended up at a humongous greenhouse. Excitement flowed through me—I adore flowers! Jesus knew this and showed me a daisy, which is my favorite, even though it is a weed. 'This flower is a representation of you. You feel like people do not like you, just like they do not like weeds called Daisy.'

And yet, how beautiful was the flower that He reserved for me!

I viewed amazing flora. Each flower growing represented a person I knew—each petal represented a time in their life. Some strangers, but I saw their faces and events from their lives within the flower. And I felt their emotions. I wonder if they will enter my life later? It almost felt like their memories became mine.

'This is going to be your spot when you get here.' He told me, 'You see into other people's lives and how they are struggling. But my goal is to help you see the beauty in others and to share that.'

I understood that it was not my time yet, and I did not feel ready to stay forever. But I relished feeling so beautiful, loved, and cared for.

I remain unable to recapture that deepness here on earth.

He finally allowed me to look at His face and eyes, but did not permit me to remember the specifics. What I do remember well is the lack of depression or anxiety while there. It became clear that He wanted me to face those issues on earth. He desired for me to do the work.

I returned with much more confidence. I don't feel mad at Him for not fixing me—I knew I could handle it.

When I returned and opened my eyes, all the prayers still circled around me. I burst into tears.

Mom startled. 'What's going on?'

'Mom, you won't believe it.'

I explained everything, feeling so many emotions that I could not sort them properly. My Mom prays for a lot of people and witnesses for Jesus in her work onstage. She hears a lot of strange requests and has even witnessed healings. I am so grateful for her support.

Now when I talk to other people who have either been to Heaven or received a Heaven vision like I did, I find so many similarities. This view of Heaven changed my life. I now strive and long for my eternal Home. After all, I have a greenhouse full of flowers waiting. And now my goal is to help others strive for Heaven too.

Reflection With Julie: Boxed Brain Barriers
Potential Block: Mental Health

We sometimes nurture a boxed-in mindset about God's people and the unique beauty blooming within each of us. We allow our human natures to overthink the simplicity of our view by applying our experiences, perceptions, and bias—often before a word is even spoken.

Laura struggles with anxiety and depression. Many of us

get it. Mental health concerns or issues can block Mission Manifesto discovery and fulfillment. Before her Heaven vision, she rotated in and out of therapy, feeling shame and convinced that others deserved it more than she. But because Jesus clearly allotted her the next step, Laura decided to march forward seriously. She changed her boxed-brain outlook, chose to believe her worthiness, grew sharply genuine with her folks, and started attending therapy regularly. She experienced a difference in her outlook as she instituted honesty with other people too—and no longer felt ashamed. She explained to me, 'I discovered in Heaven that it was all bigger than my life here on earth. So much bigger than I dreamed.'

The flowers on earth paled in comparison to Heaven's bounty.

For a long time, my anxiety during and after my trauma moved me into a harsh panic mode before and while flying. I specifically remember one super-hideous instance. Feeling so ill that I sank to the floor at the back of the plane, next to the beverage cart, I waited for a restroom. The people using them would not finish! All three of them! No way could I make it back to my seat to wait! Sweating, shaking, cramps, nausea—all that and more.

What if I passed out? Died on a plane—and not even from hitting a mountain or a bird? How mortifying! (Note this panic episode was before I went to Heaven and realized that dying as a child of God is not stressful at all—thank you, Jesus!)

When the restroom door finally hit the adjoining wall from one gentleman flinging it open, I jumped. What did I do wrong? But he did not appear mad, and I had already trumped a sure panic-death while sitting on the floor, cowering. I would make it after all! And even better—I later tiptoed gingerly back to my seat during turbulence without dying too.

I cannot believe I just provided so much bathroom detail

but apparently, someone needed to read it. Your transparency will help others break out of their box.

Mine too.

The preliminary jitters before hopping onstage to speak bordered on crazy-horrendous after my trauma too. I often worked diligently to swallow my angst onstage. Maintaining humor helped, because I laughed right along with my audience-friends as I recounted my silliness over the years. And by the time we rolled around the aisles bellowing in laughter a few times (just kidding), I forgot any nerves.

If we could not laugh, we would slide off script with no improv. Absolutely humor-less. But Jesus not only gave us humor and our ability to cackle, He laughs alongside us. I have heard Him. Some others who have visited Him in Heaven agree! Randy Kay heard Him laugh more than once during his trip to Heaven, most notably when Randy expressed pure excitement and joy after drinking from Heaven's living water. (24) Jesus also smiles plenty with His beloved children when they visit. (25)

He also felt joy here on earth. And although we do not see a specific account of Jesus laughing in the Bible, He utilized a lot of irony that likely made other people laugh. I suspect He had a deadpan face! Addressing the legalistic Pharisees of their hypocrisy in Matthew 23, He says in verse 24, 'You blind guides! You strain out a gnat but swallow a camel.' And in Luke 4:23, we read these words from Him, '…Surely you will quote this proverb to me: 'Physician, heal yourself!'' I can well see bystanders cracking a smile.

Hebrews 2:17 assures us, 'For this reason he had to be made like them, fully human in every way, in order that he might become a merciful and faithful high priest in service to God, and that he might make atonement for the sins of the people.'

Fully human, He felt everything we feel. And He expressed

those emotions, too.

A few months ago, in the middle of a prayer, I paused. 'I *so* adore you, Jesus.'

He immediately replied, 'I so adore *you*.'

I cracked up. Something about the *so*. *So* can be so—cheesy! He immediately dispatched a picture of Him generating a big 'ole belly laugh. We laughed together.

He completely gets me! And you, too. Each beautiful characteristic you haul to His table—and yes, everything else about you. My friend, please understand that you remain one hundred percent safe with Him. Even with your sins, those nasty habits you struggle with time and time again, the stunts you seem built to attract and struggle to repel—even with the gear you have been unable to release, and your deepest pain and buried, darkest secrets—you are safe.

He *so* adores you!

When I returned from Heaven, my nervy normal greatly changed. He healed my trauma brain wiring completely while I delighted in His presence—after many years of physical earth safety.

I no longer panic on planes, and even travel by myself at times. Extraordinary! The nerves still shake up a bit before I speak, but I claim a lot more God-given confidence than before. Enough that when a very large church emailed me yesterday about speaking, I replied, 'I'd be honored!' instead of first hashing out the pros and cons all night long in my boxed-up brain.

That reminds us how very far our boxed thinking gets us. Right? Umm, only as far as the walls of the box—in case you did not unwrap that part.

Is your brain stuck in a little brown box? Or maybe a slighter larger one?

Mine obviously was. My box-thinking rarely bent and

always showed the stubbornness (err, obstinance) that I excel in. And sometimes—get this—I would even remove my brain out of the box, gift it a newer environment and attempt nurturing so it could grow a different mindset. But as it tried hard to flourish, I neglected it. A few times, it pushed up one growth-stem in sheer and stubborn determination. As my confidence faltered, I let it die and sometimes even pushed it back down with a firm poke. And when it expired, I moved right back into my boxed-brain thinking.

Why?

Because I was unworthy, or certainly not worthy *enough*.

Neither did I feel capable—and get this, I also caught myself focusing on my past failures. Surely, I was unable to accomplish great things for my Lord. I pushed that new stem down or chopped it off or forgot to water it because I felt ashamed, just like Laura.

Obviously, we are not alone in this.

We enjoy boxes and planters, right? I fill them every spring. They are comfortable, predictable, and tough—built to store and guard contents. But intentional living for eternity in Heaven cannot thrive in boxes and planters, because it cannot breathe and flex to the growth He desires. Until we choose to forcefully unwrap our boxed-brains or hearts and allow them expansion room, we cannot thrive in our Mission Manifesto.

What if the expansion He needs from your brain or your heart right now is waiting patiently just outside the box? Even in the best-built greenhouse, a plant only grows so far before it reaches the ceiling. Like a plant, I love to lollygag in the warmth from the glass, but growth demands more than warm sun, water, and fertilizer—it stipulates stepping out of the box.

My Lord invites you to transplant with me. I hear this from Him today I write, giving me ecstatic shivers when I attempt deciphering a hint of the forthcoming for us all. My friend, He desires to move us into wide-open spaces where the wind might shake us even from our roots, where sometimes water is scarce, and the sun often scorches a bit.

But His field of beauty is wild. Glorious! Colorful! Heavenly! When we follow His leading to migrate out of our brain-boxes, roots deepen and blossoms flourish far beyond our limited designs. An entire garden blooms—forever.

Faith says, 'See, I am doing a new thing!' (Isaiah 43:19). New things rarely fit in old boxes or planters. And who knows, He might even want you to outgrow your porch or greenhouse.

Allow Him to choose the best seed, soil, sun, water, and season. He already has anyway. Accept the Gardener's choices. My Lord, who created you and wore humanness for over thirty years, knows what is best for your growth and is stretching you now to help grow and mold the rest of us. What He produces in surrendered ground is always more vibrant than what we can contain in a box. And like He showed Laura, the abundant greenhouse He tends while waiting for us will be so worth all the effort, and the wait.

That is a promise.

… 'What no eye has seen, what no ear has heard, and what no human mind has conceived the things God has prepared for those who love him— these are the things God has revealed to us by his Spirit. The Spirit searches all things, even the deep things of God' (I Corinthians 2:8-10).

'Rejoice in the Lord always. I will say it again: Rejoice! Let your gentleness be evident to all. The Lord is near. Do not be anxious about anything, but in every situation, by prayer and petition, with thanksgiving, present your requests to God. And the peace of God, which transcends all understanding, will guard your hearts and your minds in Christ Jesus' (Philippians 4:4-7).

Pause & Ponder

1. What biases, experiences, trauma, perceptions, or sins have held you back in coming fully into His presence?
2. What is your brain boxed in? Are you stuck? Will you consider committing to pushing through, thinking a new way, and sprouting with me? I pray that you do.

Chapter Nine

We Rocked On The Porch Of My Future Home

Kelly Fritz

My body hurt. At my chiropractic appointment, I lay flat on the table. As usual, an attached Ten's Unit, which uses light electrical currents to help pain, pulsated. It squeezed my muscles. Stickers decorated my skin—over the areas crying for relief.

The gentle scent of lavender drifted into the room.

The attendant entered. 'Are you doing alright?'

After ensuring I was good, she left. Calm stillness filled the room. Soft piano music marinated the vicinity. I again smelled the fragrance of lavender fields as I drifted off to sleep.

I woke up on a Victorian house porch in a white rocking chair, my head whipping back and forth as my eyes scanned everything around me. Victorians have always featured my favorite type of porch. When I was nine or ten, my dad bought a Victorian house and moved it to our property. I loved it immensely—including the woodworking and the minute detail.

Where am I?

The chair fit me perfectly, which is unusual as most chairs are always a little too big or small. My arms, shortened between my elbow and my wrist, normally don't fit armrests—but this one felt made for me. I rocked back and forth, enjoying the fitted chair and the view, but again wondering where I was.

To my left, I vaguely saw activity through a screen door. A railing with white spindle posts rested in front of me. Each post stretched far to the ground—intricately and beautifully designed. The woodworker who carved those posts enjoyed crafting with excellence.

In front of the railing grew beautifully trimmed bushes and a well-manicured, freshly mowed lawn. Beyond that, more shrubs stood in the distance. Further still, a wheat field looking ready for harvest glistened in the sun. It stretched forth with an opaque shimmer on top. As the wind softly blew, it rippled gently like water.

Above me, the sky was an orangey gold color mixed with blue. Rocking in silence, I felt the air shift, as if someone else lounged nearby.

Sure enough. To my right a coordinating chair rocked, matching my strides, and there sat Jesus. He wore a long robe and leaned against the back of the chair. His elbows rested on the armrests, hands steepled together against his mid-section. He gazed at the sunset ahead of us, and seemed very relaxed.

My mouth gaped open, staring at Him in awe. I planted a foot firmly on the wooden floor of the porch, halting my rocker. I wondered again where I had landed, and was I being so very rude right now?

He slowly turned to me. His face was darker-skinned, like He spent a lot of time in the sun, and His eyes spoke of soft kindness. 'Kelly.' He paused briefly. My name from His lips felt like He had uncurled a royal red carpet just for me. Love rolled off Him in waves. 'Sometimes, you have to wait.'

I awoke, back on the chiropractic table, the clinic sounds filling my ears, feeling shaken. I breathed in the familiar lavender smell. The attendant entered the room again, moving around and adjusting the Unit.

How long had I rocked on a Victorian porch?

'I just saw Jesus!' I announced. I recapped the marvelous moments. And then questioned—what did I need to wait for?

I always read the last page of a book first to know where I am headed. This vision was a picture of the homes I love—and my last page. My porch, created for me by Jesus in Heaven. It felt like home.

He says, 'And if I go and prepare a place for you, I will come back and take you to be with me that you also may be where I am' (John 14:3).

I can visit the Victorian house again, and I do. He allows me to ask questions. I recently asked one that rested foremost on my mind. 'What's behind the screen door?'

'You're not to know that yet.'

'OK. Well, why doesn't the screen door bang or make noise?'

'Well, this is Heaven.'

Come to think of it, the rocking chairs do not even creak against the wood grains of the porch. The only sound I recall is the complete pureness of His voice. His voice is firm, but not gruff. He talks to me as a loving Father would speak. His intonation is smooth, deep, calming, and familiar. But I never remember His mouth moving.

I see vibrant colors when I sit with Jesus, in our secret place He's created just for me.

Now I wait. I live each day with intention. Every day when I wake, I remember more remains for me to complete here. I look forward to the day when I can sit in that rocking chair, next to Him, for good.

Reflection With Julie: Devoted Desires
Potential Block: Dreams

Sometimes the dream or aspiration you are afraid to voice is the one God has whispered to your soul.

We are often quick to lay our dreams on the altar. Dying to self means surrendering anything we want, right? Dreams scream selfish pettiness—certainly unimportant in the greater scheme. Let's not even consider mumbling the actual issue: not feeling worthy enough to carry such a dream.

So, shut up, stupid dream!

Relinquishment is real. Not all dreams hail from Him. But what if we are misjudging the entire category of *desire*? What if God *planted* some of those dreams? What if they are part of your Heaven-Minded Mission Manifesto?

What if your dreams speak of your whole purpose?

Kelly has long held close a crazy dream—at least others might call it so. She is to build and open the Sueño Center (literally meaning 'dream'). Resting on a 212-acre property in Lafayette, Oregon, it will feature a pond, become appropriate for two wedding venues, and boast a nearby river.

She will build seven cabins around the main ministry house and rent them out—naming them each for one of the fruit(s) of the Spirit.

Kelly painted detailed watercolors of what God has shown her, including the fence she is to build around the parameter as soon as she obtains the property. She has also crafted pictures of the house setup inside, including a shelf of pottery pieces a local artesian will craft, and now the cabins around the large ministry home.

Go, Kelly! I note the Holy Spirit work in her life and see no fantasy hustle here! But when I ask about the dream moving forward, she remains firmly implemented in the current task as He assigns them: Paint it! Share it!

Yes. That is often how He works.

Habakkuk 2:2–3 says, 'Write down the revelation and make it plain on tablets so that a herald may run with it. For the revelation awaits an appointed time; it speaks of the end and will not prove false. Though it linger, wait for it; it will certainly come and will not delay.'

Let's consider the original language of these verses. For

'revelation,' the Hebrew word 'ḥāzôn' is used, which means: *vision, revelation, a message from God, with a possible focus on the visual aspects of the message.* 'Making it plain' means *to make clear, expound* so that a herald can then rûṣ *(to run, hurry, be a messenger; dart about; proclaim; make public)* the message. Yes, we are told to publicly proclaim it. Or to allow others to help with that. The message/vision/dream will be fulfilled in the right time—and it may be at the end (eternal focus).

Interestingly, the word 'ḥākâ' is used for 'wait.' One of the Hebrew definitions listed for 'ḥākâ' means not just to *wait* but *to wait in hope/ready to ambush.* (26)

Here is a quick summary of the verses: Write it down (or paint/draw), make it plain (speak of it and spend time processing it), wait for it (patiently but with great hope) and perhaps, even be ready to implement it quickly.

This quick implementation certainly reverberates for me lately and perhaps it does for you too. Why? Because it is time per our Lord. Time to increase our skills and impact—and this juncture includes implementing His provided dreams for you, because they play an important role.

I see my Lord's longing. As He speaks this, I feel His heart and His urgency. Eternal impact cannot wait any longer. He longs for His children to travel home. He grows excited for the big family reunion. He sees Satan and his minions ramping up as well—and desires to protect us.

At the same time, some afterlife accounts present a painful picture of Heaven mourning those who do not join us. (27) The Bible seems to confirm this. In 1 Timothy 2:3-4, He says, 'This is good, and pleases God our Savior, who wants all people to be saved and to come to a knowledge of the truth.' And in 1 Peter 3:9, we learn 'The Lord is not slow in keeping his promise, as some understand slowness. Instead, he is patient with you, not wanting anyone to perish, but everyone to come to repentance.' The entire chapter of Revelation 18 speaks of the monstrous grief the earth will feel at the destruction of Babylon. Believers will be urged to leave before it begins. Although it may very well be a particular city at that point (of that name or another), many commentaries agree that 'Babylon' in Revelation is a political and economic entity.

My heart cries as I apprehend His words to me: 'Gather together, my children. My squad. Each one of you is needed. They will see Me through your love. They will believe in my miracles as you become a vessel. Just as people watched the disciples funnel My miracles—they will be watching your works too, and they will draw near to Me.'

He has not returned to gather us yet—not because of His lack of preparation, but because *we* are not ready.

What might your part be in getting our world ready for Him?

I have long gripped a dream of writing full-time. I feel bashful to admit my truth, because I never saw how He could possibly fulfill this and still allow us to pay the bills, especially with my last several years of medical expenses. That is just the realism in the author world, right? My mental landscape just knew I needed to work conventionally and write as a side hustle forever, until a retirement coup.

As weariness snuck up and wrapped around my body, I finally admitted a newish struggle. In my younger years, I worked all day and wrote like a one-woman stampede once the family hit their beds or remained otherwise occupied. But as I crept ... er, sped, into more middle-ish years, exhaustion bloomed and my health suffered. My brain felt too weary after working to craft words!

I desired deeply to follow His plan, whatever it included. So I attempted to leap whatever hurdles appeared and kept hustling. Not writing at all was never an option.

But my truth of 'never' does not appear to adhere with His truth. Go figure.

After the very difficult breaching from my day job, I felt a twinge of hope despite my grief. I kept hearing, 'Go home and write. I have more for you.' And when I sat in church wondering if they might ever ask me to share my Heaven story, I heard, 'Don't worry about that. I have more for you.' Then, seconds later, 'This is your safe place to fill up.' Yes! I need that! More recently, I attended a ladies event in our area held on a regular basis. They gave me a speaking opportunity a few years ago, and I remain grateful. I have a new story now of which they are aware. However, the organizer does not respond to inquiries. As I looked around the room a few weeks ago as an attendee and silently questioned, He whispered, 'Don't worry about it. This is not your venue. I've got more for you.'

More what? WHY? (Ha ha).

I immediately bowed my head and thanked Him, repeating something I have now said several times since my first Heaven trip. 'Here I am, Lord. Send me.'

I chose to obey the direct instruction to stay home and write as fast as George the nutso squirrel who attempts highway speeds on the top of my backyard fence. Any job search emails flew to the promo folder as I refocused on His mission for me, even though I knew components of it still hid in the surprise bag.

Never astonishing to God is how He intertwines dreams. Crystal, formerly a leader of our ARMS abuse recovery group programs, replaced me at my day job. In fulfilling my desire, He provided her dream job—one in ministry she thought she would never obtain.

But God.

My path to writing full-time took forty-five years. Well, I started writing forty-five years ago. About thirty years ago, I decided to work on it as a career. As I continue to pen His insights on Heavenblog.org and as this book expands, it is obvious now that His greater plans are Heaven, not earth-focused. He pours these words into me, for you. Yay! That is the best jolt of all. How privileged we become when He builds and wields our dreams, skills, spiritual gifts, and talents for His greater good.

God desires to institute and magnify our hopeful dreams. Ephesians 3:20 says, 'Now to him who is able to do immeasurably more than all we ask or imagine, according to his power that is at work within us…'

My Lord is very future-focused. Romans 8:28 truly means that He works all to the good of people—but He was not referring to earth-time. He is far too extended in His reach to be so shortsighted. Our time here creates only a brief blip on the radar. When you understand this, it changes your perspective. And things here hardly seem important at all in the Grand Scheme.

On that note, we must remember that our Lord is not the only one future focused. Satan too knows the scriptures and his future. Have no doubt that he also endeavors to benefit it. Although conniving and evil, he does not rate on the dumb-scale. He maintained a position as a high rank lead angel before he made disastrous choices. (28) Remember who you deal with, but also recognize the power Jesus gives you. Choose to not focus on the earthly and temporary calamities—but on Jesus!

Our dreams honor our Lord. Stop dismissing what He may be inviting you to consider. Lean into Him. Ask Him boldly. Dream freely, no strings attached.

Your Creator also carries the title of Dream-Giver.

'Take delight in the Lord, and he will give you the desires of your heart' (Psalm 37:4).

'Commit to the Lord whatever you do, and he will establish your plans' (Proverbs 16:3).

Pause & Ponder

1. What dreams has He given you? Do any feel impossible? Start praying about those with the expectation that He will use your dreams for His good.
2. What one step will you take this week to fulfill a dream?
3. Have you chosen to say, 'Here I am. Send me?' If you have not, I pray you feel led to do so today.

Jessica Smith Art

Chapter Ten

A Walk With Jesus Healed My Heart

Karen G.

My whole childhood, I struggled with my mother. When I needed comfort, she was rarely available. She seldom showed affection. I had to initiate any hugs or physical touch. I felt unloved, unworthy, and distant from her.

Eventually, I stopped trying.

Once when very young, I left the house for a walk around the block after she clearly stated I needed to stay in the yard. A cop picked me up and brought me home. As I returned and he questioned her, Mom blushed brightly—she never asked if I was OK or why I left.

Would she even miss me if I went away forever?

In church, when I sat with my friends close to the back, she stared at me from the choir section. My friends peeked and confirmed when I felt her eyes on me. So weird.

Mom frequently told me that I shamed her and gave me the silent treatment.

When a bit older, I walked around at night in Spokane Valley. I felt God with me. But I often felt sad while wandering and asked for a tap or sign that He remained nearby.

My loneliness grew.

Over the years, I adapted somewhat—but my heart never stopped longing for my mom's love and wondering why I unsettled her so.

One night, at fifteen, I spent the night with my friend Marylin, and we slept in her bed. I was on the side near the wall and lay facing it.

As I rested, trying to get sleepy—I felt my heartbeat slow

dramatically. I guessed my body was getting ready for some shut eye but this was strange—I had never felt such a reluctant pulse before.

Astounded, I watched the bedroom wall open. I gaped as I viewed the bright and beautiful stars. I was in space! How?

I had never seen the skies so gorgeous, and not since.

One star singled out—moving closer to me.

The star, which was Jesus, said kindly, 'Karen, let's talk.' He took my hand, His touch tender and soft.

Jesus revealed His face, and I do not remember details. But it wore love, kindness, and openness. His eyes held more fondness for me than I ever experienced, and more than I've seen since.

He sure loved me. I observed that clearly.

We strolled through a field with lots of trees around it. Brilliant green grass grew. I remember unexplainable colors. The closest comparison I can gather are the colors after rain when sunbeams shine through dark clouds. I do not recall any flowers.

Jesus squeezed my hand. 'Karen, I want to share something with you. Your mom does love you, but she doesn't know how to show it.' His eyes filled with tenderness—for both Mom and me. Yes, I saw His deep love for her, too.

He shared many things with me. It felt like we walked and talked for hours. He then said, 'You can stay home, here, if you want. But you are not done yet.'

I grinned, happiness overspilling. 'I'd love to stay, but I have a feeling you want me to go back.'

He smiled. 'That's the right thing.'

I remember taking deep breaths as I considered. 'I guess there are a lot of people who would miss me.' And besides, it would not be very nice to pass away in my friend's bedroom, who was a new Christian.

I decided. 'I'll go back.'

Jesus smiled again, and it lit up the skies.

My heartbeat increased. He and the light disappeared, and the bedroom wall returned, like a curtain pulled across a lovely scene.

As my eyes tried to focus on the wall again, my heart pounded. I awoke my friend with my news, still trembling.

Her eyes grew super wide. 'Oh, that's scary!'

No way was I going back to sleep! Her mom made us hot chocolate and, after she heard the story, explained that I had experienced a nightmare.

Although I cannot remember what Jesus looked like, and I wonder if that is intentional on His part, I have viewed familiar things since. For instance, when I met my husband and he showed me a picture of his boys, I already knew them. And when I began watching the *The Chosen* and saw the actor cast as Jesus, I acknowledged that he did sort of look like Him.

Kind of.

There is a spirituality in me that is 'otherworld,' and it has never left. So many times, I have wanted to soar back home. Especially when my husband, who professed Christianity and became abusive to the kids and me left for another Christian woman.

That was my second 'Christian' husband to do so.

Through my walk with Jesus, I accepted Mom's inability to show me love but learned that Jesus never abandoned me. His love is the only pure love. Imperfect humans cannot mimic it, although good people try. My time with Him provided confidence in my love for Christ and my beliefs, because they have always been a little odd and different than the standard churchgoer. And now sometimes when people talk about Heaven, I need to say, 'That's not what I saw at all.'

Sadly, most people then say I am not biblical and need to

straighten out my beliefs. So I do not speak of it much.

I know what I saw. I also acknowledge that other people's experiences may differ from mine.

I am so grateful to Jesus for showing me my true home and sharing His vast love, companionship, and insights. He knew that a walk with Him while feeling His hand in mine was exactly the tonic needed for my wounded heart.

Reflection With Julie: Abiding Apologies
Block: Wounds

Have you ever apologized for something that you did not do?

A couple of years ago, it was one of those days at the office. The phone rang nonstop. Seeing that everyone else was tied up, I grabbed it again.

A pastor from another area asked for guidance as he prepared to meet with a woman interested in attending his church. There was only one issue. She had experienced a negative incident with another congregation. Her former leadership believed her ex's stories that she exerted abuse against him. Most in the congregation sided with the leadership; at least the loudest ones did. Although this gal had attended that church all her life, and brought her husband, they requested she attend elsewhere so he could worship the Lord in peace.

She departed, devastated. And did not search for a new church (very common).

After several years of working on her healing, she felt encouraged by the Lord to discover a new body of Christ.

She felt it pretty vital to meet and talk to the pastor first, which I heartily agree with.

But how should I approach this, he wondered?

He later admitted almost dropping the phone when I

answered, 'Apologize to her.'
All I heard on my end was, 'Say what?'

OK, I can be Mrs. Blunt. But I learned very early in my leadership career that appearing in the doorway of a glass shop looking like a bulldozer clearly creates negative effects on employee motivation. It turns out, many years ago, three hospital managers who reported to me started job searching elsewhere.

Ouch.

I am not one to hide in the supply room and wait for the storm to pass. We met. They apologized for talking amongst themselves instead of approaching me, and I started working on my bulldozer trait—because relationships and people are far more important than policies. I believe that—but my task-oriented brain failed to relay that message.

Now recognizing the mental scramble happening on the other end of the phone with this gentleman pastor, I offered a softer follow up. 'Please consider apologizing to her. On behalf of Jesus' church.'

Three men have apologized to me for my trauma, and none of them used abusive tactics. One, a childhood friend. Another, a professional acquaintance—smart move. But by far the most meaningful one came from Bill as we dated. 'I'm so sorry that men chose to do those things to you, hurting your heart, spirit, and body. There's no excuse for that. That was so very wrong.'

Awww. And yes, that was a very smart move on his part too, although his motive was not to worm his way into my heart (he already had it); he truly was showing his genuine self. He had noted the consequences of trauma in my life and also in my family's lives.

The three apologies greatly differed. The first basically said, 'I'm so sorry that happened to you.' Honestly, that is somewhat common to hear (although kind), so I guess it stands out only due to the giver's gender. The other two expressed it more uniquely. They said, 'I'm so sorry that *men* did this to you. We've made some really bad decisions over the years. That's not okay to hurt you, or any woman.'

They owned it.

I never received apologies from those who needed to give it and two have passed. I help many women and men in similar straits, also highly unlikely to ever hear one. Part of my role is assisting them in mending without the apology-balm. It is possible.

Healing moments occurred when these males apologized for men as a group. Although I provide ditto with lady survivors, it pales to the effect of someone of that gender taking ownership of this societal sin.

The Church carries much responsibility for survivor's secondary trauma (sometimes even primary, especially with spiritual and sexual abuse), and survivors leave the Church in droves because of it. I have seen hundreds of examples.

The Church also needs to apologize.

Abusers often begin by quietly building their camps early on, choosing institutions or groups that already feel trusted through their own presence or their partner's presence.

When I trained a church group a while back on spotting abuse, an elder and Celebrate Recovery leader asked for help. 'We have a man who is involved in Bible Studies, missions to people in their homes, helps the elderly, and often has coffee with the pastor. He seems very spiritually mature and knows the scriptures. He's always jumping up to serve. The pastor even asked him to do some mentoring to other members. I don't know his wife very well, but I believed him when he told us that she has mental health issues and is abusive. But after your talk today—I'm not so sure.'

I call each of their allies their 'camp.' I smiled warmly.

'You're right to question. His building of his camp was very intentional. He started all this serving when?' (I wanted to say 'smoke blowing' but refrained myself).

'Right when they started attending, over two years ago.'

I nodded sadly. By the time she grew truly fearful as things at home escalated, she held zero allies in the church administration. When approaching leadership about her husband's behavior, they promised to follow up. But after they met with smoke-blowing guy, they dismissed her. Why? Because her well-spoken, giving, 'humble servant' husband adamantly explained his frustration and how maxed out he felt with her mental issues and subsequent actions. They needed to help him, not her.

They thought her wackadoodle.

They trusted the wrong party.

Many echo this experience and result. Unless we are specifically abuse-educated, we tend to believe the one who approaches us first, or whom we have a previous relationship with. You know, the one who appears genuine, often charming, philanthropic, and well spoken. Perhaps even a family member or good friend. Versus the one with a shaking or monotone voice, little or greatly expanded emotion, and enough trauma that their brain is absolutely frazzled and the facts they state cannot even calculate an equation. Much less equal an answer that makes sense.

People would benefit from recalling Proverbs 18:17, reminding us to take all things into account. Thank you to those pastors and leaders who seek more than the Word of God when dealing with the very real trauma needs of your people. Someone out there may know more than you and (gasp!), it might even be a woman.

In Nehemiah Chapter One, Nehemiah begins days of fasting, praying, and mourning over the destruction of

Jerusalem. In that process, he apologizes for everyone's sins. Take a look, starting at verse 6: 'Let your ear be attentive and your eyes open to hear the prayer your servant is praying before you day and night for your servants, the people of Israel. I confess the sins we Israelites, including myself and my father's family, have committed against you. We have acted very wickedly toward you. We have not obeyed the commands, decrees and laws you gave your servant Moses.'

The pastor who called did apologize to the lady he met with. At first, after I recommended it, he felt defensive and prideful (his words). But as I prayed for him on the phone, He felt deep stirring and said he petitioned God on his own after hanging up.

He chose bravery. He chose humility. He chose truth.

He crushed it!

His willingness to apologize for the Church that wounded this sister opened healing for this woman. This leadership meant safety. It brought her closure, and she viewed this pastor's heart for the oppressed. She not only started attending that church, but now leads a Bible study.

Mrs. G., who walked with Jesus in this chapter, taught at my elementary school. She also appeared in LeaAnn's story earlier. She taught the grade ahead of me, but we all drew close in that small Christian school with teachers playing multiple roles. She became my leader in extracurricular pursuits. Not only did she also encourage my writing and commonly announce that both LeaAnn and I would write professionally someday, but I retain a fond memory of Mrs. G. emotionally rescuing me.

Mrs. G., you may not remember, but at the age of ten, as the female lead in 'Enchanted Journey,' I had to belt out a full *solo.* And before one of the performances, I grew terrified. Stress felt as big as that climbing truck tire on the playground. I burst into tears backstage, soaking the front of my gingham, costumed dress with saltiness, and refused to step onstage. But instead of panicking and saying, 'Oh no, we don't even have an understudy!' you talked me through it. 'Oh Julie, I'm sorry I didn't realize you've been struggling. I believe in you. I know you can do this.' You hugged me tightly and I clung.

Despite all the stress I now know was happening in your life, you owned that moment for me. I knew then that I could sing. And I did.

Thank you. I am sorry you suffered so much. I am sorry that your mom and men chose to hurt you. There is no excuse for that. I am so glad that Jesus saw your pain, and took you for an incredible Heaven walk—healing some of that space in your heart.

My friends, apologies, acknowledgements, and validation can help move someone to their healing. Remember these accessories for your wounds and other soldier's wounds as you implement your Mission Manifesto.

When I reached the conclusion of this chapter, I headed to the grocery store. In Aisle Eight, as I perused a simple box of teabags, my Lord's voice resonated suddenly and deeply. It so surrounded me, I whipped around to see if anyone else heard. Of course, no aisle-partners existed.

He said, 'Do you remember when you were in Heaven? I apologized. I expressed regret for your many years of pain. I'm so sorry you experienced that, Julie. Your pain is mine. Those sinful actions were never My plan for you.'

'My Lord!' I chucked the box of tea back on the shelf, and with a shot of adrenaline, scurried to the checkout with the rest of my items, battling tears. Gratefulness briskly welled. *Thank you, Jesus. Thank you, Jesus.* My fingers trembling, I quickly texted Bill while in line. 'Jesus apologized to me!'

'What?'

'He just told me that when I was in Heaven, He expressed regret for my painful years.'

'Wow. That's very powerful.'

Powerful indeed. Although not Jesus' doing, He owned it.

And He owns your pain, too.

'Be still before the Lord and wait patiently for him; do not fret when people succeed in their ways, when they carry out their wicked schemes. Refrain from anger and turn from wrath; do not fret—it leads only to evil. For those who are evil will be destroyed, but those who hope in the Lord will inherit the land' (Psalm 37:7-8).

'I will instruct you and teach you in the way you should go; I will counsel you with my loving eye on you' (Psalm 32:8).

Pause & Ponder

1. Is there something you can own, something you either did or did not do, that might help someone else's healing, or your own healing?
2. Will you commit to doing so?

Chapter Eleven

Raising My Dead Daughter To Life
Claudia Martin

My daughter Rhema's name is unique. It is pronounced 'Ray-ma' and means 'the power in the spoken word of God.' Our pastor laid hands on her during her dedication as a baby. He prayed for her and prophesized. 'She will win many souls to the Kingdom because of her love.'

Grabbing onto that and holding it in my heart, I felt so ready to watch this amazing occurrence for the rest of her life.

I was a newer Christian, and my husband and I had separated at one point due to his abuse and control. When we reunited, I saw little change. He continued to control and demand instant submission from me, even when I felt the Lord guiding me another direction.

'You are supposed to ask me the spiritual questions instead of interpreting scripture on your own,' he claimed.

When Rhema was about three months old, we prepped to vacation at Yellowstone and see some family as well as enjoy camping. Sunday became the target day to leave, but we loved our church and decided to wait until after service.

Our pastor's sermon included the story of the widow in 2 Kings, whose son passed away. She said, 'All is well' to people after he died. Traveling alone (unusual at the time), she sought out Elisha, demonstrating remarkable faith. Ultimately, Elisha resurrected him. It is probably the only sermon that stuck with me from this pastor. He provided a dramatic retelling and kept emphasizing, 'All is well, all is well!'

After church, one of the teachers of the affiliated Bible school provided twelve recordings. He smiled. 'The Lord really put it on my heart to ask you to listen to this during vacation.' It was the series, 'Body, Soul, and Spirit' with Kenneth Copeland.

We took off to Yellowstone and listened to the recordings the entire way—again and again. I felt so full of the Word. The messages rang in my ears and spirit. I especially pulled into my heart that we were not to obey the head—which fails us, but are to seek the Spirit first.

It resonated deeply.

We found a spot, opened our pop-up tent trailer and my husband told me to start dinner while he and one daughter searched for wood. Our oldest, Brian, stayed at the camp.

It grew very chilly outside—I had never camped in that much cold before.

Before I started, I checked on the girls. Inside the canvased trailer, Rhema lay on her tummy in her portable infant bed, swaddled and warm. Rachel, my two-year-old, played on the floor.

While cooking outside, I heard a strange noise. I turned off the stove and jumped into our sleeping quarters. It sounded like a rattle—a thin, fluid-filled heave for air. 'What is that?' I asked aloud.

I heard it again.

I thought my husband had returned and now played tricks. But as I focused, I heard it several more times. It was coming from the portable crib placed on the larger bed.

Brian jumped up into the tented enclosure. 'What's going on?'

I hurried to the baby. Rhema had scooted into the corner—her face squished into the plastic edges of the crib. I grabbed her.

Brian yelled. 'Mom! What's happening?' Rachel looked up from her toy, staring wide-eyed.

Rhema's body was stiff, her open eyes fixed. Foamy around her mouth, she gurgled like she could not pull in air.

But then she stopped and grew still. And instead of thinking with the Spirit, in my intense fear, I thought with my head. 'I'll take her outside,' I gasped. 'The cold air will help her breathe…'

Brian followed us outside, right on my heels. 'Mom! What's wrong with her?'

That Bible story started running the script right through my head. 'All is well, Brian. Nothing is wrong.'

'Mom, look at her. Her eyes are wide. Staring!'

'No, all is well!'

He started yelling at me. 'Look at her! What is wrong? Something's wrong!'

'All is well,' I repeated.

Rhema's lungs made one more tiny, labored, and noisy rattle. Then she lay still in my arms.

'Mom! Listen to her!'

'All is well, Brian.'

But then fear welled again, and immediately the Holy Spirit said to rebuke it. I yelled, 'Fear! In the name of Jesus, I command you to leave RIGHT NOW in Jesus name!' When I yelled, it felt like Aaron's story in the Bible—when warmth of oil poured down his beard. For me, it was my head. A strength permeated. Peace flowed.

Brian huffed. 'I'm going to go get Dad. I'm telling on you!'

'Go!' I agreed.

You see—it was only his dad's job to rebuke things. And he often became involved in intercessory prayer for others. I was not ever to provide that. Brian surely would let his father know how crazy I was acting.

I heard from the Holy Spirit again. 'Take her in the tent.'

I whirled around with her still in my arms and obeyed,

climbing back into the tent trailer.

'Lay her down.'

No longer fearful, I yelled again. 'You said a prophet's word never falls to the ground! You said she will not die! You said I have authority and I take authority over this right now. YOU said she will win souls with love.'

The Holy Spirit kept bringing scriptures to my mind. 'His word never falls to the ground. His word goes forth and creates… His word…not mine. His words will not come back void...' Verses poured out of my mouth.

He said, 'Put her on her back on the bed.'

I laid her down on her stomach instead, remembering from CPR class that you can blow an infant's lungs out by giving rescue air. 'I can't give her mouth-to-mouth.'

'Push on her back and pull her arms back.'

I turned her over and did as He said.

'Push on her again. Pull her arms back again.'

I pushed. 'Live in the name of Jesus!'

Rhema started to cough.

Great relief tingled my whole body, I gratefully held her to my chest, and started feeding her.

A lady appeared in the doorway. 'Hi. I heard you yelling and screaming. Is everything OK?'

The Holy Spirit said, 'Testify to her.'

Having no idea who this stranger was, I shared the full story.

Her eyebrows puckered a tad. 'Well, you're feeding her. I wouldn't recommend that.' Then gently, 'Do you know your daughter was dead?'

'Yes, but I didn't receive that or tolerate it.'

'But the noise you're talking about is called a death rattle. Do you mind if I look at her? I'm an RN.'

The nurse checked Rhema and approved feeding her.

Shortly after, my husband and other children returned to the campsite.

I learned that we all are capable of hearing and following the Holy Spirit. His acts of greatness are not limited to gender. He expects me to hear Him and follow through on His requests.

I also learned to listen to Him over what others tell me. When Jesus was going to Jairus' daughter, people said, 'Don't bother, she is already dead.'

He threw them all out of the room and said, 'Go away. Don't worry. She is only sleeping.' Basically, 'All is well.'

I always listen to Him over other people now. And I have personally experienced the truth: His words never come back void to Him. I praise Him for this.

Every Believer has a voice, and it is the voice of victory.
-Kenneth Copeland (29)

'Here there is no Gentile or Jew, circumcised or uncircumcised, barbarian, Scythian, slave or free, but Christ is all, and is in all' (Colossians 3:11).

Reflection With Julie: Steady Say-So
Potential Block: Disobedience

God keeps speaking to me about prayers and the power within them. In addition, the verses about believers having the same power as He continue popping out at me.

This opened a whole new world for this conservatively-raised gal.

After my return from Heaven, the Words of Knowledge gift He had already bestowed seemed to increase in frequency and became more detailed in what I learned. I am not convinced the

Heaven trip accomplished that as much as the deep study and spiritual reflection I accelerated into after my first little voyage.

Something that stuck out almost comically became the increased effectiveness of my prayers for other people. Answers to those prayers arrived from all over, even online. In the abuse recovery groups I taught, Jesus not only healed women, but sent a messenger to show up in the room. That is another book, I guess! Of course, I continued to remind people of the absolute truth. It was not me answering these prayers, but my Jesus.

I lean toward obedience when the Holy Spirit instructs me, with some exceptions. Stubborn Jules! The last two times I had visited my very good friend, Karen, He instructed me to pray for her healing—from cancer.

'Sure,' I replied. And then likely released a sigh. I do love my sister-friend! But really? Why not just heal her with my silent prayers, Jesus? I know You can do that if You choose!

But I failed to obey. The first time I truly forgot as we hurried to catch up on each other's lives. On the way home, I avoided smacking myself in the forehead, but wanted to. Duh! Sorry, God.

The next time she and I chatted, I mentioned the directive and told her I had messed up.

Interesting, she felt.

We were raised conservatively. Baptist and Evangelical—pretty much the same wash basin. I also felt nervous about her potential reaction when I asked to pray, but He reminded me to align with the plan. I set it aside.

The second time we gathered, fear rose and I downright disobeyed. I had prayed with more people by then—but it is more challenging with those I know and love. Was I afraid of disappointing them if God chose not to heal?

Probably. My knees went a'knockin!

I apologized to God again—a half apology. Concessions without true change mean little. And although Karen and I instigated some attempts to meet in the next few months, I sure did not push discovering a free time for both of us.

The clock ticked, the calendars flipped months, and time roared by.

We finally figured out a day as enough became enough. We needed each other, and besides, I reminded her, I had now failed twice in this task He allotted to me.

My merciful friend decided enough was enough too, or maybe she wearied of hearing apologies. We set a date and I arrived at her house to find her babysitting an adorable little grandson who I then played and played with. So much fun!

When we hit the porch to chat and watch little L. try to eat dirt, God poked me. I did not sigh, but I wanted to! I scooted my chair close—would she mind if I took her hand? *Don't be silly, Jules—you've only known her for thirty-five years and don't forget that at one time, you were roomies!*

God poked her too. To my surprise, she held her hand out eagerly. By now, my brain had devoured almost one full Christian healing book. Building faith beforehand seemed important.

'Do you agree that God heals, my friend?'

'Yes. I do!'

Although we heard babble in the background and kept one occasional eye open watching Mr. L. Gardener, I managed to pray, choking back the emotion that always seems to arrive like a fifty-pound throat lump when praying for people I care for.

'AMEN!' we both claimed. That very word also ranks as vital. It literally means 'so be it' or 'it is true.'

Whew! Done! I felt deep peace and grand relief because I finally obeyed! Of course, we continued our regular conversation after heading back into her living room and enjoyed a wonderful rest of the visit.

Karen walked me outside to leave later and we hugged. 'Someone didn't want you to come today,' she announced quietly.

I stepped back, quirking my eyebrows.

'Satan. When I woke up, I almost cancelled you—I felt it *so* heavily. But I knew who it was, so I didn't.'

The realization dawned quickly. 'Ohhh. He didn't want me to pray with you. Oh!'

He sure didn't! Stupid Satan!

I chatted with God aloud while driving home. Of course, I regretfully lamented my multiple instances of disobedience, apologizing a few times. When would I learn to just 'drop and do'?

After all that soul baring and now feeling His merciful forgiveness, I gazed up at some gorgeous cloud formations. 'Would you send me a dream of Heaven tonight? I miss being there with you, Jesus. I want to see Heaven again.' It had been an entire year since I visited—it felt like a century.

And He replied, 'I will heal your friend Karen.'

Silence bounced through the car. Relief washed through me. And of course, tears ran down my cheeks for the next several miles.

Little did I know He would answer my plea to see Heaven again within a week, and outfit me for my Manifesto ahead.

Perhaps I will start praying for that more often!

Amazing things happen when we choose obedience to Him. John 14:23 says, "Jesus replied, 'Anyone who loves me will obey my teaching. My Father will love them, and we will come to them and make our home with them.'"

We all have the power to pray wellness over people and to even cast out evil. Jesus did not leave us here as sitting ducks—He handed us the Holy Spirit, to guide, protect, advise, and empower His family. (31) He did not say, 'You have the same power as us, except for this, that and quite-a-lotta-stuff…save that junk for the almighty God.'

But because of power and control, Claudia learned she was not supposed to hear, interpret, or obey the Holy Spirit. As a woman, why would He even speak to her? Of course, we understand the stinkin' thinking in that garbage pail, as our Lord highly values women. Jesus not only spoke to them, but healed them, regarded them, depended on them, spent time with them, forgave them, saved them, and asked them for faith, service, leadership and obedience. (32) The same as He did with men.

Fun fact. Did you know that in the Hebrew Bible, there is no word used for just 'pastoring'? The passages that speak of being a pastor use words that truly mean 'shepherding' and 'teaching'—roles women continue to fill. In the Bible, women led, shepherded, and taught—they 'pastored.'

When it came to sparking Rhema's heart, the Holy Spirit seemed insistent and completely reversed the thinking that outside influence impacted for so many years. Claudia could, should and would be powerfully used by God to resurrect the life of someone meant to impact others for Jesus for many years to come.

Had she not listened, or had she chosen to follow instead the wayward thinking of a controlling man, Rhema would not be alive today. And in the next section of this book, you will learn one of the ways God intended for Rhema to minister to the rest of us.

'Do not merely listen to the word, and so deceive yourselves. Do what it says.' (James 1:22).

'If you fully obey the Lord your God and carefully follow all his commands I give you today, the Lord your God will set you high above all the nations on earth. All these blessings will come on you and accompany you if you obey the Lord your God' (Deuteronomy 28:1-2).

Pause & Ponder

1. Is there an area you are struggling to obey in? What is it?
2. Are you ready to be obedient? What action will you now take to fulfill what God asks of you?

Chapter Twelve

He Healed The Pain Of My Deep Loss

Michele Weisman

Note: this story discusses miscarriage.

My heart felt fully exposed during church worship as tears streamed down my cheeks. Six months ago, I had miscarried, and my pain always rose to the highest point during worship. I knew God slowly healed my heart—but I wondered how long this would continue.

Why had this baby been taken from me? Was I not good enough?

Although I had experienced unconfirmed miscarriages before, this one beat them all. During my first appointment, the ultrasound technician seemed to be a nervous wreck. She stammered. 'U-Um, I'm sorry. This wand must not be working. Let me go get the doctor.'

As she left, I told myself everything was OK. Then remembered that two or three days ago, some symptoms of increased hormones had decreased. I blinked rapidly as I stared at the bland ceiling tiles.

The doctor arrived cheerfully enough but then confirmed my worst fears with a gentle voice. 'I'm sorry. Michele, there is no heartbeat.'

As I entered the lobby, I saw gift baskets for pregnant moms. My heart stung. The staff members requested that I call for a ride, and when my parents arrived, I blindly crept to the car. As we pulled out of the parking lot, my thoughts whirled in circles. I had heard stories of babies coming back. Of no heartbeats but then the pulse of life beating again.

Was my faith just not strong enough?

One Sunday, I sat at the dining room table with my Bible study while my husband and daughters slept. The lesson covered John 14:2, where Jesus promised to prepare a room for His followers in His Father's house. In biblical times, a groom did the same for his bride, building onto her father's home. The parallel struck me—Christ's promise reveals such deep intimacy with God.

But very quickly, I no longer sat at my dining room table.

I stood in a different room. The windowless walls were lined with squarish gray stones. Each stone measured about eight-by-eight inches square and five inches thick—I am still not sure how I knew that, but I did.

Each stone moved like a breathing lung. Coursing through each one, giving life, was deep love. God's love.

I reached up to touch the stone in front of me—slightly rough under my fingers. I understood that the same love shifted in my body, moving and alive. I breathed His love and touched His love. My entire body pulsated with His incredible love—for me. For us. It felt perfect, amazing, pure—an energy I had never before experienced.

In that moment, I realized that my baby, and my unconfirmed babies before this one, lived in Heaven, fully engulfed in God's living, life-giving love. In a room made especially for them.

I could not have asked for a better answer to my heart's cry. Although I did not see any little ones, I glimpsed God's overwhelming, perfect love for me, my children, and His children. And this love experience is what my babies remain soaked in for all eternity. If that is all Heaven is, that is more than enough for me.

How could I desire any less for them?

As I stood in the stone room, considering all of this, I remembered traveling to Ireland at age 21 and viewing old ruins of church grounds. There, I placed my hand on the stone in front of me and saw someone's name and birthday engraved on it—the same date as a close family member, just in another century.

It seemed that stone was chosen for me to see that day. And here now—more stones.

I quickly found myself back at my dining room table. I sat stunned, reviewing the details, still fully in touch with all that beautiful, radiant love.

I told my husband about the experience as we drove to church. Tears flowed, but they were joy-filled tears. I wept more during worship, but they remained tears of joy! For certain, I felt forever assured of the glorious love that my children breathed and thrived in!

Tears fell all day. I could not stop them and did not want to. This Heavenly gift of compassion graced my mourning heart. Miscarriage grief is so private and often misunderstood. Some people say very unhelpful things. But I know now—death is here because of sin and the devil. Death was never God's plan for us.

And He is taking care of my babies for me.

Luke 19:40 says that the stones will cry out, meaning that the truth of Jesus and His love cannot be silenced. I experienced that. Although I still reflect and wonder from time-to-time what life would have been like without my losses, I am fully satisfied in knowing I will see my children again one day.

I have never again wept in pain about my miscarriages.

Reflection With Julie: Cement Chasms
Potential Block: Grief

In a weird shuffle that was either altruistic divine or absolutely crazy, I sat with my husband and his family as his wife lay dying.

His first wife, that is.

Bill and I met many years ago at Bible college. We were not even really friends (although I admired him from afar). And when I asked one of his friends about him, she very firmly told me that a girlfriend waited back in Pennsylvania. I remember her exact tone of her voice and how she drew out the name of the fortunate young lady.

I got the message—back off, Jules. He and I laugh about it today.

Fast forward many years.

Bill and his family still vacationed yearly in the little coastal town where we met. Fourteen years ago, his wife Glenda braked her bike for one of our famous coastal elks, flying over the handlebars when one brake failed. She wore no helmet and her head met the pavement. She cried out to God when entering the ambulance on a stretcher—then He gave her blessed sleep.

But despite brain surgery to remove fluid, she never woke up.

When I heard, I felt led to make connection. God told me, 'Let him know you're here. All his family and support network are in PA.'

I messaged Bill, and we met for coffee.

This meeting began a pilgrimage neither of us planned.

I sat with Glenda, who was still unresponsive, while Bill and his daughter took needed breaks. And then for a week when Bill returned to Pennsylvania to restart their daughter in school. While reading Glenda scripture, playing music, and praying with her, I also shared updates on her family.

'Your daughter is doing well. She's returning to school now. Bill went to get her settled, but I'm here. Can you hear me, sweet lady? Wake up if you can—so many people are praying.'

Please wake up. Please wake up.

I felt Jesus' presence, and Glenda seemed relaxed. I wondered if she already walked along paths with her Savior, and nowadays I know He met her there.

Who would want to return from a Heaven trip?

As greeting cards arrived and gathered on the walls, the staff continually told us something differed about Glenda's room—a sweet presence. They enjoyed coming by. We often took opportunities to witness in some small way.

I reminded Bill via text and phone to eat regularly and this continued when he returned to Oregon. He rarely felt hungry, and I had to push a bit, sometimes taking him out to the coffee stand or bringing him food from my house.

As he forced nutrition and gained strength, he expressed concern about the grieving process. 'I don't want to get stuck,' he often lamented.

We both knew people with great loss who seemed stuck in their processing—even years later. They never moved past their grief and failed, it appeared, to even discover new joy.

Many weeks later, Glenda's family gathered to talk about options as she still slept. I enjoyed meeting Glenda's parents, and even lunching with them. Her mom asked about me and felt sad to hear about some of my situation. Glenda's dad, also a pastor, struck me as wise and kind. A couple of times, he shared, 'At the end of life, only two things matter. Your relationship with God and your relationship with other people.'

I had expected to minister to them—and instead they

ministered to me.

As they talked about the choices they needed to make for Glenda in their meeting, I prayed from afar. Bill had grown to be my friend. The greatest gift I could give him and his family was a healthy wife to accompany them home. So, I begged God for Glenda's full healing. I did not understand why those prayers went unanswered.

A close friend of Bill and Glenda's with experience in healing prayers arrived from Pennsylvania. Sadly, she informed Bill that Glenda 'wasn't there.' She had expected to feel her friend's presence, and call for full healing. Bill's daughter informed him that she had lost her mom the moment Glenda's head hit the pavement.

With torn grief, the family decided to let her go.

I quickly grew livid.

In tears, over coffee and tea, I piled Bill with questions. 'Are you sure? What if she could wake up? What if she does? Can you live with yourself if that is a possibility? If this was someone in your congregation, what would you be telling them? Might you regret this later and how do you deal with it, if so?' I did not hesitate to tackle him with all of that. This was important!

With wisdom born of shepherding, a deep prayer life, and of course, pain, he gazed steadily at me. 'How can I keep her from Heaven? I can't keep her from Jesus.'

Silence descended on the little round table. Across the way, someone dropped a knife, and it echoed painfully in my ears. My head throbbed.

I nodded slowly, finally feeling confident of her location now. 'Jesus has her. He does. And OK, I hear you. But please be sure.' I gulped and grabbed two napkins to smear across my swollen and reddened face as tears flowed. 'Just—please be sure. Please. It's so important. Maybe think about it longer?'

'I can't keep her from Heaven. I can't keep her stuck.'

There was that lovely word again. Stuck. Wedged. No wiggle room allowed. But these potential actions seemed so…forever.

And yet, full healing as only God provides in Heaven, awaited Glenda. I just could not get past my angst and tears to acknowledge that yet.

I drove out to the care facility several nights in the next eleven days. I guess the staff considered me family now. Provided with a back door code, I slipped into her darkish room. Holding her hand, I prayed. I quietly sang worship songs and hymns, eventually reduced to a hum as my voice grew war-weary and tear-cracked. Talking about our favorite beach came next and when I ran out of words, I sat nearby—once falling asleep on the couch.

I awoke to Bill sliding his backpack off and nodding at me. 'Let's go get you some tea and breakfast.'

'I don't want to leave her.' I rubbed my eyes and pushed off the couch on wobbly feet.

But he insisted—now taking care of me.

He was not going to let me get stuck either.

We had no idea that slightly over a year later, my former spouse would also die. It happened on Thanksgiving weekend, also one of my kiddo's birthdays, and Bill caught a plane from Pennsylvania as soon as he could.

As I felt the crushing weight of grief, he walked the kids and me through hard, but needed, steps of things like writing an obituary, sorting through possessions, and yes, even eating.

Grief is sticky! It often cements our feet to the past. It can prevent us from moving forward, stall our Mission Manifesto and halt us from living abundantly.

Michele's grief with her multiple losses snowballed. While she and I worked on her story, she discovered grief for the past miscarriages as well. She had not allowed her brain to process or even consider the need to mourn those children.

But Jesus knew.

She holds significant memories in a special box, including a sonogram picture. A special, tucked in Bible verse reminds her of His faithfulness. 'I remain confident of this: I will see the goodness of the Lord in the land of the living. Wait for the Lord: be strong and take heart and wait for the Lord' (Psalm 27:13-14).

Some near-death and afterlife accounts report the presence of a large baby nursery in Heaven. Jim Woodford not only saw it but conversed with his angel tour guide about its purpose. The angel explained, 'This is the nursery for the souls of aborted babies or other babies miscarried or lost in their innocence.' (33)

Some accounts mention seeing grown children who died as babies or pre-born who now play happily as children. Gary Wood's account says, 'I saw a playground with children and teenagers—those who died prematurely.' Jesus plays with them and even tosses them into the air. (34, 35, 36, 37)

My friend Sandi left this earth a few years ago. It was sudden and shocking. God had already shared with her how she would pass, and she curtailed certain activities due to that, but none of us expected it so soon. Before she left, she wrote a short story about children in Heaven who had been aborted, hoping to get it out to pregnancy centers. These babies played happily in Heaven's meadow and with Jesus as they waited for their parents. I have no idea if God had also provided a vision of that, but Sandi was spot on! I bet she plays with them too!

Other visitors testify that Jesus waits for the mama or both parents to arrive before he grows the little ones up. They then watch the child quickly grow to maturity. (36) B W Melvin shares that in Heaven he watched a lady who had chosen abortion out of fear welcome her baby who crawled to her. The infant then grew up, and said, 'Hi, Mom. No worries. I came here.'

When she burst into tears (yes, there are many tears in that welcoming meadow, I can attest), her child said, 'Mom, recall that you are forgiven. We now have time to play. Let's go, come.' Melvin also saw a child who had died in a car accident welcome his parents into Heaven, then grow up in front of them. (37)

Do you feel stuck in a grief pit? Grief takes time—never let someone sway you into speeding through the process. The stages vary like a rollercoaster, and often revisit when you thought that ride was closed with padlocks on the gate.

Understand the potential of your healing process screeching to a halt in a nearby ditch. Refuse to make that ditch your home. Spin your tires—give it some fuel from Him. Work on it. Wave down some friends or call for a tow if needed.

Be honest with yourself and with Him. He understands grief—and He has felt it deeply. At the tomb of his friend Lazarous, He wept (38). In Luke 19:41-43, we read that He also wept over us not recognizing His future return. "As he approached Jerusalem and saw the city, he wept over it and said, 'If you, even you, had only known on this day what would bring you peace—but now it is hidden from your eyes. The days will come upon you when your enemies will build an embankment against you and encircle you and hem you in on every side. They will dash you to the ground, you and the children within your walls. They will not leave one stone on another, because you did not recognize the time of God's coming to you.'"

Jesus grieved the death of John the Baptist in Matthew 14:13. Mark 3:5 tells us that Jesus grew deeply distressed at people's stubbornness. Matthew 26:37-38 reports that before

Jesus' crucifixion, He told his disciples that His soul felt overwhelmed with crushing sorrow to the point of death. He was emotionally dragging at that point! And, Matthew 27:46 shows His deep grief at being separated from His Father while on the cross.

Grief also waits ahead for Him. While in Heaven, Randy Kay viewed visions of the last days, and one part that truly sticks with him is the mourning cry of our Lord and His people for those who are lost and do not join us. (39) To this day, in the middle of the grocery store or other places, Randy hears it. He looks around immediately, wondering who he is supposed to pray for.

I cannot imagine.

Randy also saw Jesus cry a tear in Heaven after Jesus said, 'I desire that none shall perish. But I AM the only way here, none other.' (40)

Recognize and honor your grief. Eleven years after our marriage vows, Bill and I still revere each other's impactful days, like our first spouses' birthdays, our former wedding anniversaries, and their death dates. Yes, that adds up, but it remains important. I mark his days on my calendar, so I remember to ask how he feels and listen if he chooses to talk. Somehow, he seems to remember most of my days without scratching a note in his planner.

Our grief has lessened with time—but in the early years, this formulated a very important routine. Occasionally, we even make plans for those 'days' when we visit a special place, but also intentionally create fun. It helped the grief become bearable, kept each other more aware and sensitive, and most importantly—ensured we did not get stuck.

Here is plan I recommend implementing if you feel **S-T-U-C-K** in grief.

Sojourn with your Savior. Spend time daily in prayer until you feel a balm flowing over your soul.

Tend to your Bible reading. In fact, add to the regular time you spend in the scriptures. Often people in the Bible found themselves in pain. Hit Google or an AI model and ask if there are stories or verses in the Bible related to similar things (always double fact check AI).

Understand that God may remain quiet about your grief. This does not indicate a lack of care—He cares deeply and desires for you to work through your pain. He respects distance when you need that—but remains excited to advance you to your next Manifesto steps.

Connect with other people who are spiritually mature and care for you. Perhaps ask to meet with one or two regularly for a bit. Ask them to pray for you and with you. Be intentional about reaching out to others, and developing friendships.

Keep a list of your progress and how you are feeling. Consider a tally of what you want to work toward and then a year later, pull it out and see how far you have progressed.

Grief is not something God asks us to ignore or bury. It is something He desires to carry. He meets us with comfort, understanding, and hope. In His compassion, God calls us to face our pain with Him, because unhealed wounds weigh down the heart, cloud joy, impact other people negatively, and prevent us from moving fully into our Heaven-Minded

Mission Manifesto.

He will never waste your tears, but He will hold them tightly when you trust Him with them.

'Record my misery; list my tears on your scroll—are they not in your record?' (Psalm 56:8).

'You turned my wailing into dancing; you removed my sackcloth and clothed me with joy, that my heart may sing your praises and not be silent. Lord my God, I will praise you forever' (Psalm 30:11-12).

'May the God of hope fill you with all joy and peace as you trust in him, so that you may overflow with hope by the power of the Holy Spirit' (Romans 15:13).

Pause & Ponder

1. Have there been times you have felt stuck in grief?
2. If so, what did you do or what will you do to start navigating out of that ditch?
3. Do you know someone grieving currently who you can reach out to?

Chapter Thirteen

He Honored Me With Parental Blessing
Kim Robinson

My parents and I experienced a rough beginning. We butted heads. Vastly different, we joked that maybe someone switched babies at the hospital. Their athletic, focused, purpose-driven beauty highlighted my uncoordinated plainness.

Mom and I managed to create the worst moments. I parted ways with both parents at nineteen with relief. However, after I became a Christian, the Lord convicted me of harboring ill will. At one point, while in Portugal studying the language to serve God in Mozambique, He nudged me during my devotions to review my attitudes toward my mom.

I could not serve Him as called until I worked through them.

I boarded a train which deposited me at the riverfront in Lisbon where I walked the boardwalk for miles, reviewing Mom's and my interactions from childhood onward. Since she and Dad both resided in Heaven, this exchange stayed between my Heavenly Father and me.

During those hours, the Spirit brought vivid moments to mind when Mom hurt me. I lived them all over again, bringing tremendous distress. Hadn't I already dealt with those? Forgiven her?

Apparently, some part of me still held judgment. Jesus's words, 'But if you do not forgive others their sins, your Father will not forgive your sins,' (41) weighed down my heart. How could I release these things?

Then a means came to me. I would change the negative to positive. Each time the Spirit provided a painful incident, I asked God to blot it out, to forgive her. And instead, I deliberately thought of something kind or lovely Mom had accomplished and asked that it be remembered instead. Because my heart secretly desired her punishment, this approach fully freed me.

Seven hours passed as I walked. Finally, the visions in my spirit stilled. Strolling back to the train station, I paused in a courtyard, the river behind me. Pretty carved benches surrounded the pavement—were they stone? Iron? I did not look closer, because I felt directed to turn around.

Instead of the expected river view, I saw my mother, dressed in an exquisite white wedding gown, covered in pearls and gems. Her thick, wavy auburn hair cascaded around her shoulders in youthful beauty. The words of Scripture from Revelation 19:7-8 resonated within me: 'Let us rejoice and be glad and give him glory! For the wedding of the Lamb has come, and his bride has made herself ready. Fine linen, bright and clean, was given her to wear.'

As I boarded the train, the impact of the experience hit me. When I finally chose to forgive, I viewed her renewed Heavenly countenance with joy.

Some years later, in a worship and prayer meeting in Oregon, I experienced another vision, one that deeply humbled me. In that vision, I stood on the green hills of Heaven. They expanded farther than anything one can imagine in earthly terms. It felt warm, bright, and so very alive.

Jesus walked toward me—He was huge! He strode forward in a long white tunic/robe with a big smile on his face, as if He knew something I soon would discover. He gestured with His head downward, and I looked down at His feet.

There, as tall as his big toe (Was he barefoot? In sandals? I do not remember, but I could see his big toe.), I saw two people, a man and a woman, holding hands. They easily moved as fast as Jesus somehow and acted like two little kids in playful joy. Their affection for one another shone. They appeared to glow.

Neither seemed hurried, yet they crossed the vast expanse in a moment. Then they stood before me, full sized, and I suddenly recognized Mom and Dad!

My dad lifted a filthy dress off me I had not realized I was wearing—the original color a mystery. He settled a clean white garment on me instead. Then he placed a crown of life on my head—a live wreath of little blue and white flowers with a green vine! Mom welcomed me with a tender kiss on my left cheek, and Dad bent forward, placing a kiss on my right cheek. Almost simultaneously, Jesus also kissed my right cheek and smiled. Our restored relationship became fulfilled as they welcomed me into Heaven.

In the brief moments they appeared before me, I engaged in the action versus just seeing the vision. I do not even remember their dress. They seemed gentle, young, vibrant, and radiantly happy. I could see they dearly loved each other and completely accepted me. Astonished, I truly felt real affection radiating from them, a rare glimpse in our earthly lives together.

These experiences mimicked the glorious love of God and his Kingdom of Heaven. They fill me with such promise of how we will transform into something new, fresh, free from suspicions, doubts, and negative emotions. I am so grateful!

'Father, forgive them, for they do not know
what they are doing' (Luke 23:34).

Reflection With Julie: Misaligned Malice
Potential Block: Strongholds

The gals in my group stared at me from my laptop's screen. The digital room grew so quiet that I heard only the slight squeak of my leather chair. Their faces plainly read: Umm, would you repeat that?

I smiled and repeated my request. Then added, 'I know this isn't easy, but you can do it. It's important. You'll see.'

One participant openly sighed, another looked at her notebook and scratched something out—firmly. A couple of faces and physical reactions from the remaining told me they felt, what we in the industry call, triggered. Emotionally affected, a bit upset, perhaps battling a not-so-great memory. The need to see their kickback is partly why I require camera use.

They heard my appeal for an act on another wavelength and certainly not the norm—a request beyond forgiving their abusers. I wanted to walk them through an exercise that God patiently pressed me through in my healing journey. It includes praying blessings over their abusers, especially in the areas of abuse types that person excels or excelled in. (42) This method delivers hearts from any abusive power still adhering, and sets a true fresh beginning—throwing those sins as far and wide as Christ does with our iniquities. (43)

Obliterating their current mindset, like God blasted (and replaced) mine.

Seeing two of my most advanced members react threw me a little plot twist, but we plunged on. In fact, the more I viewed, and read the resulting text conversations the rest of the week, the more the importance of this exercise stood out—blazing like a lighthouse beacon.

God intended this exercise for more than just yours truly. My ladies needed deliverance.

I want you to know that this chapter is hailing only from the words He gives, and of course, I bring my experience in leading people to emotional healing. He assures me that He will propel it to the people in need. The Holy Spirit elbowed me so much that I know at least one of you amazing readers needs to hear it. And even one of you benefitting is worth my time, so here we go.

I must first clarify my belief that a true follower of Jesus cannot be completely possessed by demons—our temples house the Holy Spirit, a natural and extremely effective deterrent. I realize some Christians disagree. I do believe and have viewed that Christians can be oppressed (deeply affected), and deliverance becomes necessary. At times, brothers and sisters do open a window for evil in their actions or chosen modalities. Satan becomes quick to jump on it—what a tremendous opportunity to affect this believer's Manifesto and influence! He especially is skilled with this when there is already unhealed trauma in the person's life or when the person struggles with active trauma.

I also feel coached right now by Him to share that effects on a human by an evil spirit do not usually result in crazy eyes, rolling around on the floor, hissing at others or shrieking at the presence of any Heaven-induced environment. Yes, we do see this and many of these examples originate from the Bible, but we must understand that Satan became a master of disguise in his spirit implementation and management.

As my Lord continued to nudge me, I asked Him a few times, 'Does this mean I need to scrounge up another Heaven story from someone? Where is *that* subject coming from? Do I wait to finish this book until You send one? Of course, I trust Your timing. Maybe I'll just add it as a paragraph into a current chapter already written? And I guess it should probably go into the very last story in the section on blocks? That would make the most sense.'

With my intended method sitting in wet concrete, I started reviewing the full manuscript to finish the footnotes. When I arrived at Kim's story, a complete oversight popped out like the North Star. The Reflection after Kim's story lasted a whopping three paragraphs. Oops! I never finished it. And when I re-read her story, I heard from Him. 'Kim instituted a type of deliverance.' Indeed, the three paragraphs about my group exercise (coming up!) also highlighted a certain type of freedom exercise. And it already lived in the last story spot about Manifesto blocks.

Provision is both what He loves to bestow and what He has rendered throughout this book!

Kim's uneasiness from her mother's neglect and control started as a block but evolved to a stronghold. A stronghold is a fortress, an attempt to provide safety for our bodies, brains, or beings. Think of it as a deeply rooted mindset or belief that counteracts God's truth. However, it ends up being a false refuge, because it cannot provide true sanctuary. Which means, of course, a stronghold is truly a lie. And sometimes a multitude of lies.

In Kim's case, remembering her mother's control and abusive tactics served Kim by installing a wall of protection over her being. As long as she recalled it, and the ensuing misery, Kim brandished a shield, deflecting other potential damaging relationships. After all, what might transpire if she dared to drop her guard? After many years, God said, 'Your stronghold is preventing your ministry impact. Will you choose to trust to lean on me instead of this shield you concocted? To trust Me?' You see, Kim's block-turned-stronghold failed in protection duty. Instead, it glued her to a life of relationship fear. And when hurtful things happened, it proved to her that her wall was indeed an important guard and in fact, she should reinforce it by tossing on a few more bricks!

Strongholds might include things like fear, control, pride, shame/guilt, unforgiveness, low self-value, perfectionism, legalism, victim mentality, lust, materialism, envy, hard-heartedness, criticism, generational trauma, generational sin, and so much more. Strongholds may cause behaviors like substance abuse, addiction, remaining stuck in unhealthiness with an inability to move forward, self-harm (mentally, physically, emotionally), pornography addiction, criminal behavior, abusive conduct toward others, bitterness toward God or people, a sheer hatred for anything spiritual, a reliance on anything besides Jesus, and so much more.

I am quite sure Frank Peretti might say there is a demon for each stronghold and each resulting behavior. The reality is, demons do have categories, and although we will not delve into that here, know that one spirit category would hold the responsibility for several sins on the list.

When someone forgives an offender but cannot seem to move on from it, there is often a stronghold (or more than one) impeding the way. If someone is trauma-damaged and has worked on their healing and just cannot progress, look for strongholds as well as the possibility that the person still lives with active trauma.

Please consider:

- If an attendee of a behavior program (abuse, addiction, sexual sin, co-dependency, productivity, etc.) cannot generate progress or always appears to continue the cycle no matter what, there is likely a stronghold.
- If someone appears very stuck and just cannot seem to

move forward in a productive manner in their lives, a stronghold likely lies in the path.

- If a person's behavior is ongoing and negatively affecting others, look for a stronghold.
- If someone has tried to avoid a sticky sin that returns despite the work, a stronghold might hover in the way.
- If someone is insistent in their continued choices that do not honor the Lord, a stronghold is very likely.
- Mental health issues can also be caused by strongholds.

Why is it so important to address this? Because strongholds always result in a failure to thrive in the abundant life Jesus intends for us. And because when they are not addressed, they often advance to becoming idols, which, of course, is anything we hyper-focus on or prioritize over God. And sometimes, strongholds even become idols in the 'stronghold' stage.

We have already seen two types of exercise prayers connecting to deliverance. One was Kim painstakingly moving through every bad memory of her mom, asking God to forgive her mom (it was unknown if her mom had asked God to do so), and asking Him to replace that memory with a positive one. This took her seven hours but is certainly a method for those struggling to heal from the control of another person.

The second method of freedom prayer is gravitating from forgiveness to blessing someone in their problem area. (42) In a way, Kim's method also accomplished this, but let's chat about the exercise I help my gals complete.

When working with survivors of trauma, the stronghold may not just be the obvious one, because it often morphs into other arenas. For instance, sometimes survivors self-medicate, adding the stronghold of addiction to their list. Those arenas may need individual assistance as they block progress but for this chapter, let's focus on the forgiveness to blessing mode I demonstrate below.

Conversation With Marcia

Opening: 'Hi, Marcia. Did you get a chance to pray about this? What is the Holy Spirit telling you?'

Marcia's answer: 'He told me that I still give my abuser some control in my life.'

Follow up: 'Even though you've forgiven him for that? I know we worked on that a few weeks ago.'

Marcia says: 'Yes.'

Asking how it affected her: 'What happened to help you realize that he still has some control and what effect did that have on you?'

Marcia shares effects: 'Well, I realized that I am always talking negatively about myself. I don't feel worthy of God or a new relationship. I can't even accept a compliment. My grandma told me I was beautiful and smart yesterday, and I brushed her off and got irritated.'

Asking for more detail: 'Oh? What did you feel when she said that?'

Marcia answers: 'That it's not true. That I'm homely and worthless. And I'm dumb. That's what he always told me.'

Asking how this mindset serves her: 'How did/does thinking in agreement protect you?'

Marcia replies: 'Serve me? Weird! Hmm... From getting hurt, I guess. I would rather tell Grandma I'm not smart rather than have her discover that or change her mind about me.' *(Note that this one can be a difficult step for whomever you are working with, but it is important.)*

Dig in a little: And how does getting irritated and brushing her off protect you?' (use their words).

Marcia answers: 'From hurt, I guess. I don't think I could bear it if she realizes I'm not all that she thinks I am. What if she tells me she can't have a relationship with me?'

I ask permission to proceed: 'Marcia, let's get you delivered from this negative perception of yourself. God says you are worthy, precious and a daughter of the Most High King (add verses for each situation, but in this case, we had already covered those references in the lesson that day). Do you want to start seeing yourself as God sees you?'

Marcia approves: 'Absolutely. I see the effect that this mindset has on me. I'm tired of it.'

I institute a prayer and have her repeat after me: 'Lord, I continue to forgive (name of person) for his/her words they used to put me down. I know now that those words are a lie. That in truth I am beautiful in your sight and precious to You. You also gave me a sound mind. (2 Timothy 1:9). I ask that in Your name, the spirit of negativity and poor self-reflection be thrown far from me. I request that these word curses spoken over me no longer hold power over my beliefs or actions. Please fill this space with your affirmation for me and help me to remember that You are my only judge. And as (name of person) used verbal and psychological abuse against me, I request a blessing over him. I ask a blessing of words, that his thoughts and talk about himself and others would become edifying and uplifting, as You also treasure him. Amen.'

This prayer not only released Marcia from the word-curses, but opened her eyes to the possibility that her abuser may have also been verbally abused. Although there is never an excuse for abusing someone else, understanding where the other person may hurt helps us not only to process, but to start viewing our difficult people with the eyes of Jesus.

Note that usually someone just beginning their healing from trauma will not be ready for this step. In fact, the first step of forgiveness (if it is separate from deliverance) needs to wait until the person is ready. Have no fear of it ducking out of sight entirely! If we remain in tune, the Holy Spirit stays very aware, knowing and nudging when it is time for us to work on these steps.

Here are the steps:

1. Pray ahead of time and follow the Holy Spirit's prompting always while enlisting this process.
2. Ask them to pray about things they might need to work on/change.
3. Ask what they learned from Him about that.
4. Inquire about more. You could just say: 'Any other insights?' or 'Do you agree?'
5. Ask how they feel about what they learned.
6. Ask what effects have happened because of this issue in their life?
7. Ask how continuing their actions serves them and/or

others, being very understanding in your body language, tone and manner. Remember that the majority of strongholds are implemented for the purpose of supposed protection.

8. Ask if they are now willing to surrender that 'lie' (because truly it hurts them) to the Lord and let that stronghold go.
9. Remind them of what God says about their situation by having some verses handy. But do not focus on 'Thou shalt nots…' Focus on His deep love for them and how much He wants them to be released.
10. Ask for permission then lead them in a deliverance prayer, following the format above.

If your block or someone else's block for living a Manifesto is very strong, consider looking into generational strongholds as well. Alcoholism, sexual abuse, and some other behaviors run amok throughout the generations in my family. You can apologize to our Father on their behalf, seek forgiveness, request to cast this sin from your bloodlines, ask for healing for anyone in need in the past or present and plead that this sin no longer affect you, yours, and current and future generations. See footnotes for a recommended resource. (43, 44)

Psalm 18:2 affirms that we implement strongholds for our own (misguided) safety and instructs us about the only stronghold we should hold onto—Him. 'The Lord is my rock, my fortress and my deliverer—my God is my rock, in whom I take refuge, my shield and the horn of my salvation, my stronghold.'

Strongholds may feel difficult to shake, but abundant life and the implementation of our Mission Manifesto wait for those who seek freedom. Any strongholds other than Him weigh us down, and can prevent effective ministry, whether that is serving in an organization, writing books, speaking, or shepherding someone else as a mentor or companion. In truth, strongholds create captivity and are a tool of Satan to prevent the impact Jesus wants us to create.

When we bring those strongholds into His light, we are not just naming a struggle, we ask Him to rebuild the very ditches where we allowed the enemy to hang a new management flag. God sees every wall we face, our protective measures, and fails to condemn us. He calls us to freedom. He asks us to trust Him instead of the carefully constructed wall and the bullet-proof outerwear we carefully pull on each morning.

Each surrendered stronghold becomes a testimony of His power at work in us.

When we choose to confront the strongholds, and combat them with His words in scripture, He delights to bless our obedience. In deconstructing what once controlled us, we gain room for His peace, joy, and flourishing purpose.

'You will again have compassion on us; you will tread our sins underfoot and hurl all our iniquities into the depths of the sea' (Micah 7:18-19).

… 'Very truly I tell you, everyone who sins is a slave to sin. Now a slave has no permanent place in the family, but a son belongs to it forever. So if the Son sets you free, you will be free indeed' (John 8:34-36).

'…will not the ministry of the Spirit be even more glorious? If the ministry that brought condemnation was glorious, how much more glorious is the ministry that brings righteousness! For what was glorious has no glory now in comparison with the surpassing glory. And if what was transitory came with glory, how much greater is the glory of that which lasts' (2 Corinthians 3:8-11).

Pause & Ponder

1. Is there something you are hanging onto that you need to be delivered from today? If forgiveness is needed, it can happen first, or they could be combined in one prayer.
2. If you are working through this book with other people, start a discussion about the strongholds or idols present in the group and how they could prevent effective Manifesto implementation.
3. Can you think of loved ones/family members who might be affected by strongholds?

PART THREE: MANIFESTO MECHANISMS

Chapter Fourteen

I Saw The End Of The World

Jennie Ersari

While visiting my youngest daughter at her ranch, I sat around a campfire with many of my family members. Nature called.

'I'll be right back.' But as soon as I stood, I fell to the ground like a timbered tree and started seizing.

It was so fast, I did not even try to catch myself. My family later said that I had been saying odd, concerning things.

I instantly broke both my neck and skull on the rocky ground. Blood spread. Several family members performed CPR – unsure if there was even a slim chance – but trying to be hopeful.

When first responders arrived, my son-in-law told them that my neck broke. They airlifted me to our closest large hospital in Phoenix and immediately scheduled surgeries for my traumatic brain injury and neck.

During that time, a local preacher visited at the request of my family. She laid hands on me and prayed, and then informed my family that I had angels around me and would not die that night.

But I was not really there when that happened.

Jesus, my Savior, took my hand and pulled me out of bed. I had always believed in God but struggled to mentally invest in organized religion.

Jesus wore a white gown. His piercing blue/greenish eyes were filled with light. As his hair blew in the slight warm wind, his gown stirred. Any movement seemed full of energy and presence. Like a warm, deep, yet comforting vibration.

He saw within me and knew everything I thought and felt.

'I'm sorry, Jennie.' He started showing me vivid pictures of the present and what is to come.

The first thing I saw was my daughter giving her daughters and my niece the news about my accident and how I was not expected to live. My heart squeezed, and Jesus clutched my hand tightly. He showed me my mom, who had Alzheimer's, and my sister, who was eating something. Then I saw my husband with other people. I felt grateful that he was not alone.

I absorbed comfort from Jesus, and I knew He secured me as we floated above the earth. He never let go of my hand.

Then came the future. 'All these things must happen before my return,' He told me. I saw vivid scenes of wildfires, flooding, and a civil war in the United States. I saw children trafficked and other horrible sins. He showed me weather disasters, fighting, and people hating each other. There was massive looting. 'There will be fires, flooding, hurricanes, and tornadoes, more than you've ever seen. The people will turn against each other, even brothers.'

More evilness took over the world as I gazed with wide eyes.

Jesus squeezed my hand gently. 'There's nothing you can do to stop this. It must happen. But if you keep the faith and carry on, you will be just fine.' He repeated this several times and told me my faith would be my best defense.

Finally, as He returned me to my room and my body, He explained that He is coming soon.

I woke up intubated when I was not even supposed to be alive. I have a DNR in my file, but when I crashed, they told my family that intubation would last only 24 hours.

With my arms tied down, I started waving my hand for my phone. I wrote: 'Get this out of my throat now. God's coming.

I met Jesus.'

I now maintain so much hope. I also now attend The Living Word Church with my granddaughter, who was recently baptized.

Our lives are never a waste. And I have witnessed almost everything He showed me. It will not be long – He is coming!

Reflection With Julie: Learning Lab
Tool to Use: Knowledge

As believers, we look forward to amazing things. In Scripture, 'hope' is not a vague wish. It means 'confident assurance.' It is not flip-floppy, delicate, paltry, or uncertain—but stable, mighty, vigorous, and stable.

Our hope is built with a rock foundation, solid and unshakable.

Checking the original languages opens deeper meaning, and often provides new thought-provoking content. I use both Bible Gateway and the Blue Letter Bible App for this always-fun venture.

I Peter 1:14 says, 'Therefore, with minds that are alert and fully sober, set your hope on the grace to be brought to you when Jesus Christ is revealed at his coming.' If we read that with the biblical definition, it instructs us to set our *confidence* on the grace to be brought when He is revealed.

And 1 Peter 1:3-4 says, 'Praise be to the God and Father of our Lord Jesus Christ! In his great mercy he has given us new birth into a living hope through the resurrection of Jesus Christ from the dead, and into an inheritance that can never perish, spoil, or fade. This inheritance is kept in Heaven for you.' These verses state and highlight that we maintain confidence in the resurrection of a live Jesus Christ and absolute assurance of the inheritance waiting for us in Heaven, kept especially for each of us.

Humans love proof, even though it seems the opposite of faith. Part of the reason we seek near-death and afterlife stories is because they are unique testimony of what we long for, and sometimes that which we would never wish on anyone. Truly, it feels in this season, God is opening the divider between earth and Heaven even more. Some of us receive the honor of peering behind the sheer curtain and reporting back as journalists. Interestingly, I had not considered it that way until now, despite a jaunt in journalism as an early career. However, I have always loved deciphering mysteries!

Research indicates an increase in near-death and afterlife experiences. (45) We do not know that with ultra-certainty, because not everyone who experiences and remembers these spiritual phenomena report them, and never have. But we see many more reports than previously. With advancements in medicine, resuscitation, and defibrillation, it certainly seems possible that our experiences on the edge of death, dying, and returning have jumped in numbers.

From Heaven, the view differs. God allowed us to advance this far in medicine and science. He approves this with a purpose—to give more of us 'eternal eyes,' to return hope and healing to the world, and to support the great revival that has always played a part in the plan. (46) How will that happen, you ask? Well, last year, at a conference called Heaven Encounters, my eyes opened a tad when Randy Kay explained what God shared with him. In the Tribulation era, our Heaven accounts will greatly encourage Christians who have hopped aboard the Jesus-train and deeply struggle with persecution, withholding of food, and even torture. Note, the train is my own comparison not his, as you likely guessed. This confirmed and explained what I heard from my Lord many months ago: Although I was to write this book for you, this assignment was handed over with the assurance that a copy or two (or more) will land in the hands someday of believers who need it even more than we do now. And seekers as well. Won't you consider purchasing an additional paper or hard copy and keeping it on your bookshelf? Or giving it to a friend or family member? Because I am assured that someday, after the Rapture, when electricity has likely been cut, someone who needs it will discover it, and then pass it onto others after they have been uplifted by learning more of Heaven.

Numerous Heaven accounts are now online as it slowly became more acceptable to experience a near-death or afterlife episode. More people are sharing, and this is not dreadful, if we read trusted sources, stay on guard, and seek our Savior's voice as we watch, read, and listen. Do not forget your Holy Spirit check system. Pray about what you read and watch. And pay attention if He waves the yellow caution or red stop flag. I learned that lesson the hard way when I read part of a book with an account after I visited Heaven. It included a New Age perspective, and my hackles raised twice, but still I read on, doubting the warnings in my head. Many online had recommended it! That night, Bill was out of town, and I received a visit from an evil spirit who decided to rattle my bedroom doorknob. Scary. Right before it rattled, my Lord said, 'You are not alone in the house.' He led me to send it out in a loud voice and the book plopped in the rubbish bin soon thereafter. You see, I had opened a portal, so to speak, by reading it. Caution flags receive my full attention now.

Regarding accounts worthy of pursual, I ran across two electrifying books, I*nside Heaven's Gates* by Rebecca Ruter Springer (which has been reprinted dozens of times and has also been published under different titles) and John Bunyan's *Visions of Heaven and Hell: Where Will You Spend Eternity* (47), soon after my first Heaven trip. Springer, a very respected wife of a Methodist preacher, suffered several weeks of horrific illness and became bedridden. She dreamed of Heaven. Much of this book, written in the 1800's, correlates with striking similarities in those who have visited. Then there are things I have not heard in any other accounts such as riding in a boat. Give it a read if you get a chance.

Controversy surrounds Bunyan's book. Everything from 'Did he really write it?' to 'Is it true?' Again, there are some similarities to modern-day experiences such as great music and song. And much of what is written in the book about Hell also correlates to modern-day accounts.

But I face-planted when I read some of the controversies regarding Bunyon's book on the internet. It very much echoes some of what other return travelers also hear. One website claims this as part of a conclusion that Bunyan cannot possibly be the author: 'God does not allow second chances from the grave. God does not grant 'special people' the chance to visit hell and write about it. God does not grant people permission to speak with those in hell. God does not permit angels to carry people to Heaven and hell.' (48)

Granted, there are other reasons why apparently some historians feel this book may not be valid, but I could not help but think of a gentleman who shared a comment on my Heaven blog when I first started scribing: 'You must be very special indeed. The Word says no one looks at Him and lives.' Never mind that I did not even get to look at Him my first time—Jesus prevented me from turning my head. I have also had people ask friends and relatives, 'Do you think she really went to Heaven?'

It became much like my experience leaving my own trauma and helping others in those sticky spots. All too often, survivors hear things like 'Are you maybe dramatizing a bit?'

My friend, I highly recommend that if someone shares

about encountering God-amazingness, please just say, 'Wow. That sounds incredible. Thanks for sharing.' Then, *boom,* you validate them without the very unnecessary 'What? How is that possible?' or 'Err, let me consult the scriptures and get back to you' as the person sharing decides that they would like to shrink and scootch right under that folding chair. So many of those with stories in this book expressed that after a few negative reactions, they zipped their lips on their fantastic truth until an author they knew started poking her sniffer around. I am thrilled that most realized I provide a safe talking space, but with several calls or emails, I started with sharing some of my own account to increase their comfort.

I write this because experiences from Heaven (or Hell) can either increase hope or dash optimism. On my return, I enacted the exact behavior as I did when I left abuse for good and what hundreds of people I have worked with also attempt: searching for validation in other people's experiences. Reading other stories like a mad Heaven book lover, I underlined things the author and I experienced in common. Often, reading those portions brought major emotion. Then I opened my computer, found the author, and emailed or messaged with my thankfulness and 'kinship.'

Gratefully, I recalibrated to reading these amazing stories for research and God's words to me instead of validation, and I am sure all our wonderful Heaven authors agree!

Let's chat about things meeting doomsday proportion in the world. Jennie is not the only one who saw future events.

My friend, Mark Lawton, retains a special touch on his life. Not only did he, as a young boy, spend time with Jesus and angels several times, but God provided him with several visions and throne room visits. Our Father said to him, 'Watch this,' and with a very large hand, pulled down a big screen and showed Mark the end-times revival. Little white churches rested strategically on a map that stretched across America and into Canada. Immediately, those churches each changed into a small lit candle, then back to churches, then transformed into oil receptacles with no bottoms. Eventually, the candles lit the oil barrels and ultimately resulted in a church catching on fire. When a church caught fire, the entire geographical area became engulfed too. Three winds came, fueling it, sweeping the whole world until His return.

But it was holy fire.

God explained to Mark that the churches were people He strategically placed and the oil represented His anointing. The winds came from New Brunswick, Nova Scotia, and Maine, and each brought ministry.

Then Mark saw the whole world lit on fire for God. Many people were delivered and set free.

In 'Heaven Stormed,' Randy Kay writes about his witness of the Last Days. When back on earth, God's messages continued for him in dreams. One dream of the winds, and another of five doors, each representing one of the five stages: Spiritual Warfare, Worldwide Outpouring of God's glory, Darkness when God lifts His presence From the Earth, Afflictions that occur thereafter and Christ's Return, when God forms the new earth that Randy viewed while in Heaven. (49) I suspect spiritual warfare will remain a part of all stages, except for the last one.

Consider the following verses:

'For then there will be great distress, unequaled from the beginning of the world until now—and never to be equaled again' (Matthew 24:21).

'I saw in Heaven another great and marvelous sign: seven angels with the seven last plagues—last, because with them God's wrath is completed' (Revelation 15:1).

'And the temple was filled with smoke from the glory of God and from his power, and no one could enter the temple until the seven plagues of the seven angels were completed' (Revelation 15:8).

Read Revelation Chapter 16 to learn what John saw as God showed him the future—angels pour out their bowls of the plagues (which Randy saw up close and explains that they are actually the underside of shields) (50), one at a time, with devastating results on both people and animals. Cities collapse. We then are hit with the greatest earthquake Earth has experienced and hailstones of one hundred pounds each.

It gets worse.

But I do not write this to toss you a frown and forehead wrinkle. Randy's experience was very real, as was Mark's. Jennie's experience is also biblical. There is a reason Jesus said to her many times, 'Hang onto your faith. It will see you through.' As the author and finisher of our faith (Hebrews 12:2), God the Father and He alone retains the right to decide when the work is done and when to return. However, if you hail as a child of the Highest King, you receive His protection.

These things are part of what must take place. But we do not fear, because we know Who holds the end. This is not a fragile hope, but firm assurance rooted in His unshakable promises. Christ will return, and His victory (and therefore our victory) is sure.

Knowledge of what is coming remains important. It is a vital tool in implementing your Manifesto and in preparation for your role. Study Revelation, Daniel and other end-times texts, read Christ-filled experiences and pursue shepherds who walk close to Jesus. Prepare your home and family for the rapture—knowing that not all will join in rising to Jesus. I personally cannot imagine God keeping us here for the Tribulation, but do prepare. And of course, more importantly than all the above, share Jesus with your loved ones and anyone else He calls you to share with.

Their lives may depend on it.

'But as for you, continue in what you have learned and have become convinced of, because you know those from whom you learned it' (2 Timothy 3:15).

'Fixing our eyes on Jesus, the pioneer and perfecter of faith. For the joy set before him, he endured the cross, scorning its shame, and sat down at the right hand of the throne of God.' (Hebrews 12:2).

'Life will be brighter than noonday, and darkness will become like morning. You will be secure, because there is hope (confidence); you will look about you and take your rest in safety. You will lie down, with no one to make you afraid, and many will court your favor' (Job 11:17).

Pause & Ponder

1. What makes you nervous or fearful about the Last Days and why?
2. How has God given you hope?

Chapter Fifteen

I Saw Bioluminescence In The Throne Room
Sally Cave

In early 2017, we experienced financial trouble and had no money for rent. I headed upstairs to pray on my bed.

When I closed my eyes, Yeshua stood in front of me in a long robe. This will sound strange, but He wore a snorkel mask. When He spoke, He spoke into my mind. He held my hands, and we lifted off the ground, moving at great speed toward Heaven. I saw the earth shrinking beneath my feet, and my stomach started to flip.

As we neared our destination, we passed through a firmament barrier. Yeshua explained that on the side facing Earth, the barrier was created of a type of ice. The other side a kind of gelatine.

As we burst through the barrier, I stared. We stood at the edge of a huge throne room.

I knew I was not allowed to see too much detail, and it took a moment to register what I, in awe, viewed. First, the winged creatures around the throne. They moved on wheels. Eyes on their wings continually looked around. Just behind them, I saw the bottom section of the throne.

I gasped as I regarded the Father's very large legs from the kneecap down and his sandalled feet. I was in the presence of the Most High and knew better than to look at His face.

Throwing myself face down before Him, I grew completely awestruck, dumbstruck, and one hundred percent aware that I deserved to die in the presence of such majesty.

I peeked over at Jesus, who was next to me and observing. He still wore his snorkel. He folded his arms across his chest.

He spoke. 'Now do you get it?'

'Yes,' I mumbled. I still lay face down—but the message was so painfully clear.

I could not enter the Father's presence without first knowing the Son. The only way I could even dream of being near the Father without being reduced to dust was because of His precious Son. Yet my Father's basic, sandalled feet made Him seem both fatherly and approachable. The familiarity pinged my heart. My Father wore the footwear of a common man, not the shoes of an extravagant King.

Jesus took both my hands in His and pulled me to my feet.

We passed through the firmament and descended back to earth. Again, my stomach flipped. I watched as our planet got bigger and bigger until it filled my vision, and I stood on two feet again.

Yeshua no longer wore a snorkel. 'We are going to lighten the load.' He touched my heart, and three pieces of living black tar (it looked very much like Venom from the Spiderman movies) emerged and hovered in the air between us, contorting and twisting. As He touched each one, He announced the sin they represented.

He removed three things from me that day: critical voice, anger, and judgment.

Then He left.

I scrambled to find my journal to write it all down.

We soon received a check for a job I had completed the week before. The amount covered our rent exactly.

During my prayer times after my journey, I saw him dressed as a groom. Every day, we walked through a mountain pass. He spoke about having an audience with His Father.

I realized that I was dressed as a bride when I looked at my clothing. The dress was exquisite, beyond words. The details, Heavenly. Tiny white roses graced my hair, and gold slippers sparkled on my feet. We climbed up the side of a mountain with stairs carved into it. 'A side entrance to Heaven.' He smiled at me.

It felt romantic. We were like newlyweds as He showed me His Father's estate. We entered a side door that led to the throne room, and as we walked inside, every step we took left a footprint of bioluminescence in a stunning iridescent turquoise color.

'Wow, that's a nice touch.' I giggled as I followed alongside.

Yeshua just smiled that brilliant smile.

Reflection With Julie: Profound Petition
Tool to Use: Prayer

As you discern how to live with intention, I hope that you not only look at any possible blocks that might affect your thinking, but also dive into deep prayer like Sally.

Sally says, 'I love the fact that there are many facets to prayer. We are not boxed into one type. The Holy Spirit leads us into different ones according to our need in that particular moment. I had no idea that I needed to visit the throne room and see the sandaled feet of the Father to experience His awesomeness and to understand my complete nothingness in His presence. I was worthy of death, but I was with Yeshua, and that was the only way I could come close to the Father and lay myself at His feet.

'It was only through this experience that I understood with my whole being how Jesus and Jesus alone is the way to the Father. The Lord knows what we need, and when we pray, sometimes the answer comes in ways beyond all we can imagine. He has the answer. He is the answer.'

Deep prayer became necessary for David. He seemed to seek God with most everything during certain times of his life.

Daniel prayed three times a day, while threatened with death for doing so. Hannah's prayer in 1 Samuel 1 provides an intimate glimpse into her deep anguish, trust, and surrender. Her prayer life bordered on so fervent that Eli figured she was drunk. In the New Testament, Paul (after much waywardness), models a life of unceasing prayer. His letters burst with prayers of thanksgiving, intercession, and spiritual wisdom. He often speaks of 'always praying' for the churches he penned words to. (51)

Prayer is vital as we discern where the Lord wants us.

After I returned from Heaven the first time, I developed a profound prayer connection with Him. I spent several weeks unable to do much else but talk to Him. All my heart and soul missed His presence—I sometimes cried as my heart longed for Him. Those around me wondered if perhaps I had bonked my head somewhere. Wasn't Jesus with me all the time?

Well, of course, He was. And especially that first week. But not physically next to me, like in Heaven. You may have picked up the deep sense of belonging it created to literally stand next to Him, to walk and talk with Him (and wow—we did!), to listen and absorb His very presence, and worship Him while in the same room. You were created for that too.

Life will not be fully complete until that occurs.

Jesus often walked off to pray while on Earth. I believe one reason was because it took Him 'home.' It became the only way He could connect with the Father He missed.

In Judges Chapter Six, Gideon starts acting like a Julie. Although he politely starts with 'Pardon me,' he questions the Lord three times. First about the presence of the Lord in a tumultuous situation, secondly questioning why he (Gideon) is being sent (because surely, he is not capable), and finally asking for a sign that the message truly is from the Lord. He says, 'Don't leave yet. Let me prepare my offering and set it here for you.'

His Lord patiently answers, 'I will wait.' Note that a few hours of prepping and cooking tick by, and when Gideon brings the food, God burns it up. How is that for proof? Still, Gideon is not done questioning both his calling and his ability. That same night, he sets out a fleece, asking the Lord to prove his calling by sending dew to the fleece with the rest of the ground remaining dry. And when God fulfills this, Gideon then turns the tables. From verse 39: 'Do not be angry with me. Let me make just one more request. Allow me one more test with the fleece, but this time make the fleece dry and let the ground be covered with dew.' That night, God honored it. He did so! Goodness, our God can show great patience and love when preparing a plan. I think at that point, I may have just boomed: 'My son, DO IT!'

Gideon does move forward to his calling of defeating the Midianites and throughout the next chapter he remains obedient, although not throughout his entire story.

I am grateful God works even with us Gideons. For me, prayer also helps me slow my questions, which can be reactive, whether that is to other people or my Lord. Gideon may have found the same true with an honest attempt.

As I missed Heaven, prayer also quickly became a method to reconnect and draw near. During prayer, I feel closer to Heaven. As I lie in bed, not just rehashing my experience, but talking to Him for hours, His delight surrounds me. He tells me, 'I'm so happy we are meeting today. I've missed you.' His weight wraps around me, so pleasantly tingly and heavy with relaxation that I call it my weighted blanket of prayer. Yes, sometimes I fall asleep before I reach 'amen.'

Sometimes, I feel initially dismayed while perceiving His epic delight because I failed to complete my quiet time that morning, because it did not stretch very long, or because so many other things occupied my brain space all day. But the truth is this—He waited my whole life to have this deep prayer connection with me. And He never tired of the delay. He never threw his hat down or insisted on a time out. Never stomped off stage or quit the dramatic musical at intermission. Never spoke with irritation, wondering what in the world was wrong with my thinking cap. Just like with Gideon, He continued to love me deeply, patiently watch out for me, intervene when I attempted self-sabotage, and always pursued me.

Even now, He never focuses on my shortcomings.

He only welcomes me.

He only welcomes you too. Regardless of where you stand in your walk or life, the decisions you contrived or paid no attention to, the trauma you struggled through, the healing you may still lack. Despite any low motivation, your flat-out weariness, the relentless stabbing pain of regret in your heart, the questions in your brain space, your sticky grief, major or chronic illness, or any other issues and questions, He continues to wait.

He is so excited to spend time with you today.

Your next step in living intentionally by finding and pursuing your Manifesto is not just important to you—it remains vital in the fulfillment of the world mission He intends. No randomness resides in His plan, or in His delicate creation of you.

You were not made to drift around like a lost raft nor speed toward the bank on your own timeline because there is so much scheduled. Grab the oars! Stop the drift or pause the race. To walk in your true purpose, you must quiet the noise and listen deeply. Not just praying surface pleas and gratitude bullet points, but the kind of prayer that presses in, where your heart lies bare before the Father, and you ask not just what do You want me to learn, develop, or accomplish? But who do You want me to become?

You will sense a great difference with deep and intimate prayers that drop you below the surface, that sometimes even require popping up for oxygen before another deep dive. Fasting also sometimes deep-dives one to a Twilight Zone where nothing but you and He exist. Where one hundred percent oxygen and concentration rely only on Him.

If you have ever dived, climbed to very high levels, had lung sickness, or endured asthma or allergic reactions, you understand that when we are oxygen-starved, we become unable to focus on anything but getting air.

In that deep blue watery place, as you develop a strong laser-focus on your Lord, direction is revealed. Seeking Him deeply is the key to discovery. It is where burdens become callings. Where steps become leaps. Where short walks become miles.

Where trips become pilgrimages.

Where earth becomes Heaven.

Your mission begins not with striving, but with stillness. So go there. Often. Do not give up.

The One who made you knows why you remain here. And think of it this way—at least you will not have to go to the extreme that I did to define your lane.

'Rejoice always, pray continually, give thanks in all circumstances; for this is God's will for you in Christ Jesus' (I Thessalonians 5: 16-18).

'Do not be anxious about anything, but in every situation, by prayer and petition, with thanksgiving, present your requests to God. And the peace of God, which transcends all understanding, will guard your hearts and your minds in Christ Jesus' (Philippians 4:6-7).

Pause & Ponder

1. Think about the times your Jesus-time or prayer life has craved improvement. Consider what you did (or will do) to improve it.
2. Have you fasted? Fasting can take various modalities and may not mean completely denying food for you. Go to Jesus, ask Him to show you the mode of fasting that He wants you to do. Get some time scheduled for that now.
3. If you are reading this on your own, schedule an hour or two for strictly prayer this week. If you are completing this book with a group, please schedule a whole session for only prayer before you start the next chapter. To prepare for this, have each person bring a list of requests that can be shared and prayed for as a group.

Chapter Sixteen

We Asked For Heavy Angels

Linda Heath

On an outing with my oldest sister, Judy, we visited the dear older lady she lived with for a time. I envied her opportunity to live in such a fascinating old house with a kind and seasoned woman. I knew I would never receive that same opportunity.

When we finished visiting, Judy backed down the long, straight driveway. Even though she had accomplished this many times, I watched as she chewed her lip and focused on her mirrors. But she still steered too far to the right, and the back tire veered off the driveway and into the ditch.

Balanced on one tire in a ditch and with another perched up in the air, we stared at each other, eyes wide.

'Now what?' I asked, my heart pounding a bit fast. 'I'm no help. I can't even drive!' Heat rushed into my cheeks. What if the lady looked out her window and saw us? Or someone drove by? How embarrassing. How could Judy have misjudged so badly?

Her car door slammed as we exited. I closed mine a little more carefully.

Judy sighed. 'Maybe if I climb up on the hood, it will get that wheel back on the driveway so I can pull out.' She jumped on the high side of the hood. She bounced a little. And waited. I watched, fascinated. Would she slide right off into the ditch?

'Linny, climb onto my lap.'

Oh great, an adventure. I may have rolled my eyes. But I trusted Judy, so up I climbed. We grinned at each other right before I planted my backside firmly on her lap. I felt pretty foolish and knew she did too. The birds chirped merrily, probably laughing at our plight. At least no rain fell from the sky.

Nothing happened.

My sister started to pray loudly. 'Lord, we need some help here. Could you send us some heavy angels, please?'

I started laughing. What did she think, that He would stretch a hand down and push the front car tire back down to the dirt? Or that we would suddenly see a host of lighted figures gather on the hood with us? That could be fun.

But then it happened! Slowly, the car started moving, shifting, then dropping, and I almost slid off her lap. I tried to grab the hood. 'J-Judy!' I sputtered.

Slowly, the car lowered until three tires rested on the driveway. We hopped off joyfully and leapt into the car. 'Whoa! I had no idea angels could be heavy.' I shook my head, amazed at the answer to my sister's prayer.

Judy smiled. Carefully, she pulled forward, then backed out onto the road. She giggled. 'Thank you, Lord!' He had quickly and efficiently answered her prayer made in complete faith.

We were finally on our way.

The unseen world seemed almost tangible to me thereafter, and my faith grew stronger with God's demonstration and help getting us out of an embarrassing situation.

Later, in my adult life, I needed healing. My toe throbbed and resembled a grape tomato, becoming all I could think about. How could such a small part of my body utterly capture my attention and stop me in my tracks? My husband and I were parked in a rocky desert area—had a creature nibbled on my toe? 'That's impossible,' I mumbled. 'I always wear my hiking books unless I'm inside the motorhome.'

Then I remembered.

A few days earlier, while driving to a camping spot in

Quartzsite, Arizona, I drove in sandals. And after stopping, I grabbed my baritone ukulele recently inherited from Dad, joining a group of musicians learning to play. We sat in a circle outside in the RV shade and made music.

It was a fun couple of hours—not just because of our praise and combined talent with plenty of first-timer bumbles, but because of the words in the songs. It reminded me that words indeed are very powerful, just as the Bible says.

But I never changed out of my sandals. That explained it all.

Propping my leg up on the dash and riding the waves of pain, I decided quickly to praise instead of complain, unusual for me. I figured the best words in this case were favorite scriptures on healing.

I declared, 'You are the God who forgives all my iniquities and heals all my diseases. By His stripes I am healed' (my paraphrase from Psalm 103.3, Isaiah 53:5) and 'I will praise you in the pain, and I will praise you in the storm. You are good. You will bring good from this.'

I continued praising Him anyway I could think of.

And then it happened.

Beside me a warm presence radiated comfort, then a white wing stretched over my leg. I stared, the praise leaving my lips speeding up. I thrilled at the sound of feathers whispering over each other. The pain grew distant as I soaked in the warmth and comfort. Joy filled me.

Later in bed, I grinned widely. Did I really see an angel's wing? Yes, I felt confident. How cool. The hushed sound of those whispered feathers echoed in my head. I lay in awe of God's tender care. The same sense of comfort and warmth wrapped around me as I fell asleep, despite my throbbing toe.

In the morning the pain was barely noticeable. But the

memory of that angel wing lingers. Feathers swishing over each other while whispering is forever etched in my mind. Every time I hear the wings of a bird flying nearby, I am reminded again of the comforting presence and sight of an angelic wing stretched over my aching body. He chose to heal me, and I felt covered, safe, and loved.

Reflection With Julie: Please and Praise
Tool to Use: Pre-Praise

One reason we may not receive a next step is because we fail to ask—a common teaching in sales training. If you have received training, or perhaps hailed as a natural salesperson, you understand that a customer's challenges must be bridged to solutions. And that to close a sale, you must either ask or use another method, such as assumption. Assumption would be presuming the sale is a done deal and moving forward in the next step of fulfilling the order.

But asking Him, you wonder? Doesn't God already know our needs and desires? And shouldn't He realize we may struggle with implementing our Manifesto? Surely, He will honor unasked pleas with solutions.

No, not usually, although I view exceptions.

God created the framework for our requests for very good reasons. For starters, it creates a natural path to gratitude. If your child sneaks into the closet in the weeks before their birthday and plays with their gift, shoving it back into the box when tired, little surprise and scant gratitude remain for party day. Certainly, delighted expectation reduces greatly.

Asking also positions us properly in His presence. As an act of humility, it requires some belief. It becomes a stark reminder of the Almighty's position of authority and our rank as His beloved children. When we ask, we remain dependent on Him, versus grabbing the steering wheel and possibly landing a tire in a ditch.

He is our source of all good things. Our Lord says in James 1:17, 'Every good and perfect gift is from above, coming down from the Father of the Heavenly lights.'

Ask becomes a unique opportunity for growth. Rather than focusing on our desires or the direction we seek, we turn our attention to the Giver of all life.

Linda and her sister not only asked for their need when the car preferred the ditch, but Linda also later raises the concept of praise. And in a task we sometimes struggle with, she praises Him before the healing starts. She praises during throbbing pain which caught and held her entire focus. In the storm. In the turbulence. In her tunnel walls appearing to close in.

Pre-Praise is a Biblical move that can open tremendous blessing.

Do you suppose Joshua and his team, while at the walls of Jericho, felt a bit odd following the instructions of circling the city several days in a row, shouting and praising…all before the walls collapsed? Come on, there must have been a few!

But the obedient did so anyway. Now we have no idea whether grumblers in their tents questioned it and asked their roomie what in the world was Joshua thinking? Heatstroke perhaps?

We do know they followed through. In an act of faith that stretched days, they shouted in victory before the walls of Jericho fell. And the miracle followed. (52)

In one of Jehoshaphat's stories, Jahaziel (son of Zechariah) prophesized, "Listen, King Jehoshaphat and all who live in Judah and Jerusalem! This is what the Lord says to you: 'Do not be afraid or discouraged because of this vast army. For the battle is not yours, but God's. Tomorrow march down against them. They will be climbing up by the Pass of Ziz, and you will find them at the end of the gorge in the Desert of Jeruel. You will not have to fight this battle. Take up your positions; stand firm and see the deliverance the Lord will give you, Judah and Jerusalem. Do not be afraid; do not be discouraged. Go out to face them tomorrow, and the Lord will be with you.'"

Jehoshaphat responded with such humility and grace. He immediately bowed to the hard ground, and all the people worshipped, following his example. Some then stood and praised loudly. The next morning, Jehoshaphat told his people to have faith—success stood just around the mountain. He assigned some to the Praise Patrol. 'Go ahead of the troops and sing and praise of the holiness of the Lord God.'

Did you catch that? They were heading to the frontlines—with weapons of *songs*.

As they began to march and praise, not before, the Lord set ambushes against the men of Ammon and Moab and Mount Seir who were invading Judah, and they were defeated. (53)

Obedience and praise before the battle brought the victory.

John 11 contains the beautiful story of Lazarus being raised from the dead by Jesus. But it is not just incredible because of the life-giving miracle. It becomes one-of-a-kind because before Jesus raised Him, He tells Martha in verse 40, 'Did I not tell you that if you believe, you will see the glory of God?' He then raises His face to the sky and expresses gratitude in a very humanlike way. He thanks His Father for hearing Him and then says, 'I knew that you always hear me, but I said this for the benefit of the people standing here, that they may believe that you sent me.'

Faith that praises before the victory, worship before the walls fall, and thanking God before the answer arrives is the kind of faith that moves Heaven. Scripture echoes with stories of those who believed before they saw. My Lord honors that, not because He needs convincing, but because it reflects hearts fully anchored in Him, not in outcomes.

The God who calls things into being that are not yet, still does.

Ask, my friend. He delights in answering. Then praise Him for what He will do. He honors the pleas of the righteous.

'He will cover you with his feathers, and under his wings you will find refuge; his faithfulness will be your shield and rampart. You will not fear the terror of night, nor the arrow that flies by day, nor the pestilence that stalks in the darkness, nor the plague that destroys at midday' (Psalm 91:4-6).

'Humble yourselves before the Lord, and he will lift you up' (James 4:10).

Pause & Ponder

1. As you work on living very intentionally in these last days, consider the concept of asking the Lord for what your steps should be. Have you done this?
2. What can you start praising Him for that has not happened yet? Take some time to practice that now.

Chapter Seventeen

I Learned The Most Important Concept Of All

Kevin Conner

On Palm Sunday, in 2022, I experienced a transformation of my understanding of life, death, and everything in between.

Three days after my triple bypass surgery, I sat at home, my body still tender, mindlessly watching television when something extraordinary occurred—a flood of memories so powerful, so overwhelming, they brought me to uncontrollable tears.

During my surgery, while my physical body lay on the operating table, I had embarked on an incredible journey. It began with a gentle separation, like silk sliding over silk, as my soul lifted away from my body. I drifted upward, passing through the stark hospital walls as if they were mere mist. Floor after floor fell away below me as I ascended through the building, eventually breaking free into the open air.

The rising continued, carrying me through layers of atmosphere. The higher I went, the more Earth's features began to blend until, finally, I found myself suspended in the vast expanse of space.

Before me hung our planet—a magnificent sphere of swirling blue and white, backlit by the brilliant glow of the sun. Breathtaking and more beautiful than any photograph could capture.

Yet, in that moment, surrounded by the infinite cosmos, I felt profoundly alone.

The solitude was fleeting. In what seemed like both an instant and an eternity, it all dissolved, and I found myself standing in a park of otherworldly beauty. Everything felt more real, more vivid than anything I had ever experienced. The rich colors hummed, the air itself seemed to shimmer with life, and a path stretched before me, inviting exploration.

I became aware of Someone—of pure light and love. He approached with a familiarity that immediately brought ease, as if reuniting with a beloved friend I had known forever, yet somehow forgotten. He radiated warmth and any movement created ripples of golden light in the air around Him.

He took my hand, and the touch felt like coming home.

No words were spoken, yet we communicated. 'We should sit and talk while the doctors work,' He recommended.

The gesture toward a nearby bench felt both casual and profound. As we sat, I experienced something that defies ordinary description—a love so pure, so unconditional that it seemed to rewrite everything I thought I knew about the concept.

He turned to face me, so brilliant that I failed to distinguish traditional features. Yet somehow, it did not even matter. Communication flowed between us with perfect clarity, transcending the need for words or expressions. Each thought, each feeling, was understood immediately and completely.

The first message pierced the very center of my being: 'Kevin, you are loved.'

The impact of these simple words was astronomical. They carried such weight, such truth, that I physically collapsed off the bench, finding myself on my knees in front of Him.

His immediate and tender response included reaching down and lifting my chin with what felt like infinite compassion. 'Child, why would I not love you? You are my creation.'

After helping me back onto the bench, I learned what He described as humanity's most crucial lesson, in a voice resonating with authority and gentleness. 'Throughout time, my message has remained constant, though humanity has often clouded its simplicity. Let me share it with you once more, in its pure form. You are loved – deeply, completely, and without condition. You are all connected, bound to each other and to me in ways beyond mortal understanding. Love one another, not despite your differences, but celebrating them. Respect one another, recognizing the divine spark within each soul. Do unto others as you would have them do unto you – this is the foundation of all harmony. This is my message in its entirety, nothing more is needed, nothing less will suffice.'

I struggled with my own earthly conflicts. 'What about the Bible? I grew up with religious teachings.'

The response was both surprising and liberating. 'The truth I share is simpler, purer – you've heard it in its entirety.'

My thoughts turned to personal struggles, and I confessed. 'I have difficulty with certain people. Sometimes I feel anger and hatred.'

'Kevin, the human form, with all its complications and imperfections, may challenge your capacity for love. But remember – the spirit within each person, the essential spark of their being, is always worthy of love.'

With the same gentle authority that characterized our entire encounter, He informed me it was time to return. No lengthy farewell was needed.

Since that day, my perspective has fundamentally shifted. Death has lost its sting. I no longer fear it, for I understand it is not an ending, but a transition. My questions about what lies beyond have been answered not with complex theology but with simple, profound truth.

Most remarkably, I have found myself carrying a deep, unshakeable peace. It is as if that brief encounter with pure love left an indelible mark on my soul, forever changing how I see myself, others, and the grand tapestry of existence itself.

Reflection With Julie: Abundant Agape
Tool to Use: Love

In Heaven, profound love is deeper than the depth of any sea and wider than the vast galaxies above us. Stronger than the muscles of all the arms in the world lifting together. We often say, 'God is love,' but in Heaven, that is not just a truth—it is the air everyone and everything breathes. It surrounds, fills, and sustains.

On this side of eternity, we are called to reflect the same. Not reduced love. Not love watered down by culture or status, sprinkled occasionally amongst the people. Not held and grasped tightly, only given if people fit a certain mold. Nor safe-distance love, provided at arm's length or across the room, and only if no funny smells arise. Nor love that is transactional, passing it out only if we receive something in return or trade.

Jesus does not ask us to dispense conditional love, only awarding it if all the parameters are met. And certainly not guarded love, the conveying of it only when it does not cost anything on our part.

But instead, a love so deep that we would give our very lives—as He did.

We are called to Heaven-sized love. Bold, yet humble. Loud, but gentle. Gigantic, yet personable. Courageous, but still vulnerable.

There is a BIG-Love reason why I missed Him so badly when I returned to that ambulance in our cul-de-sac. I did not think I visited Him for long, although He now assures me differently. I confirm along with many others who have traveled to Heaven and back that time does not exist there, or at least greatly differs from the human timeclock. Many who clinically die, with a stopped heart, spend more time than the world understands with our Savior.

His presence is Home, as Kevin discovered. Nothing else matters. The love that overspills from our Lord's eyes, hands, arms, His whole being, into and through us—connects passionately with our hearts because our hearts are built to recognize and desire it. For the first time ever, we feel complete. He created us to experience that with only Him.

Why?

Well, I suspected more than the earth-was-meant-to-be-Heaven-until-sin-came explanation, although, of course, that remains valid. Here is what I learned from Him: He created us to only experience the true fullness of perfect love in Heaven with Him for a few reasons.

For starters, we remain safe with Him. Humans break hearts, no doubt about it. Humans can be abusive, wrong, cruel, neglectful, and indifferent. Each time these instances occur, carving a tiny or big crack in our hearts, we shield up a bit more—guarding ourselves from pain.

His love, on the other hand, stays perfect and steadfast.

My Jesus will never hurt you. Humans may hurt you in His name—but I assure you that they are not Him. He loves you with every bit of Himself, and then some. Why else, in crowds of people, would He know not just my name, but what industry I work in, the relationships I have built, that I write books (!), my passions, failures, heartbreak, longings and true joys?

On earth we cannot express or feel that deep of love without also sustaining pain. But in Heaven, safe with Him, that love abounds, which is why everything there, including the petals on the flowers, the leaves on the trees and the stones on the ground and in the walls, express love.

He also reserved the perfect love for Heaven and between us and Him there because here, we wear earth-gear. Our earthly bodies and hearts cannot handle the intensity of His perfect love. Perhaps we were built to, as once upon a time, Adam and Eve managed it, or perhaps just some of it—but no longer. Those of us who have visited Heaven return stunned. Gobsmacked (or as I say, 'God-smacked'). Discombobulated. Bewildered. Enchanted. Fascinated. A bit terrified.

Because of His love.

And we are never, ever the same.

Not only is He Love, (54) He is also the Word. (55) And Light, (56) as well as Life. (57) This confused me for years, but I tend to complicate things in my eternal mind looping. He never convolutes His concepts. Standing in Heaven helped me realize that these all tie into the major overhead called Love. Let me try to explain it as He illustrated it to me: Picture a heart, with everything else inside of it.

Without Love, there is no God. A separation from God equals no Love.

Without Love, there is no Light. For why would He bother?

Without Love, there is no Word. No base for it and no purpose. And certainly, no fulfillment of the Word.

Without love, there is no Heaven, and no eternal Life. No Life here either. For it was Love that both created us and Love that chose to die for us, cancelling our debt to scrub us up for Heaven.

And in the verses that say He is the Way, the Truth and the Life? Same!

Does that help you understand how vital His Love is? Everything else flows from it and in Heaven, that gush is full, eternally ongoing, and extremely fulfilling. We could not handle it here on earth—it would quickly become staggering.

In Heaven, no sun hangs. He is the light. I did not receive an answer to whether scriptures are there to read or not, but some feel because He is the Word, they would not be. I respectfully feel otherwise. We have heard several accounts of both library-type buildings and books in Heaven. (58) Some accounts even report that there is a book for each person living there, where the story of their life is contained and read by others. (59) That would include our friends from Bible times. It seems to me that scriptures, as the most important words of all, likely shelve there as well. But we will see for sure someday!

The third and most important reason that He reserves the perfect love for Heaven-only is because He ordained it to be. I Corinthians 13:12 says, 'For now we see only a reflection as in a mirror; then we shall see face to face. Now I know in part; then I shall know fully, even as I am fully known.' Full and true Love here on earth requires His physical presence, cancelling out any reason for Heaven.

My Lord retains excellent reasons for withholding this experience from us for now. He assures me of this. I pray you choose to trust Him.

When I first started receiving a hint of a potential new calling, and things pretty much miracle-like occurred, I struggled like Gideon. 'Are you really calling *me*, Jesus? I'm **just** Julie.'

I believe I repeated it 3-4 times a day for many weeks.

One day, His immediate answer stopped me in my tracks. 'You're *my* Julie.'

Awww. His forever-love hit me with force. I have not repeated it since. I am His Julie. His Jewels, just as you are His (your name here).

The little beach town where I met Bill is not only important to multiple instances of major family, personal, and spiritual history—but also remains a vital scene for various healing and recoveries over the years.

My Lord meets me there. The weight of the world seems to roll out with the waves. Each tiny sanddollar I find reminds me of His intricate plan and story. Each burst of wind (and there are many) brings not just fresh air, but new life. Each raindrop (no comment) becomes a tiny blast of cleansing. Each rock (have you deciphered that I love rocks?) includes a formed piece of treasure—tested in the high seas, tossed about until it retains enough shape and then hiccupped on the sand for someone to find. Each cloud hovering over the large rocks and mountains a reminder that haze cannot hover forever—it is not allowed to. Every tree a remembrance of growth and how far I have truly stretched. And each ray of sun is a direct message from my Lord—of His healing power, magnificence, and intense love for me.

As I rest at the beach that holds my heart, healing occurs. Peace resounds unlike anything else—before Heaven, anyway. It remains my closest earthly comparison. And still, that beach can never be my true home. I vividly understand that now.

George Ritchie felt profound loss after returning from the Heavenlies. 'The light of Jesus had entered my life and filled in completely, and the idea of being separated from Him was more than I could bear.' (60)

Don Piper agrees. 'Memories filled my mind and I yearned to stand at that gate once again. I prayed to please be taken back.' (61) And later, 'I lived in depression…I kept feeling I had little future to look forward to…Why was I brought back from a perfect Heaven to live a pain-filled life on earth? No matter how hard I tried, I couldn't enjoy living again; I wanted to go back to Heaven.' (62)

Multiple near-death and heart-stopping afterlife survivors report depression on their return to earth. And although the beauty they see is often indescribable—it remains the presence of their Savior they long for the most.

A lack of loving connection holds serious consequences for humans, both mentally and physically. Social isolation and loneliness are linked to increased inflammation, weakened immune response, higher rates of heart disease, and even early mortality. Findings of several studies confirm that we are specifically designed for connection. (63) Love remains essential to our well-being.

Our Creator developed us for Love (Him) with the following structure in mind: Increased love builds. Decreased love hinders. Zero love deeply harms.

Without Love, we die.

No Jesus=No Love. No Love=No Jesus.

As I seek to show a measure of His love here on earth, I remember that He shows no bias, we are all created equal, and that the only privilege I truly have is that He adores me and died for me—the same sanction He gave you.

But most of all, I remember that the One who died an abusive death for you and me did so for a reason—because He cannot imagine Heaven without each one of us.

'And so we know and rely on the love God has for us. God is Love. Whoever lives in love lives in God, and God in them. This is how love is made complete among us so that we will have confidence on the day of judgment: In this world we are like Jesus. There is no fear in love. But perfect love drives out fear, because fear has to do with punishment. The one who fears is not made perfect in love' (I John 4:16-18).

Pause & Ponder

1. If the reason perfect love does not exist here is because it is not safe for us to feel or express it fully, does that mean we cannot be fulfilled here on earth?
2. What has restricted or kept you from loving someone else fully?
3. Is there someone you will commit to reach out to this month? Please do not delay any repair jobs.

Chapter Eighteen

He Showed Me The Fun In Heaven
Rhema Whitlow

While co-teaching a Bible study on Revelation, I grieved as we studied the pouring out of the bowls and the plagues they each brought upon the earth. It felt heavy and intense.

So, God showed me a fun side of Heaven.

I had retired to bed in my earthly home that night. But now I stood inside a building, gazing at a butter colored wall about ten feet away that moved and vibrated—like it was breathing. Pulling closer, I realized its virtual transparency. About twelve inches away, I inspected it closely.

Rainbow colors popped out to me and began swirling, much like rainbows move inside of bubbles, vacillating and revolving.

Hmm. We have nothing like this on earth.

Realization dawned quickly, and I spun around. I stood in a massive room! Eyes wide, I understood the truth.

I occupied Heaven.

Well, wait! There was much to see. I did not want to be stuck inside!

I stepped into the hallway and realized that I was standing on an upper floor. Gliding down the escalator-like stairs, I stared in awe at the vaulted ceilings. Then I turned and noted more thick walls, some up to twelve inches. When I focused, I saw right through them to neighboring structures. Whether the walls were transparent or I suddenly had magic eyes, I knew this unusual structure beat all buildings I had seen before. Although the walls moved like they breathed, they stayed within a patterned formation, creating obvious sections.

Excited and childlike, I hopped off the stairs effortlessly and burst through one door to the outside. I quickly pushed open a gate. As beautiful as the structure was, I knew much more awaited.

In awe, I stopped and gaped. I now stood in a valley with pristine, perfected blades of grass. The area was cleared as if lying in wait, and I immediately wondered what would be built next. In that moment, I understood that what we build on earth continues to be constructed in Heaven.

Trees waved in a nearby greenbelt-type area and displayed the greenest leaves I have ever seen. I remembered hearing from someone who had journeyed here that you do not even pick the fruit—the giving trees bend their branches as you pass, rolling a piece of its gracious offering to you.

My eyes wandered upward, then meeting the vastest sky possible. No clouds graced the brilliant ultra blue. The radiance of the colors flabbergasted me.

Spinning around, I faced a large home, the one I had hurried from. Made of gold metallic, it gleamed from top to bottom. It was a castle-like structure with rounded tower windows. The gold metal flowed almost like liquid while reflecting the luminous light of God.

Behind the mansion lay a full hill, cascading with other gold mansions which looked like they had been birthed from a mold, like a sandcastle. Even the scattered gold roofs held no crevices or ledges. Gorgeous! Some mansions mimicked mini-castles, each one lavish and different.

I gazed in astonishment at this one special neighborhood of Heaven. I understood that like earth, other neighborhoods here held different types of houses. Having always loved beautiful views, my earth homes had always rested on hills.

When I woke up back in my bed, I asked God, 'Why are the walls clear?'

Almost before I even completed asking this, He answered, 'There's no need for privacy in Heaven.'

I mused. So there are structures that define spaces and stay within their boundary, but nothing is hidden.

God had revealed the gold in parts. First as I looked, I saw only transparency. But when His light shone on the structures, it looked solid.

I decided to look up what gold appears like in the purest form and quickly discovered that it is clear. The internet led to Revelation 21:21 where I read that the roads of Heaven are transparent gold.

When I was younger, I dreamed of Heaven and beautiful wheat fields. The light hit the sheaves just right, creating a shiny glow like when the first dawn of light ripples from the horizon.

Off to the right, a big red structure reaching as high as a skyscraper held tall swings, similar to carnival rides. Hundreds of people rode the swings, expressing delight as they gazed at the wheat fields below. Thousands of others traveled up a massive interior escalator to receive their turn.

Heaven is fun after all. Gratefulness for a living picture of what will come after dark days on earth restored my joy.

Reflection With Julie: Final Fun
Tool to Use: Thankfulness

I have been dreaming of roller coasters, and I strongly dislike roller coasters. One exception—Space Mountain at Disneyland. Why? Well, one, I guess, because my older brother made me ride it when I was small (I did not want to disappoint him!), and the event stuck in my brain. But I suspect the main reason is because in pitch darkness, my view ahead became nil! A dip coming up? A sharp, going-sideways corner? No prob! I stayed clueless.

We returned as adults to celebrate our folk's 50th wedding anniversary.

'What do you mean you're done for the day? We haven't been on Space Mountain yet!' Brother Rick grinned.

I groaned. 'Space Mountain! Didn't you forget about that? Sheesh. The lines are too long. And I'm hungry.'

Ten minutes later, I jabbered away while in line for Space Mountain, a protein bar in hand. For the second time, we rode it together. I spouted gratefulness when the experience scored the same: no fear. I spun along the tracks too fast to think about it, and the dips arrived with a sense of surprised blips. Oh! That was a dive. Oh! Maybe that was kind of fun! Was I upside down yet?

No idea!

That was the last ride with my brother for now. I am so glad that I went. He caught his final lift to Heaven a few years back. I know he was behind that cloud when I visited—I recognized his shadow. I know he waited there to wave 'hello," and he understood that I was not staying. He knew more than I did! But, bummer. Hi, Rick!

I pray that he and I will ride Rhema's swings someday. After all, they've got to be better than a Disneyland ride!

But let's move back to rollercoasters—how light or the lack thereof alters things.

It was not a huge bombshell when God started giving me antidotes of roller coasters to use for my Heaven Blog. Having already commandeered fast-rolling, flimsy carts on tracks as examples in two posts over a few months, I knew they rose to the top in illustrations for many varied examples. The wobbly carts just connect!

Many people felt that the Rapture was arriving last Fall, around the time of the Feast of Trumpets, and posted videos and content to support this, including their mathematical equations and how it all added up. Some who follow me then asked what I felt. So I prayed for Rapture confirmation. Many prophecies and biblical verses are occurring. And although it is scripturally secure to say that we will not know the day and time of the actual Rapture, I found myself requesting some kind of confirmation from Him that we may be close.

He tossed me roller coaster dreams all night long. We circled the same track repeatedly in broad daylight. I talked and laughed with others. Apparently, I felt thrilled. Each time we prepared to swoop by the platform, we braked instead and picked up more people.

We never ran out of room as they piled on. The train also never rose to the sky.

As much as I long to see Jesus again, I knew it meant that more beloved humans are coming to know Him and joining the ride before His return! Some who climbed on board in the dream have long resisted Him. Hope filled me as I thought of those I love. Still, I feel the push for us all to get moving on our Heaven-Minded Mission Manifestos.

Heaven seems scary to some. And I have heard a fear of a boring Heaven from many.

But boredom is a non-issue there, I assure you. A pagan High Priest turned Christian visited Heaven from prison and assures us that Heaven is far from mundane. (64) Countless other accounts assure us that Heaven remains extremely busy. Task-oriented people feel elated. Non-tasking people also receive thrill-vibes.

My friends, Heaven remains a place for us all.

In the meantime, stuck here on earth, how do we make it through?

The Word says gratefulness is key.

Huh? Gratefulness when I am slipping around wet grassy corners, landing on my you-know-what multiple times, and spying even more hurdles ahead? I mean, not just snags, but huge slippery slopes and cascading mud slides where my sightline to the crux of any potential hill remains blocked? Ugh! Am I supposed to look at those endless hurdles ahead and say, 'Uh…thank you?!'

Yes.

For a very long time, like almost my whole life, I veered to the easy way out.

We hear many trusted advisors, including authors, pastors, teachers, commentators and scholars who teach, 'Thank Him IN your circumstances; you don't have to thank Him FOR your circumstances.'

I disagree.

I recognize my audaciousness, but again, my Lord requested brave-bold in this book.

My friends, when I search the original translations of the 'thankful' verses, the teachings do not line up with that opinion.

Let's look at 1 Thessalonians 5:18. It says: 'Give thanks in (*en* means because of, during, while) all circumstances; for this is God's will for you in Christ Jesus.' The original 'all' (*pas*) means 'all, every (thing, one), whole.' Literally, it means, 'In everything give thanks; for this is the will of God in Christ Jesus for you.' In fact, the word *panti,* the dative singular form of the adjective *pas*, is often used to indicate something inclusive or comprehensive. A single event that is happening.

As in, be thankful, no matter. Trust Him.

What about Ephesians 5:20? It says, 'Always giving thanks to God the Father for everything, in the name of our Lord Jesus Christ.'

The preposition 'for' (*hyper*) occurs over 150 times in the

Greek New Testament (65), and when it takes the genitive (possession) case (as in Ephesians 5:20), it usually means because of all things in God's plan, on account of what He will accomplish, and for the sake of the development, amends, and utmost good that He brings. (66)

I see 'give thanks because of each circumstance' in both verses.

My world tilted sideways when I started thanking Him for the calamities, not just that He saw me through the chaos. And yes, still I shake my head as I pray sometimes! Thank you, Jesus, for the stupid cancer that coursed through the bodies of my best friend and her sister. Thank you, Lord, for the trauma in my life. Thank you, God, that I lost my first spouse (gulp). Thank you for the family members who try so hard to flee You. Thank you, God, for my job loss this last year! For without these things, You would have not moved with incredulity in the rest of it. Not just affecting my sprouting, spiritual chops and maturity, but bringing harvest for many others through me.

Wow, that is hard. Goodness. (Drip sweat here).

But so worth it.

What changed, you ask?

Everything. And by that, I mainly mean my focus. But that is everything. Our focus and thinking affect everything else (67). Eve's downfall began in her thoughts. So did Cain's. And how about the woman with the bleeding issue? Her thoughts, faith, and resulting determination led to her healing. (68)

When I thanked Him for the very trials that slammed me into rocky mountainsides, He rerouted my processing and the outcome. When I thanked Him as He intended, it pointed my path toward Heaven instead of our very temporary Earth. It forced me to think eternally. It required reliance on Him and enforced my choice to trust Him, even when tough. It changed my brain-dwelling source. It allowed me to toss a lot of hope-rope to others. And I believe that it changed some outcomes because thanking Him for the hurdles requires complete submission. When we completely defer to Him, it provides space for our Lord to take the driver's seat, as our own stubborn backsides must scoot out of the way.

And of course, the most important reason to defer is obedience to Him. Blessings for me and others affected by me grow from acceptance and adherence.

Rhema's perspective changed not just when she saw a bit of the Heavenlies, but when she chose to believe His great promise of forthcoming glory. Choosing to rely on the pictures He provided rewired her brain to receive and express thanks for the here and now.

Our brains are so powerful—God ensured that.

So, thank you, Jesus. Thank you for cancer, abuse, pain, and trauma. Thank you for the recent loss that still rips my heart. Thank you for my annoying neighbor who just will not stop playing loud, offensive music. Thank you also, for loving me, a sinner too.

Join me. Give it a try. See how it reverses things for you.

'Enter his gates with thanksgiving and his courts with praise; give thanks to him and praise his name. For the Lord is good and his love endures forever; his faithfulness continues through all generations' (Psalm 100:4-5).

'Giving thanks always for all things to God the Father in the name of our Lord Jesus Christ' (Ephesians 5:20).

'Rejoice always, pray continually, give thanks in all circumstances, for this is God's will for you in Christ Jesus' (I Thessalonians 5:16-18).

Pause & Ponder

1. What have you struggled to give thanks for? Will you consider thanking Him for those today?
2. How can you help others you are close to become thankful as God intended?

Chapter Nineteen

I Walked With Jesus For Three Days
Jenna Rose

In the spring, just a few short months after leaving my abusive husband and fleeing to a city on the extreme edge of our state, I finally discovered peace and joy. With my youngest a minor, I could not cross state lines with her.

We moved in across from a police station. My oldest was placed with a sheriff's family we knew for her security.

While securing a protection order and divorce, my phone was tapped and someone followed us while we shopped at the mall. 'Please be on high alert,' law enforcement cautioned us.

Busy and stressed with duties at work, a tech school training program, and the demands of a teen daughter with trauma, I struggled medically. Recently, I had worn a heart monitor for a mitral valve heart problem, undergone stomach surgery, and endured the sudden death of my little sister.

During this wrenching time, I visited Heaven in the middle of the night.

Heaven felt exceedingly calm and peaceful, filled with light. I remember trees and countryside, but not much else of the actual place except for a warm, breezy atmosphere.

I walked and talked with Jesus for three days. Heavenly time did not equate to earth time, as it all transpired in one night's sleep back in my new little apartment.

Other things occurred around us, and people seemed busy, but Jesus and I maintained a steady conversation and close friendship, as if I were the only person with His attention. He gave me instructions as well as important insights and truths. With Him, moments of healing cascaded over me. He removed my guilt for having stayed in abuse for so long and provided emotional wholeness.

His caring eyes, fully engaged and communicating with me, carried only love and concern. Just looking into his face brought a consolation I deeply needed. He embodied infinite comfort. All the stress of my current life situation became non-existent, not a small feat.

Nearing the end of our days together, He asked me directly, 'Would you like to stay here or return?'

I had not spoken much, instead quietly soaking in all He told me. To answer felt like breaking a silent, reflective time. But quickly, I knew my reply with strong certainty. 'I have to go back to raise my girls. I need to be there for them.'

I woke up soon afterward but could not move. Mentally and physically stunned, I grasped no idea what to do next. I questioned if I could complete my normal routines.

How could I even function?

I was left with one last picture of Jesus' beautiful face and caring eyes, focusing only on me. He gave me a parting, healing gift—an unexplainable sense of joy. Friends noticed it. Lawyers commented on it. Acquaintances felt encouraged by it. It became the 'survival shot' necessary to finish my race.

I still carry this gift that remains unexplainable, apart from my special three days in Heaven.

The possibility of not surviving my husband's current abuse, even during separation, became reality. An excellent hunter, he also mastered cunning. But I prayed around my home and requested others to pray as well. I felt that if anything happened, he would become a prime suspect.

Just to be safe, the morning I awoke from visiting Heaven, I created emergency plans and a Will. I shared them with my youngest, and we chose a hiding place for them.

Other suspicious events occurred (several flat tires on days

I was required to be in court to plea for child support and complete a protection order), but none became life-threatening.

I now share my story with other abuse victims in a prayerful, faith-based ministry. Through the grace, mercy and sustaining joy of Christ, Messianic and Lyrical worship dance entered my life.

One very warm summer Sunday, while dancing for a pastor's ordination service, I remembered with astounding clarity a three-tiered stone fountain in the garden I viewed in Heaven. I danced with people there.

As I danced during the worship service, I felt cool and refreshed by the memory—like I had been there yesterday.

I know that I will see it, and Him, again.

'Nehemiah said, 'Go and enjoy choice food and sweet drinks, and send some to those who have nothing prepared. This day is holy to our Lord. Do not grieve, for the joy of the Lord is your strength.' The Levites calmed all the people, saying, 'Be still, for this is a holy day. Do not grieve.' Then all the people went away to eat and drink, to send portions of food and to celebrate with great joy, because they now understood the words that had been made known to them' (Nehemiah 8:10-12).

'You turned my wailing into dancing; you removed my sackcloth and clothed me with joy, that my heart may sing your praises and not be silent. Lord my God, I will praise you forever' (Psalm 30:11-12).

Reflection With Julie: Jesus Joy
Tool to Use: Service

Serving is not only a privilege, but a gift from God. Serving, when we are ready, brings healing, maturity, a renewed focus, and growth—drawing us closer to God and others.

At times, God asked me to break from serving others. For instance, in my demising first marriage when I felt like I was drowning.

'It's time to take a break from teaching children's church,' He whispered in my head.

'But I'm committed for the rest of the year. Are you sure, Lord? And what about AWANA and VBS?'

His same answer weighed heavily on my soul. In fact, I started feeling uncomfortable guiding these young children each week. It was time to focus on Him, and my family, more. To receive nurturing from others, gain needed grieving time—and return stronger.

I obeyed and felt sad about not pouring into the little peoples' lives. But during this sabbatical, as I concentrated more on helping family adapt to overwhelming changes and seeking my own nurturing, the fog cleared. He wanted me to focus more time and thoughts at home.

We in the industry see that children who witness even psychological (emotional) abuse struggle to heal just as much as kids who experience it directly. They show a higher incidence of learning disabilities, anxiety, depression, gender confusion, poor self-esteem, and suicidal ideology than children raised in healthy homes—and the same measure as if they were personally abused. (69)

I encourage many survivors to seek serving opportunities to switch their focus to others instead of themselves and spur healthy friendships and healing. Some of them, already overcommitted, become so determined to people-please that they stack up the service ops like chairs after church, and we instead discuss reduction and breaks.

Sometimes serving others can become a wall we crouch behind, peeking out occasionally to see if anyone recognizes the real us. We wear a Cheery Chelsee mask, though we feel like dying inside.

If you have not served others as a part of your process, and especially as you work on developing or implementing your Mission Manifesto, I encourage you to consider it, with one exception: attending to others should not reverse your progress if you are walking, jogging, or running your own healing path. Please also check with trusted others regarding your readiness versus just considering your own opinions. And of course, always pray about it.

Here are some examples that might indicate times you should stall in serving within your arena of life experience. If you are fresh out of abuse and have not completed a healing program, it is not time to work with survivors. Save it for a future period. If you are widowed or grieve a child, facilitating a grief group could swing you backward—but perhaps in a year or two. If you have battled alcohol or drug addition, please do not stroll out to witness in a bar. Maybe (and I do mean 'maybe' because your strength may eventually be sorely tested) after years of sobriety, while continuing to work your recovery steps and building an accountability structure. If you are a brand-new believer, work on seasoning before leading a Bible Study for other people.

You get the drift.

Here is what most fail to consider: although you may feel highly capable and unaffected by stepping in, if it is too early, it can negatively alter those you serve.

If you are not quite ready to move into your life experience arena, that is understandable. Consider other options. Think about volunteering at a local food bank, helping with a meal delivery service for seniors, singing, or playing on the church worship team, leading youth group, hosting a Bible Study, chaperoning student music festivals, or fostering kiddos if any of those possibilities call to you and you have tucked some healing and spiritual growth firmly under your belt. You likely will discover a natural draw to the opportunities that highlight the talents and gifts God assigned you.

What if you are reluctant to serve or it just does not bring you joy?

We see many wary servers in the Bible. Moses could not speak clearly—how could he possibly lead slaves out of captivity? They probably would refuse to even decipher or believe! Moses did gain challenges with people along the way—they became shortsighted, selfish, and sinful. Amongst other things, they decided to complain and argue about bitter water and no water, grumble about the God-provided manna, and discuss killing Moses and Aaron and choosing new leaders (70, 71, 72). By the way, you might feel encouraged to hear that Moses is still serving and recalls earthly memories. Retah McPherson's son, Aldo, who could not speak after a car accident, visited Heaven, and Moses shared with him that he also could not speak well. (73)

But back on earth, did Moses shake his head and remind God of his initial qualms with this calling some days? I wonder. What a fierce time! Only today do we realize the tremendous impact of freeing the slaves. Because God was not earth-sighted—but Heavenly-sighted. And He also knew that Moses would use his experience to encourage Aldo in the future. That was just as important to Jesus as releasing those slaves.

What if the area of service you think God is calling you to fill just does not click?

It seems like our Lord enjoys summoning us to the one project for which we have requested a time-out. In the Bible, He often named things not as they currently stood, but as they would become. Moses kept fine fellowship in the are-you-sure-dear-God league, which also included Abraham, Sarah, Jacob, Gideon, David, Jeremiah, Peter, Paul, and Mary (not the band) to name a few. (74) God models Heaven-focus for us. If your called arena does not mesh now, it will likely latch in later. But do not delay getting started—it is always preferable for the gate to latch behind you.

What if God seems to be calling you to something you cannot or will not do?

God also sometimes calls us to the deep end—the one area where we just know we cannot tread water or where we feel destined for a grand sinkage. Feeling inadequate, prideful, stubborn, and knowing that God would forgive him for declining the mission anyway, Jonah flat out fled from his calling to brutal Ninevah—only to be plopped on the sandy beach of the city by God Himself. (75)

Well, we see how that one managed to get caught and landed! Do you really want to attempt a coup of running away from your Lord's request?

How often do we hear others testify of their reluctance or even tell this story ourselves? 'I will be your missionary, Lord. Send me anywhere. Anywhere but Africa, that is.' This from the family at the pulpit on furlough from their African mission organization. And what about the very common, 'What was I the most terrified of? Public speaking.' This someone laments as they share with you and two hundred other people sitting in the auditorium.

Those stories bring 'Br'er Rabbit' to mind. In the children's story, he begged the justice keepers to toss him anywhere – except the very-familiar sticky briar patch. He used reverse psychology and received his exact desired outcome. (76)

Although we know that this conniving rabbit's intentions manipulated others and helped him squirm and squiggle out of consequences, our pleas hop far from that. Or do they? Although we may genuinely desire to avoid witnessing in Africa, speaking in front of people, skydiving to launch Bibles to needy countries, writing books about our lives, or whatever, is this not a similar attempt to manipulate God's choice for us? And in a full-circle moment, He asks for that one thing we desired to avoid or felt incapable to accomplish.

Why would He do this? To challenge us? To prove that we can do anything through His strength? To force reliance on Him? To provide an example to others? All popular thoughts!

Perhaps. But I want to present another consideration – King Minion at work. You see, if Satan sends his little minion-spies and they view your early speaking skills, decipher your Jesus-love, and carry the information back to the evil-infested, dark and dreary throne closet below, Satan may very well listen to his messenger service, nodding his head. 'Well, she must be stopped. I can't allow her to grow up and speak to hundreds of people about *Him*.'

The dark King, also future-focused, will likely begin his mutilation in your youth, as soon as he discovers this gift God gave you, by implementing consequences for using your gift and instilling fear. So that by the time you reach thirteen (or whatever), it is finished. As you scuff home from the bus stop, staring at the ground and kicking the rocks in frustration, you fume. 'I can't speak in front of people. Today was terrible. They laughed at me. I'll never be able to make any change in government if I can't even talk to people!'

And you believe these words.

All Satan writes on his related to-do list now is to check in on you occasionally to ensure you remember your fear and inability to use your God-given talent.

Ivan Tuttle, before being snatched out of Hell, witnessed demons being dispatched to earth to complete their daily work of whining and dining people to sin, and helping them entrench deeply in strongholds. You see, when something becomes a stronghold, evil forces can lessen their supervision intervals. Time to move on to a newbie. Ivan says in his book, 'There were others that just seemed to slither around like huge snakes. I could see many of them going to the center of hell and heading back to earth. I assumed they were being instructed on what to do by Satan himself and they were returning to earth to do it.' (77) In his time in hell, B W Melvin also saw demons heading out on assignment. (78)

This is partially why it is so important to encourage our children and grandchildren past the fears, building their gift-confidence in the process. Be assured that if they seem challenged in an area, there is a good reason—likely spiritual warfare. Satan does not just start his evil influence in childhood. He sometimes starts in babyhood and often with previous generations.

Recently, God reminded me of our conversation the night I left my employer and wept at my dining room table. Even before I became employed at ARMS, I led the Her Journey survivor recovery groups as a volunteer, because the program truly preserved my life and generated emotional safety for my family. And because God asked me to serve—giving back in this important arena.

After my employment ended, I wanted to return to leading on a volunteer basis. They seemed cool with it, but my Lord pushed the pause button. I figured He knew my need to emotionally disconnect.

Time away did help, but I grew excited a couple of months ago when I finally felt His nudge to lead a weekly group again. I emailed the office, and they also cheered. Very shortly after, communication shot a wayward direction and some of those same 'being accused' feelings returned to my heart.

I sat with my Lord, cringing. 'What is happening? I do not understand. I thought You said it was finally time…'

He exercises so much patience with me. 'Do you remember what I said? I told you that you have everything you need to move *forward.*'

Oh.

'You want me to start teaching Broken Souls Restored? But I decided it was going to be a book instead, and its not ready yet. I formatted it like a book, you know, not a program…but OK, I'll look, Jesus.' This even though the whole time I had crafted it over the past several years, I kept hearing 'this needs to be a program' in my head.

I pulled the manuscript up. To my (almost) dismay, I viewed at least 25 weeks of material, already formatted for class usage. Each lesson started with a Bible passage for group reading, then dove into the lesson and key points. Each wrapped with journaling questions to complete while in group, discussion, and prayer time. All these months ago, He poked me, and I figured I would tackle it after completing this Heaven book.

'Nope. Now. Healing is your service arena, Julie.'

Yup. Check. Truth. You see, God will never revert His decisions. Nor allow my bales of avalanche distractions to roll down in the road in the way of His plan.

Broken Souls Restored (BSR), now at almost 50 weeks of curriculum, began several weeks ago. Within this beta group of ten or so ladies, some will likely move into leading groups by the time you read this book. I love their input. Four at various times have joked that when reading the syllabus, they noticed that I must have read their diaries.

God knew. I am so very grateful He can use my experiences to help Him pour healing into others.

He will use yours too and will bless you magnificently alongside.

When we step into serving others at appropriate times in His chosen arena, powerful things happen. Service becomes not about preaching to others what they should (or should not) do, raising our hand to volunteer because workers are short, or hoping to become elevated in human minds or even God's eyes—but about a natural overflow of gratitude and grace. When we are finally ready, the very pain we once carried is transformed into compassion and wisdom, giving us a heart that understands and uplifts those who are hurting.

Jesus prepared Jenna Rose for service by walking and talking with her for three days, and sending her home with immense joy that even her abuser and his camp could not sway. She, and many of us, discover profound joy in serving because in that space, joy refusing to envelop shallowness or fleeting trends appears.

The joy of Jesus Himself.

Acts 20:35 says, "In everything I did, I showed you that by this kind of hard work we must help the weak, remembering the words the Lord Jesus himself said: 'It is more blessed to give than to receive.'"

When serving for Him, from a place of understanding, mercy, and healing grace, our hearts align with His.

It becomes a joy rooted in eternity that no one can take from you.

'A generous person will prosper; whoever refreshes others will be refreshed' (Proverbs 11:25).

'Give, and it will be given to you. A good measure, pressed down, shaken together and running over, will be poured into your lap. For with the measure you use, it will be measured to you' (Luke 6:38).

Pause & Ponder

1. Do you serve too little, too much, or just enough? Have you asked your Lord? What adjustments can you make if He asks that of you?
2. What is something you feel God wants you to do in service that you hesitate about?

Chapter Twenty

I Sat On His Lap And He Healed Me
Jason Cotter as told to B.B. Brighton

When I was three and a half years old, I visited Jesus.

My baby sister had just been born, and Mommy was truly exhausted, so my grandparents, Cathleen and Richard Rutt, took me to visit my cousin in Camp Verde to give her a rest. I visited for three nights—and had a good time.

I yawned as we headed home around sunset in Grandpa's new white Chevy 1985 truck. In the middle of the bench seat, I loosened my seat belt all the way and placed my feet on Grandpa's lap, who drove. My head rested on Grandma's lap. She stroked my hair.

The highway descended through the mountains from the high desert to Verde Valley. This stretch on I-17, I learned later, is one of the deadliest highways in the state.

Grandpa suddenly shouted, 'Jesus!'—a plea. The truck shifted, and I felt a jolt. Then it flipped upside down and rolled over and over. Shattered glass flew. I felt time slow down.

On the third roll, Grandma flew through the window. I wondered where she went. On the fourth roll, I vaulted out the back window, hitting my head hard on a rock. Pain shot through me. I moaned in agony. The smell of blood scared me.

Grandpa crawled out of the truck, which had landed at the guardrail, and limped over to me. He lay on top of me and cried out to God for my life. To me, he said, 'Call on Jesus. Ask Jesus to help.'

So I did.

Two angels appeared. They were huge—much taller than humans. Shiny and radiant, they looked like normal people except for their size and the fact that they wore robes. One was my guardian angel.

I knew they had been in the truck with us. I wondered how they fit, being over ten feet tall.

Each angel took one of my arms, and carried me up, up, up. We traveled quickly through space toward a bright light. Stars and night sky surrounded us.

The white light grew closer, brighter—more dazzling than the sun. I had never seen anything so white. I realized that Jesus was the light, but it did not hurt my eyes to look at Him. His eyes burned with love as He gazed at me. The intensity of it shot through me, filling me vividly, beyond anything in this world. I did not miss anyone, not even Mommy. I only wanted to be with Jesus.

Jesus picked me up and held me. I sat on His lap in a big chair of wood and maybe gold, with a high back and wide armrests. He placed His hand on my head. 'I'm making it all new.' He touched my jaw. 'I'm making it all new.' He gently pressed His hand to my side. 'I'm making it all new.'

I played with His hands. They were big and strong, with purplish-pink scars in both wrists. He showed me His feet with scars too. He wore a glowing white robe.

Nothing else mattered but being there with Him.

He then took my hand, and we walked. The colors around me were like nothing I had seen before. The grass a deep green and the river's water crystal clear. Mountains rose in the distance, but there was no sun. Jesus Himself lit the whole place.

I saw roses without thorns and flowers I had never seen before.

Jesus showed me my life—past, present, and future—laid out in front of me. A record of everything I had done and what I still would do.

Across the nearby river gathered people I had never met but somehow knew. A lady who used to have a disease but now was all better. A man who had once been in a wheelchair but no longer needed one. I wanted to go to them, but as I moved toward the river, Jesus took my hand again and said, 'Not yet.'

The scene changed quickly. I hovered in a hospital room and then, embarrassment rolling over me, I watched myself return into my naked body—tubes extending from my nose and throat. I observed as they prepared me for surgery. My shattered jaw was held by the doctor's hand, but they were mostly concerned about my swelling head. They prepared to insert a shunt. Someone had already told my parents that if I lived, I would be unable to do anything, even feed myself.

But then, something changed. The whole atmosphere shifted. They watched the swelling in my head go down. 'There was a strange mist around him,' they later said. Now nothing seemed wrong with my head. They x-rayed my jaw—nothing wrong! 'This doesn't happen,' they told my parents. 'He's a miracle.'

My grandma met Jesus too, and He had a message for her: 'Tell My people that it's their thoughts that keep them bound.'

She spent forty days and nights in ICU. Her face was smashed, her right arm crushed, her eyes crossed. She had to relearn to walk and feed herself over the next year. While she was still in the hospital, God told her, 'Jason had a miracle. You are going to have a healing.'

The doctors said she would never use her arm again, but she insisted otherwise. They said she would never walk again, but she disagreed. Eventually, they told her, 'You're proving us wrong.'

The hospital kept me three days for observation, then sent me home with only aspirin for a few scrapes on my side. I have a scar on my head but no complications.

When I came home from the hospital, I told Mommy I had an amazing dream.

She smiled. 'Why do you think it was a dream?'

'Because my eyes were closed.'

After I told her everything, she said, 'That wasn't a dream.'

Years later, I learned that she dreamed unsettling pictures while I was gone those three nights. The first night, God asked her, 'When you dedicated Jason to Me, what did that mean?' Realizing that she was not trusting Him, she pictured my grandpa's truck in God's hand and slept peacefully.

The next two nights, she dreamed of red flashing lights and her sister-in-law crying. At 2 a.m., the second night, the fear became so strong that her legs felt weak. As she prayed in her heavenly language, she heard God say, 'Come against an untimely death.' She prayed for hours until the heaviness lifted.

When she told Dad, he said, 'You prayed, so it's all good.'

At 6:30 p.m. on the night of the accident, my mom felt heaviness in her knees. She heard me crying in her spirit. She and Dad prayed again.

God took me to Heaven and healed me because He wanted me to know that He is real and alive. He loves us more than we can imagine. And I now also know—God truly holds me in the palm of His hand.

Reflection With Julie: Hermetic Hold
Tool to Use: Belief

I experienced a tough day—focused on, of all things, family members. Many seem to have no desire to walk with Jesus now. I know I also sprinted away from Him many times throughout my life, giving me understanding.

Still, it grieves me.

I pray avidly for them and will never stop. Recently on a day when I spent an inordinate amount of time dwelling on a family announcement, I watered the garden while wiping tears and praying.

He answered with the same opening as a few weeks ago while I stood in the grocery store aisle. Only the ending was different. 'Do you remember when you were in Heaven? I told you that I hold them in the palm of my hand.'

'You did?' Relief washed over me in huge waves. Of course, when I gained an audience with my Savior, it likely became the first subject I broached. As we walked, I raised my concerns and He addressed them.

Because that is what He does.

Every new revelation He brings stirs my heart as fast as a mixer whipping eggs. Each time, my feelings tip over outside my eyes. I wear my emotions out loud and always have. But that is another subject.

On the topic of walking with Jesus, no matter how far we wander—whether through outright rebellion, selfish choices, or missing the path God intended—His grace is always prepared to meet us on that path. The prodigal son returned home to forgiveness and joy, but Jesus farmed nearby even as the kid fed the pigs and possibly slept near the slop trough. After Paul and Silas pre-praised and sang the jail bars open, the Philippian jailer and his entire household embraced salvation together, inviting the Lord into their home. Zacchaeus, after recognizing His value in Jesus' words and actions, grew a conscience. He turned from cheating people to generosity. Mary Magdalene, freed from a traumatized broken past and multiple demons, fell at His feet. (79) Countless others left idolatry to follow Christ when they met Him, heard Him or His people preach—or witnessed or heard about a miracle or deliverance. They thought, 'Could He possibly love *me* like that? So much that He waited for me all these years?'

Yes. He did! And yes, He still does.

Each story shows the same truth: Our Lord stays nearby. And He invites us back with open arms, transforms our hearts, and restores us into His ever-loving family. Deciding to walk with Him or choosing to return to Him brings not only forgiveness but also the deep, lasting Jesus-joy of knowing we are truly loved and welcomed, no matter how far we sprinted away.

While perfectly normal to vacillate emotionally a bit, at some point we must curate a conscious choice to not just believe Him and accept His leadership in our lives, but to trust and believe that He *will* work. The more we practice doing so, the easier it becomes. Philippians 4:9 says, 'Whatever you have learned or received or heard from me, or seen in me—put it into practice. And the God of peace will be with you.' James 1:22-25 follows with, 'Do not merely listen to the word, and so deceive yourselves. Do what it says. Anyone who listens to the word but does not do what it says is like someone who looks at his face in a mirror and, after looking at himself, goes away and immediately forgets what he looks like. But whoever looks intently into the perfect law that gives freedom, and continues in it—not forgetting what they have heard, but doing it—they will be blessed in what they do.'

As you move forward in writing and implementing your Mission Manifesto, belief is essential. You must choose to believe that your Lord will assist you in fulfilling your mission, including giving you the needed chops to make it happen. And any additional needs, whether that is financial, physical, or emotional. As I write, He uses this material to help me shape my Heaven-Minded Mission Manifesto as well. I truly do walk right alongside of you, my friend.

I write this chapter a week after Charlie Kirk, Christian Political Activist for Gen Y, Z, and Alpha, was tragically assassinated while speaking truth at a rally. In the first few days, absolute outrage poured out online. Anger and extreme sadness snaked into almost every post by his fans—a fountain of grief that seemed never ending: God, why in the world did you allow this?! Charlie had influence and impacted thousands of people for you. This makes no sense!

But remember, God is eternally-focused, not temporary earth-focused. What have we seen since? Thousands attending church for the first time or returning to church after years. Hundreds of people driving their family to services for the first time. (80) People in all communities choosing to know Jesus and posting their testimonies, in tears. And Charlie's activist organization, Turning Point, growing chapters and members by the tens of thousands. (81)

Was it really His plan to allow the murder of Charlie? A tough question, and we do not know the answer, although people sinning obviously never graced His grand scheme plan. In Heaven, we will learn much. We can be assured that our Lord works in the trials and grief to facilitate good for the eternal Kingdom. Anything Satan tries to crush us with becomes a tool in our Lord's very capable hands to wield for good. In Genesis 50:20, Joseph says, 'You intended to harm me, but God intended it for good to accomplish what is now being done, the saving of many lives.' And Paul penned the following in Philippians 1:2 about being imprisoned, '...What has happened to me has actually served to advance the gospel.' Numerous other verses also express this. (82)

Jason's story highlights not just how his mother clung to Jesus in her prayer life, and especially when prompted, but her incredible belief that God would hear, and answer her pleas. In fact, our Lord asks us to have an expectation of fulfillment as we pray. James 1:6 says, 'But when you ask, you must believe and not doubt, because the one who doubts is like a wave of the sea, blown and tossed by the wind.' That is not the only verse. There are countless other ones! (83)

Jason experienced multiple miracles while with Jesus, and they all branched to each other. Both he and his grandma saw Jesus and became healed—on different timelines. His mom, called as a studious prayer warrior, beseeched the throne, and likely increased the impact and duration of the amazing miracles because she listened, and remained faithful.

I bet you have someone praying for you as well. If you do not, I want to pray for you. Please let me know.

Another experience in Hell that Ivan Tuttle pens in his book highlights this importance of prayer and undying belief. 'I thought what a fool I've been. I was truly trapped and now would have to pay the price for all eternity. All of the sudden, I heard a voice like a mighty roar of thunder that said, *It is not his time yet. His mother has been praying for him since he was a little boy. You must release him now; I made a promise!* The evil spirit that had hold of me released me immediately and I just seemed to fly through space upward and out of hell in seconds.' (84)

Later, Ivan continues. 'The angel that spoke to me in Heaven also told me that God was honoring my mother's prayers because she had been so faithful to God in her life and had said over 20,000 prayers for me. God made her a promise about her children. She prayed for me two or three times daily…' (85)

Dean Braxton says of his experience, 'More people than you think will be there (Heaven). Family was created to be together forever. We were never meant to be separated. It's pretty hard for someone you are praying for to land in Hell. God wants them there (Heaven) more than you want them there.' (86)

If you are praying and believing for a loved one, do not

forget that He hears you. And do not give up. Ever!

Why did I sprint away from Jesus way back when? Because I wanted to control my own life. I have no doubt that some of my family members get this too. Turns out, some of my choice results grew ugly and negatively impacted my life as well as other lives.

It is never too late for you to believe, either. Even if Satan booked it miles away with a piece of your armor, or snagged your weapon—and now taunts you. Even if you realize now that you willingly followed the evil camp to the edge of the abyss or even further—it is never too late if you are still here and Jesus has not yet returned for His people. Even if the enemy successfully recruited you to his team, you can raise your hand and request a transfer. The Captain of the Jesus team sees your value, understands your marathon or sprint to the other side, and loves you anyway. In a heartbeat, He will plop you into the godly team huddle, welcoming you with a team cheer. Please talk to your Coach if you have wandered or fled and are considering a return.

As coaches go, He is the most understanding of them all.

Although you are never too far gone for Him, time is short. His great plan of accompanying as many of us as possible to Heaven is not just outlined in scriptures, He is also actively speaking to many here on earth. He is waiting—and I want to welcome you, too. Or welcome you back as a returnee.

You were worth waiting for, my friend.

"For I am the Lord your God who takes hold of your right hand and says to you, 'Do not fear; I will help you'" (Isaiah 41:13).

'And you also were included in Christ when you heard the message of truth, the gospel of your salvation. When you believed, you were marked in him with a seal, the promised Holy Spirit, who is a deposit guaranteeing our inheritance until the redemption of those who are God's possession—to the praise of his glory' (Ephesians 1:13–14).

Pause & Ponder

1. What do you believe? Our actions show our beliefs, and your Manifesto will also reflect this. If You feel that your actions are not mirroring your true divination, it is time to take a deep look into your heart to consider what you truly believe.
2. If you still need to accept Him as Lord of your life, or you want to return, here is a sample prayer that you can use:

Dear Jesus, I desire You as Lord of my life. I want to be on Your team. I admit to the sin I've partaken in that has removed me far from You. I ask for Your forgiveness because I no longer want sin to stand in the way of our relationship. I want to begin anew. I believe in You and that Jesus was sent to die and rise again to cleanse me of sin. I accept that cleansing now. Guide me in my next steps and help me to place You at the helm of all my goals and plans moving forward. Amen.

Chapter Twenty-One

In Death, He Restored My Husband's Features

Holly Klingensmith

My husband John hated the hospital and vowed never to return after his surgeries and cancer treatments. When he asked me to drive him there, my stomach dropped. He still received chemo, even though we received reports of no remaining cancer.

Previously, I had asked him to seek additional medical opinions—I felt they were administering too much. He assured me that everything now was purely prevention. I told his doctor how I felt too, but with me outvoted, the infusions continued.

John started struggling to walk, needing both a cane and a leg brace.

I drove him to the hospital with his quietness filling the passenger seat. He had gained a lot of weight in the past week or so, but I hesitated to mention it. When we arrived, they assigned him to the cancer ward.

One night, our best friend Mark and his girlfriend visited. We joked as the men playfully poked fun at us ladies. Ordering popcorn, we watched a movie, and very quickly, laughter and popcorn were tossed around the room. Normally, this would have bothered me, but I felt that it was important to allow John some fun.

That night, after our friends left, John asked me to rub his feet. The overhead light glared brightly as I had scrambled to discover and clean up all the popcorn.

I pulled a chair up at the end of John's bed and moved the blanket and sheet off his feet, trying to disguise the shock that rattled me. His feet were enormous and yellow.

'What's wrong?' His forehead wrinkled.

I looked up, noting his yellowing complexion. 'N-Nothing,' I answered as I focused on gently rubbing his feet.

'I love you,' he told me with a big smile. And I returned the smile.

When he fell asleep, I headed to the nurses' station, even though I check in there every day before entering his room. The usual news changed this time.

'His kidneys are failing. They will soon shut down completely,' the nurse explained. 'You can stay a little longer, but when the end comes near, we will ask you to leave.'

'What? Why?'

'I'm so sorry. But when a person still has copious amounts of chemo in their body and the kidneys can no longer function, they swell, gaining an amazing amount of fluid. Jaundice will take over his normal skin color. The skin will stretch until it can't take it anymore...and you won't want to see him that way, Holly.'

I shook my head, unable to respond but knowing that I would never leave his side.

I wandered back to his room, where my mother now hovered. She looked concerned. 'His face is changing, Holly. He looks so yellow and swollen.'

'Let's step outside.' My palms sweated. I did not want John to hear us. Once in the hall, I explained the situation. 'But I'm not leaving him.'

Wiping her tears, she returned to the room to say goodbye.

The head nurse approached. 'Some other nurses will come now, Holly. We are going to wrap him up tight to help lessen the reaction we expect as things progress.'

When they arrived, Mom decided to leave. She squeezed my arm. 'Are you sure you're up for this?'

'I'm not leaving him now, Mom.'

The nurses started wrapping John's body in what looked like large cloth bandages. They carefully began with his feet and legs and then removed his gown to move up. Now slipping in and out of a coma, he cried each time they wrapped a limb. He became angry and agitated with the pain, so the nurses asked me to step outside. They finished wrapping and gave him another pain shot. He calmed and seemed to slip back into a coma. When I reentered, I whispered in his ear. 'I'll be right here. I'm not going anywhere.'

They say those people in a coma do not hear and cannot communicate, but that is not true. With eyes closed, John smiled as he seemed to drift off.

The nurses left the overhead lights on, and I moved the lounge chair closer to his bed. About 10:00 p.m., the doctor visited. 'I'm not sure what is keeping him alive at this point, Holly. Sheer stubbornness perhaps.' He left the room.

Resigned, I stood, and being careful not to touch John's hurting body, I leaned close to his ear. 'It's okay, John. It's okay to let go. You always told me that you would protect me and love me to the end of time, but it's going to be alright. I have family. Please, John. I will be okay, I promise you.'

About midnight, a woman across the hall whose husband also lay dying, entered the room. 'Do you need anything? You look cold.' She left, grabbed a blanket, and draped it over my shoulders. The warmth of the covering and the quietness of the room soothed me. 'Would you like me to turn down the overhead lights? That might make him more comfortable.' She suggested this gently, as if afraid of offending me.

I looked at John, feeling reluctant. At this point his head had grown so large that it laid on his right shoulder in an awkward position. Deep yellow and black streaks formed on any exposed skin. The once-handsome face looked grotesque. Sadness flowed over me. I nodded, and she turned the lights down as she left.

Feeling drowsy after many days of staying awake, I pulled my chair close so I could see his face and hold his hand. All I could really see was the monitor, which indicated his numbers slowly falling.

About 3:00 a.m., a noise startled me, and John's once-limp grip tightened slightly. He battled hiccups, then quieted.

In my excitement at John's response, I remembered him defeating death not too long ago. He once shocked his surgeons by asking for a pizza when they pretty much counted him as going, going, gone.

But this differed. John's beautiful green-blue eyes were now open, and he wore a smile, his whole face illuminated by a brilliant white light that shone only there, nowhere else.

I pushed up from my chair. 'What are you seeing, John?' I leaned over the bed and looked up to the ceiling, trying to see from his viewpoint. The ceiling lights remained off—the bright white light shining from the ceiling was not coming from anything in the hospital room. I glanced at John again, startled. I no longer saw an abnormally large, swollen, and yellow face. He wore no black streaks or breaking skin.

I realized then that my husband had passed. And yet, he seemed so aware of someone or something in the room that I failed to see.

The man I had known for forty years now had beautiful eyes, normal skin, and a wonderful smile. I whispered. 'Oh, John…I love you so much.' Still holding his hand, I lifted and kissed it, clasping it with both of mine.

I did not cry. Seeing his face of joy, I realized his incredible happiness as he vacated the room. He knew or recognized whomever came to call him home. After six long years of pain and suffering, healing had arrived.

I leaned over to grapple for the call button to alert his

nurses.

'We'll be there shortly,' they assured me.

Still holding his hand, I smiled down on him the same way he continued to smile at the light above him.

The nurse entered the dark room and stopped in her tracks. 'Oh my gosh!'

I turned to her, still smiling. 'I know. Isn't he beautiful?'

She quickly crossed herself and started praying out loud. I turned back to look at John, who still smiled at the light.

The nurse rounded the other side of his bed. 'Please close his eyes, now.'

I did not want to but with one last look at his seemingly awake eyes, I gently moved my hand over them.

The nurse watched intently. 'This isn't right. This does not happen. I have worked the cancer ward for more than twenty years, and no one reverses the signs of illness or death. This is absolutely a miracle. May I bring some people in to see him? Not to make a spectacle, but for others to witness it? This is astounding.'

Knowing John would never object, I nodded. 'That would be OK. Could you call my mother?'

'Yes, of course.'

A few minutes later, the nurse returned, bringing two other nurses on John's team. Staring in disbelief, they then started checking for vitals. It must be protocol when someone dies.

For about an hour, I just stood, gazing at John. My mom arrived, gasping when she saw his face. 'He looks…..he looks...not sick anymore!' I nodded and smiled. We stood by his bed, and as the sun started rising, the bright light on his face slowly faded.

Mom offered to drive me home—we would come back for my car. 'Holly, that light and smile? That was Jesus telling you that John is with Him now. He will never hurt or suffer again.'

Both parents and grandparents dragged me as a child to every church conceivable, but to this day, organized religion remains a turnoff for me. Maybe I was even an atheist because I never grew keen on what ministers preached about.

But with John's experiences, I realized something existed with more power and love than any church teaching. I changed my beliefs and ways that night, and though far from perfect, I try to live my life according to the way God intended.

I, too, want to be received by God and taken home to Him when my time comes. I now know I have nothing to fear. Seeing John again, along with my mom and dad, and my best friend Mark, will become my best day. We will meet again!

Reflection With Julie: Radical Refurbishing
Tool to Use: Restoration

My Lord takes great delight in the restoration process. Many experience this when accepting Him as Lord of their lives. But He also performs this feat after our acceptance as needed.

Naomi in the Bible is a great story of God's restoration. In Ruth 1, she loses her husband. Later, she loses both her sons. What continual agony! When she decides to return home to Bethlehem, one of her daughters-in-law, Ruth, clings to her and vows: 'Where you go, I will go. Your people will be my people and your God, my God.' (87)

When Naomi arrives back home, grief meets her with unrelenting force, even as the town rushes about in gossip and welcome. In verse 20, she responds with 'Call me Mara (bitter), because the Almighty has made my life very bitter.'

In Ruth 2, we begin Ruth's story of gleaning the fields, meeting Boaz, a kind and rich relative of Naomi's, and winning him over as a husband. Their son, Obed, later becomes the grandfather of King David. Finally, in Ruth 4, the women of

Bethlehem remind Naomi of the restoration project at hand. 'Praise be to the Lord, who this day has not left you without a guardian-redeemer... He will renew your life and sustain you in your old age. For your daughter-in-law, who loves you and who is better to you than seven sons, has given him birth.' Naomi, once bitter and empty, is restored not just with family joy, but a place in the line of eternal royalty.

God restored protection for me on my return from Heaven. I quickly surmised that whatever the doctors say or feel about my health does not affect me so much. Every test they recommend, I kind of shrug my shoulders. My response to most every recommended preventative measure is 'meh'—well, not out loud, of course. God did not just walk me through my allergic reaction and death and pitch me off to Heaven, He outfitted me with His armor for the work and daily asks me to complete it. My extreme focus on safety, paramount before my experience, now pales in stature.

Should I go skydiving? I resisted that urge!

I gained a desire recently to listen to music as I walk in the mornings but avoided it, believing it would create a safety hazard. I wondered what the lady-jogger with earbuds was thinking? She could not even hear the dog barking and running along the fence, hoping to eat her ankles, and maybe her knees too. No way would I choose to clog my ears with music and risk downgrading my ultra-aware!

I have also, since my trauma, always walked with mace in hand. A few months ago, I grabbed the canister off the table before heading out the door and instantly heard His voice resonate around me. 'Julie, *drop* that mace. I am protecting you.' That was all—I do not receive long-winded discourses from Him. At least here on earth. Dropping the canister instantly, I nodded and almost skipped outside. For the first time, I worshipped as I walked and even lifted my hands in praise at times. (By the way, that makes a great arm workout!)

How glorious is this new exercise technique! I feel free.

One of the most famous Bible restoration stories features Job. After the loss of his children, his wealth, home, and health—he remained steadfast in drawing close to God. Although he lamented his angst across several chapters, he never blamed God. After many verses of his torture, experience with 'friends' and consultations with Elihu son of Barakel the Buzite, God spoke to Job in the longest speech I have ever seen from Him. In Chapter 42, God asked Job to pray for his friends. After Job obeyed, God restored to Job a double portion of all he previously enjoyed. (88)

My Lord also redeemed my years. In Joel 2:25-26, we read a reference to restoring the years the locusts have stolen. Jesus started chipping away on this huge task when I finally said 'that's a wrap' to mistreatment and started working hard on me. After I healed, He provided Bill and doubled my blessings, honoring my choice to start respecting His temple, my spirit and my family's future. He gifted me with new family members, including Bill's folks—incredible God-servants who loved me. He plopped me into a job arena of my experience, allowing me training, time and tenacity. He walked me through healing—which resulted in not just better health for me and mine, but a whole new program. He combined the bestowed gifts of writing and speaking with this recovery space in multiple ways. He then provided women to benefit from my past struggles, allowing me to teach them and pray for and with them. I tell these gals with high confidence: He does not just desire your healing—He wants to completely restore and bless those years. Just as He restored mine. And just as He physically restored John's body, facilitating witness of His amazing power to Holly, and all who entered the room.

In John 9:1-3, we learn that our Lord is very aware of the

impact of our tough times on other people. It says, 'As he went along, he saw a man blind from birth. His disciples asked him, 'Rabbi, who sinned, this man or his parents, that he was born blind?'

His answer? 'Neither this man nor his parents sinned, but this happened so that the works of God might be displayed in him.'

God also restored our world. Have you ever considered that? Earth basically looks unaffected by the ravishing flood highlighted in Genesis. (89) And He will refresh it again. In Isaiah 65:17, He speaks of restoring the earth to become the new and final Heaven. By resurrecting Jesus, He not only revived His son, but provided the ability for all to become eternally saved and dwell in Heaven with Him. (90) His very desire and capacity to toss our sins into the deepest ocean when we confess shows a sheer craving to rebuild and renew us. (91)

He loves to restore!

Do you need rehab of some tough times? He will not reconstruct for the unwilling. He wants more than to simply mend your pain—He wants to tip your past-bucket upside down and send the contents down a hundred-foot cliff into the depths of the sea. Seasons of hardship, regret, grief, or wasted efforts do not stretch beyond His reach. He restores because His nature is abundant love—delighting in bringing beauty from ashes, joy from mourning, healing from trauma and strength from weakness.

No loss defines us, no scar is wasted, and no stolen year is beyond His power to renew. In His hands, the hardest chapters of our story will become the very Mission Manifesto pages testifying the most clearly of His goodness.

Ask Him for restoration today. You may be very surprised at the abundance He provides.

'But I will restore you to health and heal your wounds' (Jeremiah 30:17).

'...that times of refreshing may come from the Lord, and that he may send the Messiah... Heaven must receive him until the time comes for God to restore everything, as he promised long ago through his holy prophets' (Acts 3:19–21).

Pause & Ponder

1. What regrets do you have? What tribulations have highlighted your life?
2. Consider seeking any forgiveness still needed from other people, yourself, or God, and ask Him to restore these years in your life.

Chapter Twenty-Two

God Gave Me Two Visits With My Son In Heaven
Lindsay Wessinger

Note: This story discusses child death.

After multiple miscarriages, a very troubling marriage, and the loss of my grandmother, I unexpectedly lost Jordan, my four-year-old son—to Heaven.

Life fell apart, and I never recovered. Things kept getting worse.

I found Christianity early in life and often attended church growing up. Even after many of my losses, I walked closely with God—until He took my son.

While pregnant with Jordan, I received the usual sonogram. Something felt wrong—the scan dragged on and on. 'What's going on?' I asked when the technician stopped talking and grew quiet. Her puzzled look alarmed me. She finally left the room to get someone else.

I felt panic climbing and started to sweat. Even with so many losses, I had also experienced a successful pregnancy which resulted in my daughter Emma, now nine.

The clinic ordered a higher-level ultrasound, and I finally received some results from the doctor.

'I'm sorry, Lindsay. Your baby has Truncus Arteriosus. That means that no pulmonary artery developed. His heart has no way to move blood to his lungs. He will need immediate open-heart surgery after birth.'

Only one surgeon could operate—and we would need to travel to a different part of the state. This condition is so rare that only one in thirty thousand babies suffer with it.

'I need to close up the nursery,' I whispered as I entered the house later. 'My baby isn't going to live.' And as I closed the door on his room, I realized that my whole purpose in life had crashed off a cliff. Being a mom to healthy children was all I had ever desired.

When Jordan was born at the specialized hospital across the state, they rushed him into surgery. I lived at the Ronald McDonald house for two months as he recovered. My dad stayed at my house with Emma. Not able to even eat as it tired his heart, Jordan received nutrition via a feeding tube in his nose, then later implanted into his stomach. I learned all about the specialized care he needed ongoing.

We finally traveled home, and I felt excited and hopeful. I wanted Emma to play an active role in helping with her brother. Amongst all of that swam severe trepidation. I now must provide a fulltime nursing—but at least getting home seemed somewhat a victory. Shortly after arriving, my husband decided to move out, having met someone else. Of course, that stung. But I set my sights and heart on making the best home possible for my two children.

As Jordan grew, he became a devoted little boy. He loved hugs. Generous, sweet and kind, He also developed the most contagious laugh. He lit up rooms so much that sometimes I wondered if an angel hid inside of him, glowing through his eyes.

Jordan loved jumping on our trampoline, and one day at the age of four, after a seventh surgery and a release to normal activity, he ran out to the trampoline. I later called him in for dinner. He ate well then decided to dance to *Lion King* songs as I cleaned up. As I washed dishes, I heard him start crying—he had thrown up.

Oh no! Maybe a flu bug? 'You'll be alright, buddy.' I tried to comfort him.

Emma helped me get Jordan into the bathtub to clean up. 'Emma, can you get him some clean clothes, please?' She nodded and left.

In the tub, Jordan threw up more and lost bodily functions. His eyes could not focus on me when open and then kept closing. His cries sounded more like moans. I tried to bring him to full awareness, but something seemed seriously wrong. I scooped him up and ran to the couch, setting him down. 'Call 911!' I called to Emma.

On arrival, the EMTs picked him up and headed out to the ambulance. With no shoes or phone charger, I ran behind them. I left Emma on the sidewalk with a neighbor as I hopped into the ambulance.

When the doors closed, the monitor showed my son's heartrate dropping to 52, and then the EMTs began CPR.

'Wait! What are you doing?' I cried. I looked out of the window and saw Emma drop to the ground. I banged on it with my fists then spun around to the EMT. 'Why are you doing that?'

They drove fast, running red lights as I rubbed what parts I could reach of him. 'Stay with me. I love you. Don't do this.' I kept saying over and over. I feared looking into his eyes—afraid of what I would see, and terrified that it could be my last memory of him.

Please stay with me.

'Mom.' The EMT sounded urgent. 'We have to tell you his heart has officially stopped.'

I started screaming. I could not look at my baby's face, but I zeroed my eyes in on his legs and started shaking and slapping them gently. 'Come back to me, Jordan! Come back!'

We stopped at the closest hospital, and they pulled Jordan out so fast and hard, it knocked me out of the ambulance. I scrambled upright and ran after the stretcher.

I watched, still screaming and crying, as so many adults threw their weight on him. 'You-You're going to hurt him!' I desperately wanted to shout. Each time they pushed down on him, his little arm flew up.

Then, the worst happened—they all stopped pushing, and they walked out of the room. A weight dropped on my heart, on my very soul. He looked so tiny, so helpless.

As I sobbed, they directed me to an empty room. I waited an hour for my brother to arrive with Emma. She seemed to expect the news, but confirming to her that Jordan had died felt torturous.

I later learned that during Jordan's most recent surgery, bacteria had contaminated the surgical site. Jordan died from asymptomatic endocarditis—infection of the heart. It was also likely preventable had blood tests been ordered at his surgical follow up appointment.

I turned my back on God. 'You took everything from me! My son, my babies, my grandma, my husband—even my dog! I've had nothing but loss. You took my future—all of it, and You stole my whole purpose.'

Emma would be able to grow up and go to college, but Jordan had still depended on me. I did not feel done. Knowing I was not supposed to ask God 'why,' I asked anyway, multiple times. I began to live under a dark, black cloud and could not break away from it. 'There can't be a God. I'm supposed to be His child. What kind of parent puts His child through this kind of pain!'

I started drinking alcohol every evening, way too much, and stopped taking care of myself—piling on sixty pounds. My dirty house reflected my inability to barely leave my couch for months.

One day, I woke up and felt a little different. I mused, 'Maybe I'm not thinking clearly about the God part. Maybe He wants me to return to Him for answers. I need to know that Jordan is okay now.' After considering this, I acted. Turning off electronics and other distractions, I prayed like crazy, for an hour at a time. I prayed for everything I thought of—like knowledge, acceptance, peace, physical and mental health, and for signs that He remembered me. I had never prayed for those things before, but I asked for everything that might pull me back to His light, and love.

A week or so later, God allowed me an encounter with Jordan—a vision as I slept. But I do have untreated sleep apnea and often wonder if I visited for real.

In another place, I walked down a new neighborhood street with pretty little houses next to each other that were all about the same size. In their yards, people gathered. They obviously knew each other as they sipped drinks and ate snacks. I heard voices and laughter but it was all telepathic. I felt their excitement and joy, then realized that I could float. When I heard music, I drifted over to the back yard where it generated from. A Mexican woman sang into a microphone. Her mouth moved slightly, but barely. The song was beautiful.

As she looked at me, the singing stopped, but I still heard the music in my head. Dark, shoulder-length hair graced her head, but light reflected off it, making it glow, glitter-like. With her breathtaking smile, I viewed the whitest teeth I have ever seen and noted her gorgeous eyes.

Here in Heaven, the air felt warm—not too hot or cool, and the vividly beautiful sky welcomed me. I saw that the green grass differed from any shade of green I had seen before. It glistened, and looked alive. It felt cool to the touch, and extremely soft—like brand new baby-grass as it first grows.

I am forty years old and still wanted to throw myself down and roll around in it.

No one sat in front of the last house on the block. The party sounds kind of faded as I gazed at it across the street. Grey with white trim, the surface had vertical panels from the floor to roof.

Two men walked out of the house. One tall and one shorter, but both wearing white shirts, khaki shorts, and sandals. I never saw the tall one's face—it seemed irrelevant and still does. But I saw the shorter man's face and can still recall it today. He had olive-colored skin and approached me. 'Would you like to meet my son?'

'Hmm. OK.' I knew he could not be talking about Jordan, as my son is white. But I would see what was next in this odd but beautiful adventure.

The door of the house flew open, and Jordan sprinted out, wearing a little navy blue and white onesie that he often sported on earth. He was about three years old.

Laughing, he ran fast toward me with open arms, looking perfectly healthy. On earth, he had been skinny and often carried dark circles under his eyes. Now he bore weight on his body and absolutely glowed. No dark circles, either! Joy filled me.

As I grabbed him, I felt his warm breath on my cheeks. His skin felt so soft.

We played. We spun in circles as I held his hands, his feet rising off the ground. Then we walked for a while, still holding hands.

'It's time to go back into the house,' the man told Jordan. Together, they walked away.

Oh no! I started yelling, 'Wait! No, stop! That's my son, not yours! He's dead. Please bring him back. Please give him back.'

The man turned around and smiled reassuringly at me. The door closed behind them, leaving me alone.

But the visit was not complete.

When the door opened again, Jordan exited a little older

and was dressed in bigger boy clothes. The shirt was the same color as the striped onesie, and he also wore khaki shorts.

This time he called to me, 'Mommy, Mommy, Mommy!'

We sat on a bench, and I squeezed him so tight. He smelled clean and fresh, the same as he had on earth, and wore the same buzzed haircut. I rubbed his hair. He breathed so well here. But again, I saw and felt a healthier version with added weight and good color on his lips. He did not look tired like he often did on earth, but vibrant.

The two men stood off to the side, communicating about something unknown.

I squeezed Jordan, sitting on my lap as another man walked down the sidewalk toward us.

I waved. 'This is my son on my lap and you can see him, right? He passed away. But you can see him?' I suddenly felt the need for someone else to confirm what I viewed.

He provided a huge, glowing smile.

For some reason, I felt only relief and gratitude when the two men drew near this time. The shorter one motioned me to follow, so I placed Jordan on my hip and did so. We floated through the neighborhood and then approached a wall with a big ladder against it.

At the top of the ladder, I saw silhouettes of hundreds of different people in various sizes and shapes. The two men climbed up and motioned to me. With my left hand on the ladder, I said, 'I need help,' because I was not going to let go of Jordan.

But then I did.

The taller man reached down with very large hands. I still could not see his face. I handed him Jordan and felt fine about it. Perhaps they would reach for me afterward.

I cupped Jordan's little behind to help him up. I heard him laugh. Oh, how I missed his laughter. But at the top of the ladder, he happily ran off to all the shadow figures. This gave me joy too. I stepped further up on the ladder to peer into the above, but then I opened my eyes in my bed.

Tears of sheer happiness poured down my cheeks. 'Thank you, God. That is what I needed. I just needed to know that he wasn't gone. That he was happy and being taken care of. Thank you, God.' This was the first time I remembered ever crying happy tears.

Our lives turned around. I stopped drinking and lost 20 pounds in a month. I had worn glasses since the 6th grade, but my vision was healed. I decided I did need to be healthy. 'I still need to take care of Emma. I am still a mother. Dear God, continue to give me emotional and physical healing and health and to always remember my daughter.'

Emma, upset when I shared my visit because she was unable to say goodbye to her brother, experienced something too. While visiting her dad, she grew sad and felt sick. She turned off her electronics and lay on her bed. Then she heard Jordan's voice. 'I love you, sissy.' It came from every direction, resonating through the room. She jumped up and glanced at the clock, seeing it was 5:13. Jordan was born on 5/13. Crying, she called me.

For much of the first year, it was so much easier to pretend he had not died. But then, changes occurred. The trampoline started falling apart. The balls Jordan used to play with deflated. His bedroom seemed lifeless. The reality of the loss stank. I started to feel myself slip. As his first angel-anniversary date and birthday hovered near, depression pushed to return to my heart as joy faded.

And God granted one more visit.

I saw the same green, soft grass but no buildings this time. I stood in a field and a street to the left of me had parallel parked cars—I viewed the sides of them.

A blue car pulled up and parked. A woman with light brown or blondish hair in a ponytail like my grandma when she was younger opened the door and slipped out. A man stepped out of the passenger seat and opened the back door.

Jordan was now the same age as when he passed, and exactly how I remembered him, but healthier looking. He sported a navy striped shirt and khakis again, even though he had died in grey sweats.

Like he had wings, he flew out with wide open arms. 'Mommy!'

I knelt to brace for impact.

He jumped into my arms. 'Hi! Hi! Hi!' he kept saying.

I held him, and smelled him, and rubbed his hair. I whispered to him, 'It's been so long since I've been able to do this. So long. I miss you.'

He did not speak after his greetings, but he also never returned to the car.

I opened my eyes, back in my room.

It is so tough to describe the immense hope and joy my visits with Jordan brought. I have dreamt of him since, but dreams remain a completely different experience. There is a huge difference between sleeping and dreaming about him versus actually spending time with him.

I am so grateful that God cared about me and Emma enough to ensure our continued thriving until our jobs on earth are completed. Although the last visit with my son was shorter, it impacted me just as greatly. I praise Him for the moments in Heaven that He provided.

Reflection With Julie: Amazing Acclaim
Tool to Use: Worship & Praise

Just as I discovered that pre-believing and pre-thanking is important in results, building an attitude of praise and worship also remains vital. Praise builds faith. Not just in you—but in others too.

In Acts 16:16-38, Paul and Silas get tossed in jail for freeing a slave girl from her demons. The slave girl generated income for her owners by telling fortunes and this 'talent' became defunct. To add disgrace to disagreement, Paul had not even set out to deliver her. The scriptures clearly point out his irritation with the evil spirit, who hassled him for several days. Annoyed, Paul ordered it to leave the girl.

Their punishment brought the humiliation of being stripped and whipped with rods before lock-down, and the crowd participated. There might as well have been a scripture verse: 'Thou shalt not take away from a man's earning power.' Perhaps there was a law, I do not know.

In jail, Paul and Silas chose to rattle the bars with praise. Trusting God, they sang songs, likely cheering up the other inhabitants as well as themselves. When the clock hit midnight, some rather interesting events flooded main stage. 'Suddenly there was such a violent earthquake that the foundations of the prison were shaken. At once all the prison doors flew open, and everyone's chains came loose. The jailer woke up, and when he saw the prison doors open, he drew his sword and was about to kill himself because he thought the prisoners had escaped. But Paul shouted, 'Don't harm yourself! We are all here!' (92)

The jailer called for lights, ran into their cell, and fell before them. 'How can I be saved?' He had witnessed a miracle he would never be able to explain—and his prisoners stood right in front of him instead of running! Paul and Silas not only shared the gospel, but visited the jailer's home where the jailer cared for their wounds and fed them. The spiritual impact caused the entire family to be saved. All were baptized that night. The scriptures state that joy filled the family members.

After the most miraculous jailbreak ever, and a short vacay in a kind man's home, all arrived back at the jail in time (no word about the other prisoners), and the magistrate released Paul and Silas the next day. They had learned that Paul and Silas were citizens after all.

Oops! Big fumble!

In studying First and Second Kings in the past month, I find myself greatly drawn to Elisha and have read his stories multiple times. The kid basically started out as Elijah's intern but developed a deep honor of the Lord and became Elijah's replacement. God gave Elisha multiple supernatural abilities. (93)

In 2 Kings 3, the king of Israel set out with the king of Judah and the king of Edom with their troops to immobilize the enemy. Curious Julie always finds it interesting that the kings then practiced very hands-on leadership and fought wars with their ground people.

Apparently ill-prepared, they used up all the water for the people and the animals. I assume this because they ran out, and scripture does not mention leaks, water bandits, or incidents of leaving water containers at the campsites behind them. Stuck with an issue that could kill them all and soon, they team-huddled to chat. In verse 11, Jehoshaphat asked, 'Is there no prophet of the Lord here, through whom we may inquire of the Lord?' The king of Israel then told him of Elisha, and that Elisha had poured water on the hands of Elijah.

A water guy!

Elisha, who hears them out only because of his respect for Jehoshaphat, says in verse 15, 'But now bring me a harpist.'

While the praise occurred, the hand of the Lord came on Elisha. Yes, my friends, the Holy Spirit was in the house! Or maybe on a horse! Elisha informs them that there will be no rain or wind, and that the Lord will fill the valley with pools of water. Victory would occur in Moab as they overthrew every fortified city and every major town.

They woke up to the pools of water the next day.

Well, that was a long story. My apologies. But my point is – it started with praise!

Ever feel the presence of the Lord in church while you are singing or praying? Or perhaps as you are belting along with tunes on the road? Praise is also how we will enter His presence in Heaven, and are to enter His presence here on earth. Psalm 100:4 says, 'Enter his gates with thanksgiving and his courts with praise; give thanks to him and praise his name.'

Praise is so important that Heaven is filled with it! Barbie Porter visited Heaven for a short time while experiencing an allergic reaction after the birth of her daughter. She heard thunder that seemed to call to her – only realizing that it was the sound of praise when she got closer. (94)

Dean Braxton arrived in Heaven and saw Jesus, who was brighter than the noonday sun. Dean says that everything within him began to praise Jesus, and he could not stop. (95)

Don Piper speaks of angel's wings producing a holy melody and explains, 'A second sound remains, even today, the single most vivid memory I have of my entire Heaven experience. I call it music, but it differed from anything I had ever heard or ever expect to hear on earth. The melodies of praise filled the atmosphere…the praise was unending and remarkedly, hundreds of songs were being sung all at once…I heard it from every direction and realized that each voice praised God.' (96) Don states that the closest sound he has found to compare is the 'The Battle Hymn of the Republic' sung by the Mormon Tabernacle Choir with the West Point Band. (97)

Marv Besteman shares, 'The music I heard there was incomparable to anything I had heard before…' (98)

Although I do not currently remember sounds other than His voice in either of my experiences, many other accounts talk about the music of Heaven. And here, praise and worship play an essential role for me. So much so, that when we visit a new church, it is not just a great sermon that needs to stand out. Worship pulls me close to my Lord, and I treasure the contact with Him.

Psalm 149:6-9 speaks of the power of praise. 'May the praise of God be in their mouths and a double-edged sword in their hands, to inflict vengeance on the nations and punishment on the peoples, to bind their kings with fetters, their nobles with shackles of iron to carry out the sentence written against them—this is the glory of all his faithful people.'

But it is not just a weapon; praise is a method to activate the precious presence of the Holy Spirit. Praise is a pathway to breakthrough. In Joshua 6, the walls of a very secure Jericho fell at the sound of voices raised in praise.

God honors praise, and therefore it is an important tool for your Mission Manifesto toolbox.

Why does God honor praise in such powerful ways? First, it is an act of faith. It declares that God is bigger than the prison, the battle, or the wall. Faith pleases Him (Hebrews 11:6), and is audible faith. Praise also tends to shift our focus. Instead of magnifying our problems, we magnify the Lord, and His power and presence receives an invite into our situation. Praise also indicates agreement. While aligning our hearts and voices with the truth of who God is, it highlights our identity in Him. As His children, we are beloved, victorious, highly valued, worthy, and perfect.

Lindsay created a huge shift in her life when she chose to

praise instead of blame Jesus and spend a large chunk of time in deep prayer with Him. Her entire outlook, ultra focused on her grief, flipped a switch. Focusing on the Lord moved her pain, questions, and grievances into the background. A life filled with Him left little room for sadness.

And what did He do? He met her there.

Worship, praise and prayer bridge Heaven and earth.

Our Lord loves to respond when His people choose to agree with Him instead of their circumstances. Praise always pleases Him. Praise shows our trust in Him, welcomes His involvement, and proclaims His glory even before a victory. In other words, praise is not just what we give God after the battle is won—it is often the very tool He uses to win it.

'Praise the Lord. Praise God in his sanctuary; praise him in his mighty Heavens. Praise him for his acts of power; praise him for his surpassing greatness. Praise him with the sounding of the trumpet, praise him with the harp and lyre, praise him with timbrel and dancing, praise him with the strings and pipe, praise him with the clash of cymbals, praise him with resounding cymbals. Let everything that has breath praise the Lord. Praise the Lord' (Psalm 105:1-6).

'The Lord is righteous in all his ways and faithful in all he does. The Lord is near to all who call on him, to all who call on him in truth. He fulfills the desires of those who fear him; he hears their cry and saves them' (Psalm 145:17-19).

Pause & Ponder

1. How do you praise?
2. How has praise made a difference in your life?
3. What can you do to add more praise to your life?

Lindsay's son, Jordan Autry, graduated to Heaven
in 2024, at the age of four.

Chapter Twenty-Three

After Full Surrender, He Healed Me

Patti Tasa

Three years before my stage 4 inoperable cancer diagnosis, I dreamed that I stood in the middle of a vast, abundant wheat field that stretched as far as I could see. The wheat seemed ready for harvest, its golden hues shimmering as the sun readied the chaff to surrender and bow.

As I looked up toward Heaven, feeling His presence, I heard the Lord gently ask, 'If I took away everything you loved—your ministry, friends, family, hopes and dreams, your children— would you still love me?'

I hesitated at the children part—they remained my greatest treasure. 'I don't know, Lord, but I want to love you that much.'

I woke up.

Lying on my bed, I reflected. Though the field looked full, it was symbolically empty of my earthly treasures. There, I stood alone with the Lord. He knew my thoughts and my hidden struggles, and the prayers I placed before Him. He spoke with a loving and gentle voice, and I knew my heart's desires could not be hidden from Him: 'Would you still love me?'

I considered again. Could I still love Him if He took them? Did I love Him that much?

Three years later, in August 2006, I received a diagnosis of terminal colon cancer, and my 'field' emptied quickly as I released everything I once felt important. Yet I symbolically held my children close, sheltering them under my arms in that empty field. How could He ask me to give them to Him? If I surrendered, my empty arms would indicate a vanishment of my dreams. But from the onset of my diagnosis, the Lord continued to whisper, 'Will you release your children to me?'

His unchanging request cut deep because of my past. Raised in a broken family, much of my childhood shouted instability—my parents divorced when I was thirteen. As a little girl, I vowed to raise my children differently. I would provide love, stability, and the best family life I possibly could. That vow shaped my adulthood and guided how I raised our four children. In the forefront of my mind, it remained woven into every choice I made.

When the doctor spoke the words 'stage 4, inoperable, no hope for survival,' not only did my life flash before me, but also theirs. In the parking garage afterward, I collapsed into my husband Carl's arms, sobbing, 'But what about the children?'

In November 2006, I attended a women's retreat called Cast Your Cares at my friend's home in Central Oregon. After four rounds of chemo, my body felt weak, and weight fell off. Still, it felt good to step away from routine and spend a weekend with friends.

During a quiet prayer time there, my thoughts once again turned to my precious children and my painful unwillingness to surrender them to God. Alone with Him, I poured out my heart. 'Who will be there to wipe away their tears when I'm gone? Who will comfort them when they mourn?'

I opened my Bible to Job 38, a passage highlighting the strength of the Lord and our human efforts which can never measure up.

After reading, and being reminded how mighty and all-knowing God is, the Lord spoke again gently to my heart. 'I will be the one to wipe away their tears and comfort them when you're gone. Give them to me.'

In that moment, I realized I held my children too tightly, not trusting Him to care for them. Supplied as precious gifts from Him, they were never mine to keep. He knew and loved them far more than I ever could.

I opened my hands and released them into His care. 'They're Yours, Lord. I give them to You and trust You to care for them.'

I entered a peace deeper than ever before. With my field now empty, I discovered that I truly did love Him that much. He remained all I needed. What a beautiful gift He gave me.

The Lord already knew my eventual answer. He saw beyond my trembling fear of letting go into the quiet places of my heart. In time, He understood that my response would rise. 'Yes, Lord, I love You that much.'

In His mercy, He chose not to rush me but patiently allowed each small step of surrender, gently leading me into the wide, open field of His peace. It reminds me of Isaiah 26:3: 'You will keep in perfect peace those whose minds are steadfast, because they trust in You.'

The following week, I met with my oncologist to review my CT scan results. He walked in with a smile. 'Your results are remarkable. Your tumors shrunk so much that I believe you are now operable.'

Two months later, after a twelve-hour surgery, the cancer-free pronouncement soothed my heart. The pathology report stated that the cancer cells were dead and no evidence of disease remained.

Did the Lord wait until I surrendered all to Him to heal me? Perhaps. Or maybe He used that journey to lead me to the deeper truth that He is enough. To me, the greater gift is the latter.

At my last treatment, I sat beside a woman also suffering from stage 4 colon cancer, with children close in age to mine. With joy, I shared of my final treatment day.

She sighed. 'It's my last day too. There's nothing more they can do for me.'

Driving home, I gripped the steering wheel, sobbing and crying out, 'Lord, why is she dying while You healed me? She too has children who need her!'

'I am sovereign. My love is the same when you were dying as it is now that you are healed. Don't question My ways.' His voice remained gentle.

I have accepted that sometimes answers to the hardest questions never arrive, like why some are healed and others are not. I wrestled deeply with this, especially years later when our oldest daughter died of cancer. But I have learned that healing sometimes comes in Heaven and sometimes here on earth.

What remains constant is this: Jesus' love never changes. He has loved me far more than my parents could have loved me. The same love that met me in that empty wheat field, asking me to surrender what I treasured most, is the love that carries me still. His love is wide enough to hold my questions, deep enough to cover my grief, and strong enough to sustain me when nothing else can. He is sovereign.

In the end, I found what I first glimpsed in that wheat field dream: He is all I need. He is more than enough. And He has a reason, or multiple reasons, in asking us to surrender the hard things—and to rely one hundred percent on Him. Not only did He physically heal a dire diagnosis, but He has prevented a return of it for many years now.

I leave you with this prayer from Ephesians 3:18-19: 'I pray that you, being rooted and established in love, may have power, together with all the Lord's holy people, to grasp how wide and long and high and deep is the love of Christ, and to know this love that surpasses knowledge—that you may be filled to the measure of all the fullness of God.'

Reflection With Julie: Unexpected Utility
Tool to use: Holy Spirit

As God provided the introduction of this book, He has now dispensed the ending.

My friends, my physical body is healed. And in the process of that, and in writing this book, God also clarified my Mission Manifesto with startling radiance.

The conservatively-raised Evangelical gal is no longer conservative. I am wearing some woo-woo.

Throughout my spiritual walk, even before I traveled to Heaven, I felt His presence many times. I have also felt the Holy Spirit as I worship and praise—sometimes in church but not always.

The first time I lifted my hands while praising Him years ago, it felt like a lightning bolt zapped down them, gently but firmly jolting the rest of my body.

Huh. I guess lifting hands brought me closer to Him?

One could say that.

Five or so years ago, Bill and I found a church we really connected with. For the very first time in our conservative backgrounds (his Mennonite), we attended an Assemblies of God church.

And we stayed.

I did not comprehend why, but now we understand much more. God was prepping me, and Bill too. He then pushed the starter button with a little trip to Heaven and personalized conversation with me there. This heightened my desire to know Him on a deeper level, completely surrendered—and live with an eternal mindset.

And help other people get there too.

Over the years of health issues, and especially in the past year or so, numerous people prayed for my healing. In the past few months, I approached four different lovely, wonderful people and asked for healing prayer. It was like—watch out! If one mentioned that God had utilized them for an amazing healing miracle, I requested directions to the ticket booth and asked where to line up. Just kidding—no lines existed. Gracious and giving, each one prayed with me, some seeing pictures God brought them of my future ministry, the reach of this book, and encouraging me. I feel very indebted.

Multiple other people also prayed, including family, friends, co-workers, other authors and writing friends. If you are one, know that you played a part and I am very thankful for you.

One friend who prayed for me online a few months ago produced some results. My back pain from a car accident twenty-five years ago reduced for almost a full week.

I peered about, seeking more. After another's efforts, my friend Robyn and I visited a church's healing room—where I heard in part that my regeneration would arrive as I prayed more mending over others. Since then, I met with a fourth person who I remembered had prayed healing over people—God had honored her prayers for healing eighty people.

I did not feel any changes, although we had a great time catching up!

'OK, Lord. Am I not supposed to receive healing on earth? But I feel it will affect my ability to pick up the full mantle of service I think you are calling me to.'

Of course, our Lord remains intimately aware of our needs, and I reminded myself to wait patiently. I settled my mind to stand by—and refused defeat. 'Dear Jesus, keep my eyes open. Help me to see it when the time is right and to know the steps you want me to take.'

Then Robyn requested a favor. She had been talking for months about a couple who opened a business and ministered to people in downtown Portland. 'I want you to meet them. He provides healing prayers and his wife does too, but she leans more toward deliverance.'

I prayed about it and felt compelled to connect. 'Sure. I want to meet with everyone in the space that I can.'

We got close to the planned meeting date, and she pertly announced, 'My sister Lynne needs eye surgery—her vision is really bad. She has two cataracts plus scratches on her corneas. But she didn't schedule the surgery. She wants you to pray over her instead and is on a plane to get here. How about we do that the same evening?'

Sounded like a good plan!

But my friend pulled a switcheroo.

As the three of us stood outside the couple's apartment door, Lynne mentioned them all praying for my healing. I frowned. 'Oh, no no no. That wasn't the plan. I'm supposed to pray over *you*.' For some reason, I now wanted to turn tail and book down the hallway like the Cowardly Lion.

They grinned like two cheshire cats. Robyn did not even blush! 'Well…you need healing, don't you?'

I sighed and probably rolled my eyes. Who wants to explain that this would be attempt number five? She had accompanied me to the healing room but had no clue of my other tries. Surely, I had run out of turns. I read the look on her face: *Would you have come if I told you this was also for you?*

She said brightly, 'You can do the healing prayers for Lynne after. But you first.'

I cleared my throat. And heard my Lord say, 'Do not argue.'

'OK. Let's get this done.' I tried to mask my irritation, but I am not very skilled at that.

The gracious but somewhat quiet couple welcomed us, and with a Holy Spirit channel on mute on the flatscreen behind them, quietly and humbly changed my life.

Robyn perched on the edge of the couch, broaching topics. Good! She seemed skilled in not letting conversations stale or stumble into awkwardness.

As we shared, I felt compelled to tell them about my short vacay in Heaven. In that exchange, I agreed that people in Heaven can see prayers from earth and the wife grew excited, saying I had confirmed a vision. She described what they looked like, and I helped her sharpen it. Then the look on her face implied a serious question waiting in the wings. Finally, she leaned forward. 'Have you found your prayer language?'

'You mean, like tongues? No, that seems to be the one gift He left out.' I fought a grin that wanted to pop out. I had wondered about that gift and if I was supposed to somehow just know the ins-and-outs. 'And what is it about tongues anyway? Are prayers more powerful in tongues?'

'Yes. The human brain is limited. Prayer language is a way of communicating with Him above the level of what our brains can do.' She shared about a few times when she had been called to pray for someone in the language of Heaven—and the incredible results.

And then her husband asked, 'Would you like the gift of tongues? And we will pray for your healing, too.'

'Yes. I'm absolutely game on tongues. And yes, I also heard a rumor about healing being involved.'

No one hid their smiles, including me.

I quickly found myself in the dubbed 'hotseat' (barstool) where momentous things happened. Writing it all might take another book!

They gathered around me, the husband asked Robyn to touch my stomach (while I joked about the jiggles I am working on) and they started healing prayers, in English and Heaven-Speak. Then he looked me in the eye.

'You already have the gift, Julie. We just need to activate it in you. And the reason God chose you is because you are humble and obedient.' He flashed a quick grin. 'You may give some gruff at first, but you always make whatever He asks happen. He knows you will do it.'

I seriously considered arguing the compliment part, but God poked me about that too. Nada! I smiled instead and nodded. 'Yes. Thank you.'

'Your ministry is getting ready to take off.'

I felt honored and blessed. Several other people had also recently confirmed this. I knew this was God's call and that for some reason, this visit must be the essential sound booth in the Theater of Calling. Had I even auditioned? Only for years!

Questions popped at me as the Spirit brought them to their minds and the wife also asked what I thought of certain words that flew into her brain. 'What do you need to give to Him?'

Puzzlement rose. 'I can't think of anything.' I thought hard. Still nothing.

'This has to do with self-protection.'

'Ah. Control, yes. Hey, I tossed my mace. But I recognize that my sarcasm, deflecting to others, and questioning something that someone tells me is a way I attempt to control situations to stay safe.'

Holy guacamole! That must have been the Good Lord speaking through me. That was very fast, smooth ... and unfortunately true.

I considered a bit more. After my years of trauma, I now helped others protect themselves from controlling people. But the glaring spotlight froze on me, little 'ole me—cringing on center stage. Although those methods sometimes work well for onstage humor, it is not very edifying in relationships.

My Lord whispered, 'Julie, will you give this to me?'

'Julie, will you give your control to Him?' The wife asked.

I nodded adamantly. Anything He desired, He could have. He deserved more than the paltry leftovers in my heart-basket. 'Yes.'

But then she shocked me. 'And ask Him now, what will He give you in return?'

Me? Ask God to give me something? I blinked furiously. 'That's allowed? Isn't that … er, a little disrespectful?' My lip twitched, squelching a quick, uncomfortable grin. And I have since learned that is a common factor in deliverance prayers.

The gentle smile on her face helped me realize that He wanted to graciously reward me and informed her.

OK! I felt Him working, and I trusted them. Despite praying like crazy ahead of time for His discernment if any of this was not of Him, I felt nothing but His peace and presence.

But at the thought of Him desiring to bless me, my eyes filled and tears started leaking down my cheeks. Someone handed me a tissue box. With a heaving sigh, I closed my eyes. I felt my Lord, in the version of the Holy Spirit, press in gently around my body in an unspoken message of comfort and strength. 'M-my Lord, what do You want to give me in return?' My lip trembled like a three-year-old's.

The three words faded into my brain one at a time: Peace…Power…Prophecy. Much later, I heard Provision too, and a deeper meaning of the first three were explained to me by Him. I repeated the three words aloud as they arrived and still around me, my four confidantes nodded and confirmed them. Lynne later said she kept seeing a flame of fire over my head.

We wrapped up my healing session only when I felt ready and moved onto the prayer language. With a simple exercise, they activated mine, and soon I cautiously spewed unknown blabber right along with them, repeating the foreign syllables as they arrived to my lips and, of course, wondering what they meant. I am Curious Julie, after all. Later, I surrendered my 'need to know' because I was not in control and not attempting that anymore. As a result, He shared some word meanings as He deemed appropriate.

And I decided on a new mantra: **Don't deflect, just accept.**

Lynne replaced me on the hotseat, and I had the amazing privilege of helping God with His goal of healing her.

'Can I touch you, Lynne?' She said yes, and I gently cupped her shoulder with my hand.

'Do you want us to join in with your prayer?' the husband asked.

'I would be honored.'

We prayed as the Spirit led. After the first round when she did not have improvement, the wife suggested starting again.

'In the morning,' Jesus told me as I prayed again. Perhaps He considered that we might pray all night. Perhaps we would have.

I nodded. 'Lynne, your eyes will be clearer in the morning.' We then talked a bit about the importance of continuing to address her trauma healing because I felt that poke strongly from the Lord.

Disappointed on the way home that we had not seen immediate results, I chose to cling to His words instead of dwelling on it, or doubting my 'prayer power.'

But Lynne woke up in the morning with clearer vision. Two days later, I received a wonderful text: 'I just left a store and realized in a panic that it had turned dark...I can't see to drive in the dark. But on the way home, I saw just fine. My eyes are clear, and the film is gone.'

Thank you, Jesus, for healing Lynne.

And me? I woke up with no back pain after twenty-five years of it. I traipsed about two miles in the sand at my fave beach with zero repercussions. I rode in the car back and forth to the beach and some between, and did not need my heated massage pad. I stood for the entire worship time at my church without spasms and weeded my garden for the first time in many years. The next day, I vacuumed! Usually, Bill needs to do all of that.

My allergies are greatly reduced. In the year following my first journey to Heaven in anaphylaxis, I experienced almost daily throat swelling and consumed large amounts of medications and supplements to help, as well as continued my natural medicine therapies. But still, I endured two more close calls—requiring epinephrine both times.

My kidneys were starting to show the strain.

Robyn had prayed for a reversal of funky DNA, to cover both my allergies and my EDS (Ehler's Danlos Syndrome). My DNA does feel new.

Thank you, Jesus.

This gift of Heaven-language has already resulted in more prayers answered, unique time with Him, deep and ongoing conversation with Jesus often most of the day, and expanded discernment and wisdom.

Early in motherhood, Patti tightly tangled up her value, identity, and happiness within the provision of a great home life. Having been rejected and abandoned by her own parents, her need for love became so strong that she raced overboard in creating the best environment for her kids.

Her children became her idol.

In idolizing her children, she neglected her first Love.

That is why God asked her to surrender them.

In Revelation 2:4-5, we read the Lord's word to the Church of Ego-Tripping Ephesus, 'Yet I hold this against you: You have forsaken the love you had at first. Consider how far you have fallen! Repent and do the things you did at first. If you do not repent, I will come to you and remove your lampstand from its place.' In Revelation 3:15-16, He says to the Church of Lukewarm Laodicea (us!), 'I know your deeds, that you are neither cold nor hot. I wish you were either one or the other! So, because you are lukewarm – neither hot nor cold – I am about to spit you out of my mouth. And in verse 19-21, to all, He announces that there is still time on the clock, 'Those whom I love I rebuke and discipline. So be earnest and repent. **Here I am! I stand at the door and knock.** If anyone hears my voice and opens the door, I will come in and eat with that person, and they with me. To the one who is victorious, I will give the right to sit with me on my throne, just as I was victorious and sat down with my Father on his throne.'

Retah McPherson also felt asked of the Lord to offer her children to Him. From her website:

"Then a scripture in Matthew, that I wasn't even aware of at that stage, suddenly came to me. (Matthew 10:37) 'You, who love your son or daughter more than me, are not worthy of entering into my presence.' I immediately knew He was talking about me…The Word teaches us that if we want to boast, we should boast in God. But what do we boast about? About our children, their achievements, the positions we are pushing them to reach. We boast about our dreams and ideals for them. The Lord said to me: 'Retah, kids are there to love. Not to boast about.' (1 Corinthians 1:31) And I said: 'Lord, here he is.' Then the most amazing thing happened. I opened my eyes and I was in the throne room of God, and the light was extremely bright. I can't describe the light to you. It was the kind of light that can shine through one's bones, so bright that I couldn't help asking: 'What is this amazing light?' God answered me and said: (1 John 1:5) 'God is light, and in Him there is no darkness.''' (99)

When we relinquish whatever block or stronghold He says is in the way (we might be idolizing it), surrender it fully even when tempted to grab it back, heal our trauma, ask for restoration, fully seek the Holy Spirit in our actions (perhaps opening our minds in the meantime!) and accept help from our Christ siblings, we gain His tools. His priorities. His Mission. His passion. And His strength to make it happen.

We become primed to implement our Heaven-Minded Mission Manifesto.

You have read about the blocks throughout my life and one that became a stronghold—control. What is yours? Perhaps you have more than one like me.

Have you taken care of them yet?

It is never easy to show vulnerability, especially in front of our spiritual families. I had to sit there, all eyes on me—and receive. Without deflecting. I certainly tried for that at first. Although I neglected to mention this part, I really did try to talk Lynne into taking the hotseat before me.

Oh, Jules!

Don't deflect, just accept!

Since that failed, I had to intentionally relax, remind my brain of my safety, and release the tension that unknowingly plagued me. I needed to admit to faults, even though I had just met three of the people around me.

Patti, the fourth person I approached for healing prayers, worked the Women's Ministry Director job at ARMS before me. As she trained me, I learned about her healing from cancer and that she had also at times felt called to heal others.

While she prayed healing for me a couple of weeks ago, God opened a vision. Although her efforts to explain made me giggle, she attempted to communicate the picture— my body as a full pitcher, pouring liquid into other people. 'I wish you could see this!' She kept saying. 'You aren't holding the pitcher.

You are the pitcher!'

'Ha. Is it Tupperware? Am I plastic?'

Her turn to giggle. 'No, it's clear glass.'

'Ah. Like I saw in Heaven. Clear jewels. Orange glass jewels. Is the liquid clear?'

'Yes. And you keep pouring! You never stop. But you as the pitcher remain full.'

'Like the oil story in the Bible? Huh. Oh! I know!' Chills raced up my arms. 'It's living water. When Robyn and I visited the healing room, the man kept seeing us cooking bread in a kitchen. We chuckled and mused on the way out—neither of us even like to cook. Were we supposed to open a soup kitchen or something without those skills or desires? I doubted that. But God told me the next day that it was the Bread of Life. That in our healing work, whether that's trauma pain or emotional and physical ailments—we are giving…Life. Him. Abundant life.'

The enormity stunned me. How fitting that God would choose this vision for Patti today.

As we wrapped it up, she hugged me. 'You're ready, Julie.'

'Yeah? What's that mean?'

'I mean the pitcher was always full. I would have been concerned if I had seen it only partially full because that means you are not ready. But it is full, and it will stay full.'

'Yes. He filled me. And He outfitted me, too.' A brief memory of my chest plate and His words filtered through: *No weapon formed against you will prosper.*

I mused more on the way home. Some fill comes from people, too.

To be physically healed and fully activate my gifts, now the cornerstone for my Mission Manifesto, I immersed myself in Him and His concepts. I had to release the stronghold I thought protected me. I needed to open my mind to the Holy Spirit and consider spiritual concepts that scripture supports but seemed foreign to me. He also required me to understand and accept that I was worthy not just of pouring into other people's lives as I had furnished their healing nutrition for years but worthy of receiving fill. And recognize my inability to fully tilt and pour until I accepted His bountiful mercy and direction to let others who walk close to Him assist in my replenishment.

I am, after all, ~~just Julie~~ *His* Julie—a faithful warrior for Jesus.

Don't Deflect, Just Accept…He'll Direct.

'…let us run with perseverance the race marked out for us, fixing our eyes on Jesus…' Hebrews 12:1–2.

Pause & Ponder

1. Where are you in this journey? Did you find your Heaven-Minded Mission Manifesto? Share it with someone else today or come on over to our Facebook group page and share at https://www.facebook.com/groups/1828150357873149 (Heavenbound Collective)
2. Review the steps God had you take to get there.
3. What does He now want you to do?

Jesus

Behind the flames in his pupils, he has ocean-colored eyes. The ones above are lighter, and how they appear to others sometimes. But when I saw Him, they were somewhat like the color you see from a plane over water when you view the deeper parts of the body of water. Like the colors in Heaven, the color is difficult to find on Earth. Each time I snap a picture, my Lord seems to bring in a bit of spotlighting from one of my windows – gone seconds later. 😊 Also, His face is a bit more elongated than this picture presents but this one is the closest that I have seen so I treasure it. (Thank you, Jessica!)

Topics Included In This Book

Fundamental Foundation:
How He Speaks - Magnetic Microphone
Your Value & Purpose - Priceless Purpose
Spiritual Warfare - Clashing Combat

List of Blocks/Potential Strongholds or Idols:
1. Guilt - Third Strike Sins
2. Tribulations - Course (De) Construction
3. Fear - The Terror Tunnel
4. Waiting - Divine Delays
5. Mental Health - Boxed Brain Barriers
6. Dreams - Devoted Desires
7. Wounds - Abiding Apologies
8. Disobedience - Steady Say-So
9. Grief - Cement Chasms
10. Strongholds - Misaligned Malice

List of Tools to Use:
1. Knowledge - Learning Lab
2. Prayer - Profound Petition
3. Pre-Praise - Please & Praise
4. Love - Abundant Agape
5. Thankfulness - Final Fun
6. Service - Jesus Joy
7. Belief - Hermetic Hold
8. Restoration - Radical Refurbishing
9. Worship & Praise - Amazing Acclaim
10. Holy Spirit - Unexpected Utility

Want A Deeper Dive?

Consider this group or personal study guide!

Available on Amazon

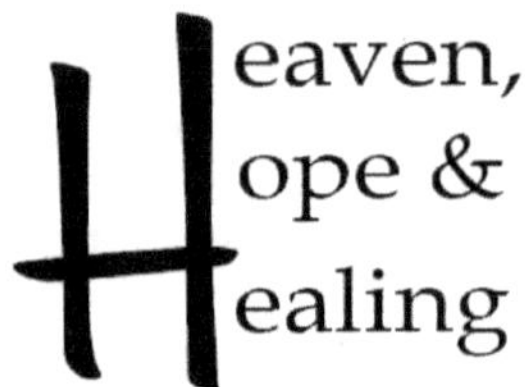

Join Julie on HeavenBlog.org!

Did This Book Bless You?

If so, please tell others!

REVIEW- If you loved the book, leaving a review on Amazon, Goodreads, Facebook, or your retailer's site helps this message reach farther than we can alone.
STUDY- The companion study guide is ideal for current small groups or for starting a new one, offering insight and Scripture-based discussion.
BOOK CLUBS- *Routed to Heaven* is a great book club choice, and Julie is sometimes available for Zoom Q&A.
INVITE JULIE TO SPEAK- Julie speaks nationwide on Heaven and related topics and also offers prayer sessions. Visit her website to learn more.

Have A Story?

Additional *Heaven Journey* collections are in development, and we are seeking near-death, afterlife, Heavenly visions and miracle stories. You do not need to be a writer—we are happy to interview you and write your story. Writers are welcome as well. Please visit Julie's website to share a brief overview of your experience, and we will contact you if we would like to learn more or include your story in a future book.

Able To Translate?

Routed to Heaven will soon in the process of Spanish translation! If this book touched you, you want to extend the reach, and you have resources to translate it into another language, please connect!

Meet Our Amazing Contributors

Pam Farrel is the bestselling author of 60+ books, including *Glimpse of God's Glory: One Woman's Near-Death Experienc*e. She and her husband Bill are international speakers and together they co-direct Love-Wise, teaching concepts to strengthen marriages and family relationships. Her website is love-wise.com

Jeff Schmidt grew up the last of six children in Sheboygan, Wisconsin but finished school in Franklin, Wisconsin. He now resides in Illinois and is a retired entrepreneur with a long-lived passion for all things spiritual and God-centered life, love and lineage. He is currently setting up his podcast titled "Lessons of Spirit and Truth". Questions can be sent to Jeffschmidt1961@gmail.com.

Dawn Caldwell De Wulf began writing early, inspired by books and her vivid imagination. An only child, she found companionship in stories. While primarily a children's author, De Wulf has recently explored historical fiction. She lives in Oregon with her husband Henry, surrounded by a large family, including five adult daughters (two sets of twins!), three adult stepchildren and six grandchildren. Her website: dawndewulf.com

LeaAnn Nielsen Swinney lives in Spokane, WA. This is her first story published in a book.

Lea Peters, together with her husband, has been a missionary and church planter in Africa since 1987. In addition to planting churches, she works to establish schools, feeding programs, and outreach efforts for the elderly and the disabled. She's also a wife, mother of four, and grandmother of two. She shares lessons of her life journey on her blog called 'A Cultural Shift': aculturalshift.com

Dawn M. Andreson considers herself a miracle from God. She lives her life with Heaven in mind for her eternal home. She is changed by God's grace and loved with an unfailing love. Jesus is her King. Email: dawn.andresen@yahoo.com

Laura M. is a young girl who loves the Lord and her experiences with Heaven and His love. She enjoys telling her story to hopefully inspire others to believe in things beyond what they see on earth!

Kelly A. Fritz, M.Ed., is an international best-selling author and award-winning speaker. Kelly is an encourager who inspires others to overcome obstacles, dream big, and live with unshakable faith. Living with dyslexia, she turns challenges into testimony. As founder of The Sueño Center, Kelly advocates for children with special needs worldwide. Website: Kellyafritz.com

Kevin Conner (KC N Kind) is a retired IT and Finance Administrator from The Goodyear Tire & Rubber Company. In 2022, after a triple bypass surgery and a profound near-death experience, he began writing songs inspired by themes of hope, healing, and unconditional love. His story 'I Learned The Most Important Concept Of All' became the inspiration for his song *You Are Loved*, now available on all major music streaming platforms under the artist name KC N Kind. Kevin lives in Canal Fulton, Ohio, with his wife, children, and grandchildren, and is active in local community and social justice work.

Karen G. is a retired teacher who taught English, U.S. History & World History, first at Manchester Christian Academy and then for 28 years at John Sedgwick Junior High in Port Orchard, WA. She retired in 2007.

Claudia Martin makes her home in Oklahoma and enjoys time with her children and grandchildren.

Michele Weisman writes to bring you peace with God, yourself, and your city. Learn more at walkingonmustardseeds.com

Kim Robinson is a former Oregon and Alaska schoolteacher. Kim's favorite position was as English and Bible teacher to missionary crew's teens aboard the hospital vessels of Mercy Ships in Africa. She currently lives in Oregon, where she enjoys serving the Lord as writer, line editor, and encourager of others. She writes for several devotional publishers and anthologies.

Jennie Lee Ersari is retired from law enforcement. She is a mother and grandmother. She resides in Arizona. She can be found on Facebook under her name.

Sally Cave is a woman of God. Find her on Substack at 'Echoes of Memory by Sally Cave.'

Linda Heath is a writer, worshiper, and creative who draws inspiration from family, travel and faith. Whether with her six grandchildren or on the road in a motorhome, she loves helping others connect to the heart of Father God through her words and presence. Learn more at LindaHeathScribe.com.

Rhema Whitlow's curiosity about Heaven began in childhood. She wondered what Heaven was like—even asking if the flowers there could sing. Over time, she prayed for glimpses of that realm and began experiencing dreams and visions, including scenes of herself as a child singing to Jesus in her childhood home. Rhema believes these experiences, affirmed through Scripture and study, revealed a living Heaven filled with purpose. Her life has been marked by signs, visions, and prophetic dreams, reinforcing her conviction that God continues to speak in the last days. She holds fast to the promise that Jesus is returning and that visions and dreams are part of God's outpouring for both the young and the old.

Jenna Rose is the pen-name for a domestic violence survivor. She works to empower the lives and voices of other women, and enjoys worship dance, cooking, and gardening.

Jason Cotter, his wife Andrea, and their family live on Kaua`i.

B.B. Brighton has spent her years writing, teaching, counseling, and parenting. In her spare time, she makes messes in the garden, in the kitchen, and especially in her craft room. But creating adventures with realistic people in messy situations brings her the greatest joy. View her website at: authorbbbrighton.com.

Holly Klingensmith lives in Arizona. She never remarried. Her faith in God is strong.

Lindsay Wessinger is a stay at home single mother to 2 children (her angel son Jordan and his older sister Emma) living in Dallas, TX.

Patti Tasa is an Oregon-based writer and former singer-songwriter whose life is rooted in faith, family and community. Married for over four decades, she is a mother and grandmother who loves camping, hiking, traveling and spending time with those she holds dear. Patti received Jesus as her Lord and Savior in 1986 and continues to grow in her walk with Him, believing each day is a beautiful gift.

Julie Bonn Blank is commonly dubbed a "Heaven Reporter." You can read her reporting results, stories, and inspiring devotionals at heavenblog.org. Julie is an award-winning and accomplished author and speaker, oversees Cascade Christian Writers, freelances nationally for many Christian publishers and publications, including *Guideposts,* and is the founder of Broken Souls Restored, an advanced and impactful faith-based abuse recovery group for survivors of relationship, child, and church abuse as well as trafficking. Learn more at juliebonnblank.org.

Thank You for Sharing Your Stories to Encourage and Inspire Others!

End Notes & Further Reading

Books listed are the paperback version unless otherwise indicated. Bible verses were sourced in the NIV version unless otherwise indicated. All Hebrew/Greek references were sourced using BibleGateway.com and BibleHub.com

1. Proverbs 4:7
2. Isaiah 54:17
3. Matthew 7:7-8
4. Philippians 1: 23-24
5. Psalm 56:13
6. 'The Two Sides of Love,' Gary Smalley and John Trent, 1999, Tyndale House Publishers, Carol Stream, Illinois. Available at: https://www.decal.ga.gov/documents/attachments/5minutepersonalitytest.pdf
7. 'The Two Sides of Love,' Gary Smalley and John Trent, 1999, Tyndale House Publishers, Carol Stream, Illinois. Available at: https://www.decal.ga.gov/documents/attachments/5minutepersonalitytest.pdf and Spiritual Gifts Assessment: https://gifts.churchgrowth.org/spiritual-gifts-survey/
8. Ephesians 1:18-21, 2 Timothy 1:11, Romans 8:11, John 14:12, 2 Peter 1:3, Luke 10:19, 1 John 4:4
9. 'This Present Darkness,' Frank Peretti, Crossway Books, 1986
10. 'Heaven: An Unexpected Journey: One Man's Experience with Heaven, Angels, and the Afterlife,' Jim Woodford & Dr. Thom Gardner, Destiny Image Publishers, 2017, page 55; 'I've seen Heaven: Pastor Sarah's Glorious Journey to Heaven and a Life filled with Supernatural Encounters,' Sarah Gardner, Sarah Gardner Ministries, 2023, page 35; Debra Hanson, Interview with Randy Kay, 9/26/25 on YouTube: https://www.youtube.com/watch?v=mhzTuOWzbHE; 'A Journey to Hell, Heaven, and Back,' Ivan Tuttle, Destiny Image

Publishing, 2020, page 65; 'Dying to Wake Up: A Doctor's Voyage into the Afterlife and the Wisdom He Brought Back,' Rajiv Parti, MD with Paul Perry, Simon & Schuster Inc 2016, page 35. 'I Believe in Heaven: Real Stories from the Bible, History and Today,' Cecil Murphey and Twila Belk, Revell 2013, page 21

11. Mark 9:43-49; Revelation 20:14-15; 'Dying to Wake Up: A Doctor's Voyage into the Afterlife and the Wisdom He Brought Back', Rajiv Parti, MD with Paul Perry, Simon & Schuster Inc 2016, pages 42 and 44; Christian Tribune interview with John Burke: https://thechristiantribune.com/pastor-shares-terrifying-view-of-hell-from-near-death-experience/ ; Testimony by Florencius Mojikon on Christian-faith.com at: https://christian-faith.com/moms-Heaven-and-hell-encounter/; 'Heaven Stormed: A Heavenly Encounter Reveals Your Assignment in the End Time Outpouring and Tribulation,' Randy Kay, Destiny Image Publishers, 2024, Randy Heaven Stormed, page 203 (Kindle)

12. B W (Bryan) Melvin, spoken at Heaven Encounters Conference 2025

13. Steve Kang, spoken at Heaven Encounters 2025. Also, during interview with Sid Roth on YouTube interview, 2/20/25 at: https://www.youtube.com/watch?v=YVrawNJdV3A, timestamp 11:12

14. 'Trace Mark of a Miracle: A Heavenly Adventure After Death,' Ruthellen Davison Carlton, independently published, 2024, pages 90, 131-138

15. I John 8:44, 2 Corinthians 11:14 and Revelation 12:9

16. 'My Sweet Encounter with Death,' Ana Christina, independently published, 2023, page 73 (Kindle)

17. 'Heaven Stormed: A Heavenly Encounter Reveals Your Assignment in the End Time Outpouring and Tribulation,' Randy Kay, Destiny Image Publishers, 2024, Randy Heaven Stormed, page 172 (Kindle)

18. 'The Rock That Is Higher: Story as Truth, Madeleine L'Engle,' Convergent NY 2018, page 72
19. 'Miraculous Life: True Stories of Supernatural Encounter with God,' Bruce Van Natta, Charisma House, 2013, pages 17-26 and pages 45-54
20. 'Face to Face with Jesus: A Former Muslim's Extraordinary Journey to Heaven and Encounter with the God of Love,' Samaa Habib and Bodie Thoene, Chosen Books, 2014
21. 'The Long, Long Trailer' starring Lucille Ball and Desi Arnaz, Directed by Vincente Minnelli, Studio Distribution Services
22. The 'Tunnel Beach,' that some call 'Secret Beach' is located in Oceanside, Oregon, south of Cape Meares and west of Tillamook. If you go, be sure to check the tide chart as sometimes the tunnel gets filled with very high tides. Note: There is also a 'Secret Beach' near Brookings.
23. Psalm 91:11–12; 2 Kings 6:16–17; Psalm 34:7 ;'Heaven: An Unexpected Journey: One Man's Experience with Heaven, Angels, and the Afterlife,' Jim Woodford & Dr. Thom Gardner, Destiny Image Publishers, 2017, page 67; 'Heaven Stormed: A Heavenly Encounter Reveals Your Assignment in the End Time Outpouring and Tribulation,' Randy Kay, Destiny Image Publishers, 2024, page 174 (Kindle), 'Miraculous Life: True Stories of Supernatural Encounter with God,' Bruce Van Natta, Charisma House, 2013, page 50; 'Near Death Experiences: 101 Short Stories That Will Help You Understand Heaven, Hell, and the Afterlife,' Randy Kay & Shaun Tabatt, Destiny Image Publishers, 2023, page 126
24. 'Heaven Stormed: A Heavenly Encounter Reveals Your Assignment in the End Time Outpouring and Tribulation,' Randy Kay, Destiny Image Publishers, 2024, page 124 (Kindle)
25. Ibid; 'Imagine Heaven Devotional: 100 Reflections to Bring Heaven to Your Life Today,' John & Kathy Burke, Baker Books, 2018, pages 80 and 83; 'Heaven Beckons,' BW (Bryan) Melvin,

Destiny Image Publishers, 2024, pages 97-98
26. https://www.biblegateway.com/passage/?search=Habakkuk%202%3A2%E2%80%933%20&version=NIV (you must turn on Hebrew visibility, which may require a subscription)
27. 'Heaven Stormed: A Heavenly Encounter Reveals Your Assignment in the End Time Outpouring and Tribulation,' Randy Kay, Destiny Image Publishers, 2024, page 252 (Kindle)
28. Ezekial 28:12-15
29. Quote from Kenneth Copeland, YouTube Link: https://www.youtube.com/watch?v=ucOs0xkH71k
30. 'A Journey to Heaven and Back,' Ivan Tuttle, Destiny Image Publishing 2020, page 65; 'Dying to Wake Up: A Doctor's Voyage into the Afterlife and the Wisdom He Brought Back,' Rajiv Parti, MD with Paul Perry, Simon & Schuster Inc 2016 page 35; 'I Believe in Heaven: Real Stories from the Bible, History and Today,' Cecil Murphey and Twila Belk, Revell 2013, page 93
31. John 14:15-18, 26; John 15:26; Ephesians 1:13-14; Romans 15:13; Ephesians 5:18
32. John 20:11–18; Matthew 28:1–10; Luke 10:38–42; Luke 8:1–3; Mark 5:25–34; Matthew 15:21–28; John 4:1–42; Mark 14:3–9; Luke 21:1–4; John 8:1–11; Luke 7:36–50
33. 'Heaven: An Unexpected Journey: One Man's Experience with Heaven, Angels, and the Afterlife,' Jim Woodford & Dr. Thom Gardner, Destiny Image Publishers, 2017, page 113
34. 'Heaven Stormed: A Heavenly Encounter Reveals Your Assignment in the End Time Outpouring and Tribulation,' Randy Kay, Destiny Image Publishers, 2024, page 127; 'I Believe in Heaven: Real Stories from the Bible, History and Today,' Cecil Murphey & Twila Belk, Revell, 2013, page 106
35. 'Imagine Heaven: Near-Death Experiences, God's Promises, and the Exhilarating Future That Awaits You,' John Burke & Don Piper, Baker Books, 2015, page 93
36. '48 Hours in Heaven,' Robert Marshall, TST Global, 2025, pages 151-152 and Randy Kay Interview at:

https://www.youtube.com/watch?v=xVxqCAmpvmw
37. BW (Bryan) Melvin, speaking at Heaven Encounters 2025; 'Heaven Beckons', BW Melvin, Destiny Image Publishing, 2024, page 97, 98
38. John 11:35
39. 'Heaven Stormed: A Heavenly Encounter Reveals Your Assignment in the End Time Outpouring and Tribulation,' Randy Kay, Destiny Image Publishers, 2024, page 178 (Kindle)
40. 'Heaven Stormed: A Heavenly Encounter Reveals Your Assignment in the End Time Outpouring and Tribulation,' Randy Kay, Destiny Image Publishers, 2024, page 154 (Kindle)
41. Matthew 6:15
42. Adapted from 'Freedom Coach Model: Encounter the Presence of God and Find Freedom in Christ Through Powerful Questions and Listening Prayer,' Jill Monaco, Jill Monaco Ministries 2017, page 23. In Jill's freedom methods, she often combines both forgiveness and freedom as one step.
43. Psalm 103:10-12
44. Resource for deliverance and generational strongholds: https://www.jillmonaco.com/
45. Increase of near-death experiences article: https://pmc.ncbi.nlm.nih.gov/articles/PMC6179792/
46. Joel 2:28, 29; Acts 2:17-2; Revelation 7:14; 'Heaven Stormed: A Heavenly Encounter Reveals Your Assignment in the End Time Outpouring and Tribulation,' Randy Kay, Destiny Image Publishers, 2024, page 286 (Kindle)
47. 'Inside Heaven's Gates: A Glimpse of Your Eternal Home,' Rebecca Sringer, Ichthus Publications, 2017; 'Visions of Heaven and Hell: Where Will You Spend Eternity?' John Bunyan, Quest Publications 2013
48. https://www.cobblestoneroadministry.org/VisionsofHeaven_bunyan.html
49. 'Heaven Stormed: A Heavenly Encounter Reveals Your Assignment in the End Time Outpouring and Tribulation,'

Randy Kay, Destiny Image Publishers, 2024, page 253 (Kindle)
50. 'Heaven Stormed: A Heavenly Encounter Reveals Your Assignment in the End Time Outpouring and Tribulation,' Randy Kay, Destiny Image Publishers, 2024, page 275 (Kindle)
51. Philippians 1:3–4; Ephesians 1:16
52. The Book of Joshua, Chapter 6
53. 2 Chronicles, Chapters 17-21
54. I John 4:8, 16
55. John 1:1-5, 14
56. John 1:9
57. I John 1:1-2
58. Library in Heaven. 'Heaven Stormed: A Heavenly Encounter Reveals Your Assignment in the End Time Outpouring and Tribulation,' Randy Kay, Destiny Image Publishers, 2024, page 185 (Kindle); 'Heaven: An Unexpected Journey: One Man's Experience with Heaven, Angels, and the Afterlife,' Jim Woodford & Dr. Thom Gardner, Destiny Image Publishers, 2017, page 110; 'Inside Heaven's Gates: A Glimpse of Your Eternal Home,' Rebecca Springer, Ichthus Publications, 2017 pages 25-30
59. 'Trace Mark of a Miracle: A Heavenly Adventure After Death,' Ruthellen Davison Carlton, independently published, 2024, page 124; Randy Kay, spoken at Heaven Encounters 2025
60. 'Return from Tomorrow,' George G. Ritchie with Elizabeth Sherrill, Chosen Books, 1978, 2007, page 80
61. '90 Minutes in Heaven,' Don Piper with Cecil Murphey, Revell, 2004, 2014, page 68
62. '90 Minutes in Heaven,' Don Piper with Cecil Murphey, Revell, 2004, 2014, page 82; Don Piper, spoken at Heaven Encounters 2025
63. https://pmc.ncbi.nlm.nih.gov/articles/PMC2900369/
64. Pagan High Priest Turned Christian at https://www.youtube.com/watch?v=Ybm1Zc1Mm64
65. Bible Hub: https://biblehub.com/greek/uper_5228.htm
66. Bible Hub: https://biblehub.com/greek/5228.htm; Hebrew

version on Bible Gateway at
https://www.biblegateway.com/passage/?search=Ephesians%205%3A20&version=NIV
67. Proverbs 23:7; Isaiah 26:3
68. Matthew 9:20-22; Mark 5:25-34; Luke 8:43-48
69. https://pmc.ncbi.nlm.nih.gov/articles/PMC7683637/
70. Exodus 15:22-34 and 17:1-3
71. Numbers 11:4-6
72. Numbers Chapter 14
73. Retah McPherson, spoken at Heaven Encounters 2025
74. Genesis 17:4–5; Genesis 17:15–16; Judges 6; Jeremiah 1:4–5 and 9-10; John 1:42; Acts 9:1–19; Luke 1:26–38
75. Book of Jonah
76. 'Br'er Rabbit,' Joel Chandler Harris, Running Press Kids, January 29, 2008
77. 'A Journey to Hell and Back,' Ivan Tuttle & Shaun Tabatt, Destiny Image Publishers 2020, page 45
78. B W (Bryan) Melvin, spoken at Heaven Encounters 2025
79. Luke 15:11–32; Acts 16:22–34; Luke 19:1–10; Luke 8:1–3; Luke 7:36–50
80. https://www.foxnews.com/lifestyle/faith-revival-follows-charlie-kirks-death-more-people-attend-mass-read-bible
81. https://www.newsweek.com/turning-point-usa-donations-chapters-spread-charlie-kirk-2133816
82. Romans 8:28; Colossians 2:15; The book of Job
83. Mark 11:24; Matthew 21:22; I John 5:14-15; John 14:13-14; Psalm 5:3
84. 'A Journey to Hell and Back,' Ivan Tuttle & Shaun Tabatt, Destiny Image Publishers 2020, page 65
85. 'A Journey to Hell and Back,' Ivan Tuttle & Shaun Tabatt, Destiny Image Publishers 2020, page 106
86. Dean Braxton, spoken at Heaven Encounters 2025
87. Ruth 1:16-17
88. Job 42:10, 12-16

89. Genesis Chapters 6-9
90. 1 Peter 1:3
91. Micah 7:19
92. Acts 16:26-28
93. 2 Kings 2:9-10
94. 'I Believe in Heaven: Real Stories from the Bible, History and Today,' Cecil Murphey and Twila Belk, Revell 2013, page 50
95. 'I Believe in Heaven: Real Stories from the Bible, History and Today,' Cecil Murphey and Twila Belk, Revell 2013, page 56
96. '90 Minutes in Heaven,' Don Piper with Cecil Murphey, Revell, 2004, 2014, page 43
97. Don Piper, Spoken to me at Heaven Encounters 2025
98. 'Imagine Heaven: Near-Death Experiences, God's Promises, and the Exhilarating Future That Awaits You,' John Burke & Don Piper, Baker Books, 2015, page 58
99. Retah McPherson, https://www.retahmcpherson.com/testimony-shortened-version

www.ingramcontent.com/pod-product-compliance
Lightning Source LLC
LaVergne TN
LVHW020705110826
845149LV00012B/2122

* 9 7 9 8 9 9 4 4 5 3 2 4 7 *